Caste and Social Stratification among Muslims in India

Edited by

Imtiaz Ahmad

AAKAR

Caste and Social Stratification among Muslims in India
Edited by Imtiaz Ahmad

First Edition 1973
Second Revised and Enlarged Edition 1978
First Aakar Edition 2018
Reprinted 2021

ISBN 978-93-5002-546-8 (Hb)

Published by
AAKAR BOOKS
28 E Pocket IV, Mayur Vihar Phase I
Delhi 110 091 India
www.aakarbooks.com

Printed at
Sapra Brothers, Noida

To Saghir

Contents

Preface to the First Edition (1973)

The presence of a caste-like system of social stratification among the Muslims of India, Pakistan and Bangladesh has been recognized for a long time but there have been few systematic attempts to examine the working of this system in local communities. This has had some unfortunate consequences for our understanding of the nature of caste among the Muslims. For one thing, in the absence of first-hand field studies, the subject has been discussed on the basis of secondary, and often highly unsystematically collected, data compiled by early British administrators and commissioners of decennial censuses in British India. Secondly, while we know something about the structure and organizational characteristics of specific Muslim groups, there is little sociological information on the social framework within which Muslim groups operate in local situations and the patterns of interaction among themselves and with Hindu castes with whom they live. Lastly, though the available evidence points to the presence of a hierarchy of different Muslim groups, there is hardly any reliable data on the principles that underlie such hierarchical arrangements. This book tries to fill these gaps in our knowledge about the structure and functioning of the system of social stratification among the Muslims, with special reference to caste, on the basis of field studies carried out by sociologists and social anthropologists in different parts of India during the past few years.

The idea for this book originated in the course of a conversation with Professor McKim Marriott during 1967-68, when I was a Fulbright Fellow in the Department of Anthropology, University of Chicago. Following some initial planning and discussion with him and some other scholars at Chicago, I approached individual scholars who had conducted field research in Muslim communities to contribute papers to this volume. Seventeen scholars were originally approached as potential contributors and they responded warmly to the invitation and the idea of the present volume. Unfortunately, not all of them were eventually able to contribute papers to this volume. I am, nevertheless, grateful for their warm response and encouragement. I am quite sure that their contributions would have greatly enhanced the value of this book and would have extended its geographical coverage.

When I invited them to write for this volume, the contributors were not requested to produce any particular type of paper, to emphasize any specific dimension of the problem, or to cast their data within any common theoretical framework. Each contributor was requested to exercise complete freedom to write on an aspect on which he had data and to emphasize the dimension which he considered worth highlighting. The only requirement was that they report the results of their particular research dealing with caste and social stratification in the communities in which they had conducted their fieldwork. Caste and social stratification, thus, provide such unity to the book as it possesses. No doubt a more precise specification as to the content and emphasis of these papers would have contributed to a greater degree of evenness and would probably have also increased the comparability of the various contributions. Such precise specification was, however, eschewed as it was felt that it might produce less realistic, and possibly even biased, results. It will perhaps be agreed that variations in methods of analysis, areas of emphasis, and the scope and nature of data reported are as significant as the results of the research reported.

The papers are presented essentially as separate, individual contributions and are not arranged according to any specific scheme or plan. Nevertheless, they fall into two broad categories on the basis of their content and emphasis. Some papers are restricted to the analysis of single Muslim castes or groups and deal with their internal structures, patterns of endogamy, and social identities without necessarily taking account of the social settings in which they live and operate. Other papers are concerned with the interactional dimension and explore the patterns of interaction amongst the different castes and groups residing in a single local community. These papers deal directly with the hierarchical and interactional dimensions of the system of social stratification amongst the Muslims.

There is a dearth of data on caste and social stratification amongst the Muslims in India as well as of sociologists and social anthropologists who have taken interest in their study. It is, therefore, a matter of some satisfaction that this collection has succeeded in bringing together papers covering most of the areas of significant Muslim concentration in India. The two areas of significant Muslim concentration excluded from coverage in these papers are Kashmir and Assam. Moreover, they deal with social stratification both in rural and urban settings. It would be erroneous, and even absurd, to suggest that these papers provide any representative picture of the social structure of Muslims in India. One hopes, however, that they will help toward the emergence of a better-informed view of Muslim groups and the nature of their adjustment in different geographical settings in India.

All the papers presented here, except for the papers by Victor S. D'Souza and M.K.A. Siddiqui, were written especially for this volume and are being printed for the first time. D'Souza's paper originally appeared in *Anthropos*. Siddiqui's paper was presented at a Seminar on the cultural profile of Calcutta organized by the Indian Anthropological Society and has appeared as part of the proceedings of that Seminar.* I am grateful to the editors of *Anthropos* and to Dr. Surajit Sinha and the Indian Anthropological Society for permission to reproduce the papers by D'Souza and Siddiqui respectively.

A collection of papers is usually a cooperative effort in every sense of the term and this one is no exception. It has been made

*Surajit Sinha (ed.), *Cultural Profile of Calcutta*, Calcutta, Indian Anthropological Society, 1972.

possible by the willing cooperation and encouragement of several individuals. I wish to express my appreciation in particular to each of the contributors for their genuine interest and willing cooperation in this endeavour as well as to their extended patience during the preparation of this volume for the press. I am thankful to Professor M.N. Srinivas, who first suggested that I engage in research among Muslims, and to Professor McKim Marriott for helpful suggestions in the planning of this volume. I am also thankful to Mr. R.C. Jain, the publisher, for putting up with the various lengthy delays in the preparation of this book and for expeditiously bringing it out, and to Miss Reeta Chowdhari for help in proof-reading. Last but not the least, I remember my wife, Karuna, who constantly reminded me of my editorial responsibilities and coaxed me into working on the manuscript whenever I seemed to shirk from it.

Originally, my plan was to include papers on both India and Pakistan in this volume. I invited six Pakistani scholars who have carried out field work in what used to be the two wings of Pakistan to contribute papers, but was unfortunately not favoured by a positive response from all of them. Dr. Saghir Ahmad, Assistant Professor of Anthropology at Simon Frazer University at the time of his sudden and untimely death in 1971, was kind enough to contribute a paper based on his fieldwork in a West Punjab village. Since his was the only paper on Pakistan, I thought it desirable to limit the volume to India and had to omit his paper. As a token of appreciation for his genuine desire for greater collaboration and intellectual interaction among the scholars of the entire sub-continent, this book is dedicated to his loving memory.

Jawaharlal Nehru University,
New Delhi.

Imtiaz Ahmad

Preface to the Second Edition (1978)

The publication of a second edition of this book is a matter of profound encouragement and satisfaction to us. It shows that the book has met an existing need and our collective endeavour has proved worthwhile to fellow students of the social structure of Muslim communities in India.

Numerous printing errors and bibliographical inaccuracies had crept into the first edition of this book. I have tried to use the opportunity provided by the publication of this edition to eliminate those errors and to have the entire book copy-edited afresh. It is hoped that this has resulted in a substantial improvement of the book.

Some contributors, who had been requested to write for the volume, had been unable to send in their contributions by the time the first edition was sent to the press but did so subsequently. The opportunity provided by the publication of this edition has been used to include their contributions as well. Thus, the contributions by Dr. Hasan Ali, Dr. S.P. Jain and Dr. A.R. Momin have been added to this edition of the book. Of these three contributions, the one by Dr. Hasan Ali has appeared previously in *Man in India*. I am grateful to the editor of *Man in India* for permission to reproduce it here. I had also planned to include a second contribution by me in this edition of the book. As it was a lengthy contribution and would have made the volume unduly bulky, it has been decided to exclude it from this edi.ion. It is proposed to publish it elsewhere subsequently.

The first edition of this book contained two contributions by Dr. Partap C. Aggarwal. His contribution focussing on the internal structure of the Meo caste fitted in well with the contributions in *Family, Kinship and Marriage among Muslims in India* published in 1976. Consequently, it was included in that volume and has been dropped from this book altogether. I am grateful to Dr. Aggarwal for having allowed me to do so, and I hope that this change has given greater coherence and thematic unity to this edition of the book.

This book was reviewed extensively and a large number of comments and criticisms had been offered by the reviewers. The contributors were sent a copy of the reviews and were requested to revise their contributions in the light of the comments and criticisms offered by the reviewers. Perhaps, I should have taken the opportunity provided by the publication of this edition to respond to some of the general conceptual questions raised by the reviewers regarding the study of caste and social stratification among Muslims in India. However, I have refrained from doing so as I feel that on a book of this kind it is the reviewer rather than the editor who should have the last word.

Several people have helped me in preparing this edition of the book for the press: Shri Nabha Kishore Rout and Shri M.F.U. Kazmi read the manuscript and checked the bibliographic references with considerable care; Shri A.N. Talwar and Mrs. Amali Mathew typed out the manuscript with care and precision; Shri A.K. Mehra, Shri Rakesh Kumar Sharma and Shri Shushanta Kumar Mohanty helped with the rather dull and tiring job of proof-reading and Miss N. Hamsa helped the project in several ways. To all of them I am extremely grateful for their help, at the same time reserving blame for the deficiencies that may still remain entirely to myself.

Jawaharlal Nehru University,
New Delhi. Imtiaz Ahmad

The Contributors

PARTAP C. AGGARWAL received his training in anthropology at Cornell University where he earned his Ph.D. in 1966. He taught at Colgate University for four years and is currently Director of Research at the Shri Ram Centre for Industrial Relations and Human Resources, New Delhi. He was Branta Professor of Anthropology at Colgate University during 1976-77. Dr. Aggarwal's major research interest has been in the areas of social and cultural change, social stratification, economic development and stigmatized groups such as the Harijans in India. He has published several papers in anthropological journals and is also the author of *Caste, Religion and Power*, *Green Revolution and Rural Labour* and (with Mohd. Siddique Ashraf) *Equality Through Privilege*.

IMTIAZ AHMAD received his training in anthropology and sociology at the Universities of Lucknow and Delhi respectively. He was a Fulbright Fellow at the University of Chicago during 1967-68 and Visiting Assistant Professor in Social Anthropology at the University of Missouri during 1968-1970. He was a Fellow of the Indian Council of Social Science Research during 1970-72. He is currently Associate Professor in Sociology in the Centre for Political Studies at Jawaharlal Nehru University, New Delhi. He has published papers in leading professional journals and edited *Caste and Social Stratification among the Muslims* and

Family, Kinship and Marriage among Muslims in India.

HASAN ALI received his training in anthropology at Ranchi University and is currently Research Associate in the Anthropological Survey of India, Calcutta. He has carried out extended fieldwork in South Bihar and among the Chinese of Calcutta, and is currently involved in research on the tribal customary law among the Korwas. He has published several papers in leading Indian anthropological journals. His research interests include social stratification among Muslims, cultural identity and mechanisms of group boundary maintenance in India.

RANJIT K. BHATTACHARYA received his anthropological training at the University of Calcutta. He worked as Research Associate in the Anthropological Survey of India, Calcutta, during 1966-71 and at the Administrative Staff College, Hyderabad, during 1971-74. He is currently Research Associate in the Anthropological Survey of India, Calcutta. He has published several articles on caste and social relations in leading Indian anthropological journals.

ZARINA BHATTY received her M.A. in anthropology from the School of Oriental and African Studies, University of London, in 1960. She held the Junior Research Fellowship of the University Grants Commission during 1961-63 and the Housewives Fellowship of the Indian Council of Social Science Research during 1972-74. She is currently Lecturer in Sociology at the Jesus and Mary College, New Delhi. She has carried out extended research on the changing social stratification among Muslims and the impact of economic development on the social system of the Muslims in Uttar Pradesh and contributed to professional journals and compendia volumes on caste among Muslims, status of Muslim women, and the role of educated women in India.

VICTOR S. D'SOUZA received his training in sociology at the University of Bombay, and is currently Professor of Sociology at Panjab University, Chandigarh. Professor D'Souza has done research among the Moplah Muslims in Karnataka and Kerala and on the relationship between caste and occupation in the Punjab. He is author of several well-known papers published in leading international journals.

LEELA DUBE has carried out fieldwork in many parts of India. Her research in South-eastern Madhya Pradesh resulted in her doctoral dissertation, The Gond Woman. As a Senior Research Associate of the Cornell University India Programme, she studied the response of women to Community Development projects in western Uttar Pradesh. At the University of Saugar, she directed a research project on the concept of Community and Community Integration in Indian Villages. She has held the Senior Specialist Award of the East-West Center, Hawaii, and was Reader in Anthropology at the University of Saugar until 1976. She is currently Director in the Indian Council of Social Science Research, New Delhi. Dr. Dube's current research interests are centred on the matrilineal communities of Kerala and Lakshadweep. She has contributed numerous papers to learned journals and is the author of *Matriliny and Islam*.

S.P. JAIN received his training in sociology at Panjab University where he earned his Ph.D. in 1967. He is currently Deputy Director at the National Institute of Rural Development, Hyderabad. Dr. Jain's research interests are social stratification, social change, and sociology of rural development. He has published several research papers in leading journals and is the author of *The Social Structure of Hindu-Muslim Community*, *Panchayat Raj and Political Perceptions* and *Panchayat Raj in Assam*.

J.C. MASSELOS undertook post-graduate research at the Heras Institute of Indian History and Culture and was awarded a Ph.D. by the University of Bombay in 1965. He is currently Senior Lecturer in Indian History at the University of Sydney. Dr. Masselos has contributed articles to leading professional journals and to R. Kumar (ed.), *Essays on Gandhian Politics* and S.N. Ray (ed.), *Gandhi, India and the World*, and is the author of *Nationalism on the Indian Subcontinent* and *Towards Nationalism*. He is currently engaged in research on the social and political history of Bombay City during the nineteenth and twentieth centuries.

MATTISON MINES took his Ph.D. in anthropology at Cornell University after fieldwork in Tamilnadu State and is now Associate Professor in Anthropology at the University of California, Santa Barbara. He has published several articles on the Muslims of Tamilnadu and is the author of *The Muslim Merchants: The Economic Behaviour of an Indian Muslim Community*.

A.R. MOMIN received his training in sociology at the University of Bombay. He was a Junior Research Fellow of the University Grants Commission during 1971-73, and is currently Lecturer in Sociology at the University of Bombay. He has contributed research papers to several professional journals. His major research interests are a unified science of man, the state of sociology and anthropology in India and the Indo-Islamic tradition.

M.K.A. SIDDIQUI received his training in anthropology at Calcutta University where he earned his Ph.D. degree in 1976. He is currently Research Associate in the Anthropological Survey of India, Calcutta. Dr. Siddiqui has done extended fieldwork in rural and urban Bengal and Manipur. His current research interests are caste and social stratification among Muslims, social change and the role of religious institutions in urban centres. He has published several articles in professional journals and is the author of *Muslims of Calcutta*.

Prologue (2018)

This book was first published forty-seven years ago. The idea that caste existed among Muslims in India was not new or novel. Empirical studies, which initially adopted the form of a decennial census, adduced considerable evidence that castes (or groupings analogous to castes, a much later categorization) existed among Muslims and could be identified through a hierarchy of status orders that had several significant attributes: source of descent, so that those claiming to be the descendants of the Prophet or one of his Companions enjoyed precedence over local converts, and association with an occupation leading to each caste confining marriages to its members. Using evidence from decennial censuses, Ghaus Ansari (1959) argued that Muslims in India were divided into three broad categories which he called the *ashraf* (noble born), *ajlaf* (mean and lowly), and *arzal* (excluded). Each of these categories was further divided into a number of groups for which, following the practice of the decennial censuses, he chose to designate as castes. Even then the book came in for widespread criticism from Muslims and scholars of South Asian Muslim societies.[1]

1. There is an interesting view on caste among Muslims which maintains that the Muslim system of social stratification has evolved independently and is seen as having no relationship with the Hindu caste system. Charles Lindholm (1965) has argued that many of the features found in Muslim society are similar to those among Muslims in other parts of South Asia, and on that basis has argued that

Muslims as a rule, while admitting that caste or groupings analogous to caste, exist among them, display a high degree of ambivalence on the subject of caste among Muslims. This ambivalence has many expressions and has resulted in two distinct tendencies among Muslims. Many Muslims, who admit that caste differences obtain among them, often advance the plea that rather than caste some other term should be used to designate Muslim castes. Ethnic groups, *biradari*s, or groupings analogous to castes have been considered and utilized as substitutes (see Madan, 1974). Others altogether deny the existence of caste among Muslims, arguing that Islam is an egalitarian religion and does not recognize distinctions of caste and status honour (Momin, 1989; Farooqui, 1989). Such Muslims refuse to recognize that Islam and Muslims are not necessarily coterminous and that there may be a gap between Islamic beliefs and ideology and actual social behaviour.

Both tendencies arise from Muslim anxieties about their position in India. Those Muslims who argue that rather than caste an alternative term should be used to designate social divisions among them are guided by the anxiety that if caste were to be used it would betray an affinity with Hindus. The Muslim community was very substantially formed through conversion from indigenous groups and the fear that it might relapse back into Hinduism has prompted it throughout history to clearly distinguish itself from Hindus by evolving diacritical distinctions which they feel are more Islamic and set Muslims apart from Hindus. Accordingly, while they are willing to admit that formations analogous to caste exist among Muslims, they would much prefer that some other term be used to designate Muslim castes.

On the other hand, those Muslims who are prone to denying the existence of caste among Muslims altogether do so because they seek

---

the Muslim social stratification found in India is an extension of the system found elsewhere. Many Muslims who do not like the word caste to be associated with religion are themselves inclined to adopt a similar line of argument. This would have been tenable had Islamic scriptural sources provided a blueprint of a system of Islamic social stratification. This not being the case, the argument fails to sustain itself. It is plausible that Islam did modify certain social practices, including that of caste. Whatever practices were not sanctified by Islam but existed in India were attenuated. Whatever practices that existed in India which were in conformity with the Islamic ethos became more rigid. Thus, purdah practices, which were prevalent even in India, became more strict and rigid and caste principles were relaxed or made less restrictive.

to project the community as a monolith in the context of its standing as a minority in India. Benur (2004) traced this dimension in the context of the rise of the nationalist movement in India. He writes:

> The Hindu nationalists, using religion and culture as the bases of nationalism, tried to push only the Hindus as the 'national' community, and the Muslims as the 'illegitimate' residents of India. The Muslim elites also tried to project the Muslims as [a] religious monolith and advanced the theory of distinct 'Islamic' identity of the Muslims. But because the Muslims were divided by the caste hierarchy, it was inconvenient for them to project the Hindus as monolith. Hence, they put forward the theory of 'unity in diversity' and argued that the Hindu culture was the 'unifying force' behind the so-called diversity of the Hindus. The Hindu elites, i.e. the Brahmanical upper classes pushed the Brahmanical value system and philosophy as the 'essence' of so-called Indian culture. The Muslim elite adopted a similar view about the Muslims, reducing everything to Islam. . . . So, it was contended that the Indian Muslims are without any caste system and they are one homogeneous community.

This tendency has percolated down to sociologists who show a remarkably uncanny ambivalence towards caste among Muslims. At the behavioural level, they are willing to concede that there are elements of caste in Indo-Muslim society. However, as soon as the discussion shifts from behaviour to ideology they recoil from their position, seeking to add caveats or hedge around the issue by unabashedly admitting that when they apply the term in the context of a Muslim group they are using it in a loose sense. Two recent studies by Husnain (2005) and Nazir (1993) exemplify this tendency. Husnain locates his discussion in the context of the question of whether the concept of caste can be applied to the system of social stratification of a community professing a faith other than Hinduism. His conclusion is bald and simple: 'It is true that the egalitarian social order of Islam stands in sharp contrast with the ideology of caste yet the "Indian Islam" and "Hindu Caste System" have been able to achieve a substantial compatibility' (2005: 2). He then goes on to offer a host of explanations for this. He writes:

> Hutton sounds convincing when he says that when Muslims and Christians came to India, the caste was in the air and the followers

> of even these egalitarian ideologies could not escape the infection of caste. Moreover, the overwhelming majority of Indian Muslim population comes from the lower Hindu castes who have been coming into the fold of Islam to escape from social persecution and the oppressive socio-economic disabilities. They were also attracted and lured by the social egalitarianism of Islam but the search for equality proved a mirage. In many cases there were improvements in their socio-economic condition yet the goal of social equality remained illusive. Moreover, in most of the cases the people embracing Islam gave up their religious faith but not the caste that was brought forward even to a new socio-religious milieu. Thus, it would be apt to say that while Islam may not be having castes or caste-like groupings, the Indian Muslims do have' (Husnain, 2005: 207-08).

No sooner than he has advanced this sociological formulation, Husnain becomes uncomfortable, fearing that he might have committed an almost sacrilegious act by declaring that caste exists among Indian Muslims, and wishes to resile from it. Cryptically, he adds:

> But in the present paper an attempt is being made to stay clear of the issue whether the model of social stratification among the Indian Muslims is the replica of the Hindu caste system or not. The author, in this paper, shall be using the term caste and caste system among the Indian Muslims in a conveniently loose manner. It is undisputed that there are groups of people among the Muslims who are organized more or less like the Hindu castes but this is also true that many of them are less rigid because Islam, theoretically at least, permits marriage between different classes of believers (2005: 207).

He does not stop at that. He grasps for crutches that would enable him to perform this summersault. He finds one in a statement of Nazir, which he approvingly quotes:

> . . . It is necessary to make a distinction between a caste system and caste labels: the former refers to a local system of hierarchically ordered corporate groupings involving division of labour, occupational specialization, unequal dependence, and recruitment

> by birth only; the latter refers to a set of non-local, non-corporate named groups which provide a ranking hierarchy, and which do not involve occupational specialization, unequal dependence, and recruitment by birth only (Nazir, 1993: 2898).

'Perhaps,' concludes Husnain, 'the "caste system' and "caste- like groupings" among the Indian Muslims with all its fluidity may be better analysed and better understood through this observation' (2005: 208).

This assumes that Hindus live under 'the caste system' and Muslims only use castes labels. Several theoretical and empirical questions are raised by this assumption. First, how is this assumption made? Is it made on the basis of empirical research? or, alternatively, is it made solely on a priori grounds. As far as I am aware, there has to date been no empirical research which can be said to have established beyond a shadow of a doubt that Muslims do not live under a caste system and only use caste labels. Indeed, if such empirical research existed, the dilemma these authors (and others) face over how to characterize Muslim social stratification in India would not exist. It exists because available empirical research has demonstrated that Muslim social stratification in India and beyond is marked by features of the caste system. It is, therefore, clear that the assumption is made on a priori grounds. As believing Muslims, committed to upholding the widely proclaimed Islamic egalitarianism as axiomatic, they cannot face up to the behavioural reality that Muslims live under a caste system. They not only assume the distinction between 'the caste system' and 'caste labels' but go on to suggest that it constitutes a viable framework for analysing and understanding Muslim social stratification in India. It is used as a smokescreen to avoid facing the harsh behaviourai reality of caste among Muslims in India.

Second, is there an empirical basis for the assertion that Muslim social organization in India is 'a set of non-local, non-corporate named groups which provide a ranking hierarchy, and which do not involve occupational specialization, unequal dependence, and recruitment by birth only' (Nazir, 1993: 2898). Nazir does not make explicit the level at which he is speaking. Is he speaking about the categorization of Muslims into the broad categories of *ashraf*, *ajlaf*, and *arzal*? If that is his point of reference, then his characterization of Muslim social organization as a set of non-local, non-corporate groups can be said to have some validity. However, it would invalidate the distinction between 'the caste system' and 'caste labels' as a similar broad division exists in the form of varna categories in 'the caste system'. Ansari used the three broad categories of *ashraf*, *ajlaf*, and *arzal* in the collective sense but clearly recognized that they were divided into smaller named groups which were distinguished from one another by occupation, endogamy, and sociability. Thus, if Nazir's reference is to the groups at this level, then his description of Muslim groups is wholly erroneous. Let us look closely at the empirical evidence in order to determine whether the distinction he posits between 'the caste system' and 'caste labels', and by implication between Hindu and Muslim modes of social organization, is confirmed by available studies.

Sociological research on Muslims in India, as opposed to lay and impressionistic writings, continues to be thin. Evidence presented in this book and subsequent research demonstrates that Muslim groups which are the point of reference here, for which the words *biradari* and *zat* are commonly used, are local and corporate entities. Even *biradari*s or *zat*s, such as Saiyyid, Sheikh, and Ansari, which are widely dispersed and found in different parts of a district, state, or India as a whole, are identified by their affiliation to a particular territory and restrict their marriages to members within that territory. Of course, how that territory is distinguished, varies widely. For Saiyads, Shiekhs, and Pathans, who resent being characterized as *biradari*s and prefer to be described as *zat*s, the association to territory is expressed by appending the name of the territory to their names. Thus, one hears of Saiyads of Satrikh, Sheikhs of Allahabad, Kidwais of Baragaon, and Kasauli and Pathans of Malihabad. In the case of *biradari*s which have an internal organization of government and social control (called *biradari* or *zat panchayat*), this territorial association is defined by the jurisdiction of the *biradari panchayat*. The Ansaris in Rasulpur, a village in Barabanki District of Uttar Pradesh, where I conducted fieldwork, were divided into concentric circles of three and thirteen villages. They confined their marriages to these thirteen villages athough there were also Ansaris in neighbouring areas.

That is not all. Considerable evidence exists to show that the *biradari*s or *zat*s are associated with particular occupations, are interdependent (tied into patron-client relationships of the *jajmani* kind), and are endogamous. This does not mean that all members of a *biradari* or *zat* necessarily practise the occupation with which their group is traditionally associated. There has been much variation throughout history among *biradari*s and *zat*s, as indeed there has been within castes, to the extent to which their members remain tied to the practice of their traditional occupation. *Biradari*s and *zat*s higher up in the social hierarchy did not usually have a traditional occupation and there was no close association between the *biradari* or *zat* and the traditional occupation. On the other hand, *biradari*s and *zat*s further down the social ladder engaged in their traditional occupations and their association with the occupation was strong. This is not significantly different from the picture of groups in what Nazir would characterize as 'the caste system'. Risley's observation makes this explicit: 'In theory each caste has a distinctive occupation, but it does not follow that this traditional occupation is practised by its members'.

The argument that Muslim groups, *biradari*s and *zat*s, are not based on birth alone is equally fallacious. Like the groups in what Nazir would call 'the caste system', Muslim *biradari*s and *zat*s are based on birth alone. There is no process through which one can become a Saiyid, Sheikh, or Julaha except through birth. That is why, when someone marries into another *biradari* or *zat*, he is not integrated into another one but retains his/her original *biradari* or *zat* association. There exists a possibility in the case of groupings to attempt social mobility and become a Sayid, Shiekh, or Pathan in the course of time by inventing a rationale and a genealogy. Where such social mobility occurs, the basis of recruitment to the *biradari* or *zat* does not change, but just becomes another *biradari* or *zat*, and comes to be known by another name, to which recruitment continues to be based on the principle of birth. This is again not significantly different from that in 'the caste system' where there is the prospect of castes changing their antecedents and name through the process of social mobility. Thus, the point that *biradari*s and *zat*s are 'less rigid because Islam, theoretically at least, permits marriage between different classes of believers' (Husnain, 2005: 208) is not empirically established. It is asserted without any substantial basis in empirical research.

This raises fundamental questions. Why are Husnain and Nazir, and a host of other researchers, who have worked on the sensitive question of the existence of caste among Muslims, so strongly persuaded to posit that there are significant differences between 'the caste system' and the system of *biradaris* and *zats*? Is it that these differences actually exist but empirical research has so far failed to uncover them? Alternatively,, is it that they are persuaded to assert these differences in the face of contrary empirical evidence for extraneous considerations? Is it that they are prone to emphasizing these differences because as believing Muslims they are familiar with the Islamic discourse that asserts that Islam preaches social equality and are afraid to take a contrary position? Alternatively, is it that asserting these differences is a defensive mechanism that enables them to simultaneously adhere to their disciplinary obligation as social scientists and their religious obligation to uphold what is commonly considered the Islamic view on social stratification? My own view has been that the tendency to emphasize differences between 'the caste system' and the system of *biradaris* and *zats* arises from some such considerations, but I will refrain from making any such point here. I would like, instead, to explore whether their starting point that Islam is an egalitarian religion and preaches social equality is theologically and sociologically valid. This is central to understanding their standpoint.

We need to ask three different questions of the Islamic text if we are to understand Islam's position in relation to social stratification and social equality. First, is Islam opposed to social stratification as such or is it merely opposed to social inequality. Second, what is the true Islamic attitude towards social inequality that existed in the society in which Islam evolved and took root? Finally, is the social equality that it proclaims, and to which reference is always made when it is suggested that Islam is an egalitarian religion, actually occuring in society or is it merely an ideal set out as the direction mankind should strive to follow. It is necessary to ask these questions in order to understand the nature of the emphasis on egalitarianism and social equality in Islam. Basic to these questions is the sociological dictum that no society beyond the most primitive can be truly egalitarian. This was the point at the heart of Veblen's *Theory of the Leisured Class* (1999) in which he argued that as societies generated economic surplus there almost invariably developed some form of social stratification. Pitirim A. Sorokin articulated this as a general statement:

> Any organized social group is always a stratified social body. There has not been and does not exist any permanent social group which is 'flat', and in which all members are equal. An un-stratified

> society, with a real equality of its members, is a myth which has never been realized in the history of mankind. This statement may sound paradoxical and yet it is accurate. The forms and proportions of stratification vary, but its essence is permanent, as far as any permanent and organized social group is concerned (Sorokin, 1959: 13-14).

On even the most casual reading of the Islamic scriptural text, we are struck that quite irrespective of the occasional emphasis on the equality of human beings, Islam's orientation is remarkably hierarchical, and this hierarchical orientation comes in a wide variety of fields. First, the relationship between believers and non-believers is conceived in hierarchical terms with the believer, the *dhimmi,* and the *kafir* constituting a clear hierarchy. Second, the relationship of Allah to the believer is conceived in hierarchical terms. It is a relationship of subordination and subservience, to such a degree that the individual believer must prostrate before Allah in daily prayers and at the same time see himself as utterly powerless in relation to Him. There are any number of passages in the Islamic scriptural text endorsing the relatively lowly position, of believers in relation to Allah, whether as individuals or as a collective entity. Third, the relationship of the wife to her husband is clearly conceived in hierarchical terms, even if the text does not distinguish between them in terms of the religious duties enjoined upon them. This is sometimes cited by Muslim feminists and Muslim modernists to argue that Islam guarantees equality of gender and does not place a Muslim woman in an inferior position to a man. However, in reality a woman is subordinate to a man and the relationship between them is seen as constituting a hierarchy in which the woman is in relation to a man in the same way as the individual is in relation to the community, and the community is in relation to Allah. Finally, the relationship between the master and slave is conceived in clearly hierarchical terms, even if the master is required to deal with the slave with kindness and merit is assigned to those who free their slaves.[2] Thus, it is clear that the framework of Islamic thinking is deeply imbued with the notion of hierarchy and social stratification.

---

2. Islam's approach to slavery added the idea that freedom was the natural state of affairs for human beings, and in line with this it limited the opportunities to enslave people, commended the freeing of slaves, and regulated the way slaves were treated. The Qur'an and Hadith repeatedly exhort Muslims to treat slaves well and Muhammad

It is true that in the Arab society in which Islam evolved there were no great differences of wealth, but there was economic differentiation between ordinary Bedouins and the trading classes. One can easily imagine that they would have differed in terms of their wealth, material possessions, and lifestyles, and Islam could not have brushed them under the carpet. It would have been required to deal with them, as they would have been reflected in their behaviour and mutual attitudes. As far as the Islamic scriptural text is concerned, it clearly recognizes such distinctions in society and prescribes appropriate forms of behaviour for each. It asks those deprived in social and economic terms to be content and to live according to their means. It is repeatedly said in the text that Allah is All-seeing and will reward the poor for their poverty on the day of judgement. At the same time, the wealthy and rich, while they are permitted to enjoy their riches and to spend them in accordance with their economic standing, they are cautioned not to be over-proud of their material possessions. They are besides asked to show kindness to those who are deprived and poor, and to part with a portion of their wealth and income to the latter. Even the poor are conceived in hierarchical terms: first come the near ones, followed by orphans, and then the destitute and the deprived. If some form of social stratification had not existed in society, the Islamic scriptural text would neither have referred to those differences, nor indicated appropriate forms of behaviour towards them. It would also not have sought to devise an economic framework for the redistribution of wealth to enable the poor to make both ends meet. It is, thus, clear that the emphasis that Islamic scriptural text places on social equality does not describe an existing state of affairs.

If the world-view of the Islamic scriptural text is hierarchical and it admits social and economic differences in society, then how should we interpret its emphasis upon social equality? One way to interpret it can be to ignore that Islamic orientation is hierarchical and that it

---

demonstrated this both in action and in words. In the event of illness it was required that the slave was properly cared for. Manumission is considered a meritorious act. The slave must not be mistreated or overworked, but be properly treated .A slave could ransom himself with his master's consent through a contract known as *mukataba*. He could take legal action for a breach of rules, and could in consequence be freed. This should not however distract us from the reality that the relationship between the master and the slave was conceived in hierarchical terms with the master enjoying superior rights over his slave.

recognizes social and economic differences in the society in which it originated and to argue that it stands for egalitarianism as an absolute value. I would argue that those who maintain that Islam contemplates no social stratification are interpreting Islam in precisely this way. Even when they encounter social differentiation and stratification, they glibly ignore it and flag the proclaimed egalitarianism of Islam as a social reality. The other way of interpreting it can be to recognize a fundamental difference, i.e. the difference between society as it exists and as it ought to exist, and to maintain that the Islamic proclamation in favour of social equality is more an ideal for the future than a description of an existing dispensation.

Gaborieau (1978) sought frankness in studying the phenomenon of caste among Muslims in India. The Muslims who entered India did not seem to be shocked by the institution of caste, and if they were not shocked it must have been that they were not unfamiliar with such arrangements. Ghaus Ansari has also noted that Islam was not egalitarian when it entered India. 'The ideal of equality among Muslims,' he states, 'was practicable only in the then prevailing conditions of Arabia. In the course of the expansion of Islam and its contact with other complex cultures the democratic forms of political organization and social equality within the community gradually disappeared (Ansari, 1959: 30).

Early Muslim rulers and intellectuals, including the ulema, did not see anything wrong with the persistence of caste among Muslims in India. Indeed, they rationalized and legitimized it as the natural order of things. Zia Barni[3] elaborated a theory that the 'merits' and 'demerits' of all people have been 'apportioned at the beginning of time and allotted to their souls'. People's actions are not of their volition, but rather an expression and result of 'Divine Commandments'. Muhammad Habib and Afsar Umar Salim Khan, translators of Barni's work, painfully admit that 'Barni's God, as is clear from his work, has two aspects:first, he is the tribal deity of the Musalmans; secondly, as between the Musalmans themselves, he is the tribal deity of well-born Muslims' (quoted in Sikand, 2005). Subsequently, the ulema employed the Islamic juridical concept of *kafao'a* to provide legitimacy to the

3. For more detailed treatment of Barni's and other contemporary scholars' views on social divisions in medieval Muslim society, see Sikand (2005), but of course reading Zia Barni in original would be more rewarding.

existing social divisions in society. The term *kufao'a*, derived from the Arabic root *kafayat*, implies similarity and refers to the unity of a social group based on intermarriage (see Falahi, 2009, for an elaboration of the concept of *kufao'a*).

There are two diametrically opposing views on the existence of caste among Muslims in India. One view is that caste among Muslims can be traced to Hindu influence, although there are two variations of this view. Some scholars suggest that the existence of caste in Indo-Muslim society is accounted for only because a large majority of Muslims are converts from Hindu castes. That when they converted they brought their pre-conversion orientations with them. Others explain the existence of caste among Muslims in terms of the interface between Islam and Indian civilization. Islam came to India when there already was an established and developed civilization. It could hope to override the indigenous civilization only at the cost of its own rejection. This set in motion a process of compromise and adaptation, with both traditions borrowing from each other. As far as Islam was concerned, it adopted elements of culture and social organization from the indigenous civilization and made them its own.

This was not unique to India. Islam, as is the case with all great world traditions, had always been very flexible in incorporating and integrating local traditions and customs. We only need to look as far as the great rituals of Hajj to find a Pre-Islamic tradition which was claimed (or rather, reclaimed) by the nascent Muslim community. Another example is the Prophet's reported commemoration of Passover (or more probably Yom Kippur) by instituting a fast on that day (actually predating the fast of Ramadan). As Islam spread throughout much of the world, many local traditions and celebrations were tolerated, if not wholeheartedly embraced by the local polity.This is of course part of the normal fusion that exists in most cultures, not least among them Islamic ones (witness the modern-day Egyptian celebrations of Shamm an-Nasim, Iranian celebrations of Nauroz, the continuation of Ismaili traditions in contemporary popular celebrations of the Prophet's birthday in Egypt, and the like.).

A second view is that in the course of its journey through Persia, Islam had already imbibed the notion of social hierarchy. As such, by the time Islam entered India the notion of gradation of social groups into a hierarchy had already become a part of its cultural inheritance and therefore it had no difficulty in incorporating the caste system in India. From this perspective, it would seem that caste among Muslims in India was not only a consequence of local Hindu influence, but a form of social organization that had already become accepted through its cultural contact with other Muslim cultures which had evolved hierarchical structures. It therefore had no difficulty in adjusting to the Hindu caste system. My personal view is that when dealing with a complex institution such as caste among Muslims in India it would be futile to argue that this can be solely explained in terms of Hindu influence or Islam's contact with other cultures in the course of its journey into India. It would appear that the caste phenomenon among Muslims must be explained both in terms of external as well as indigenous influences.

Orthodox Muslims and champions of religious reform argue that caste among Muslims in India is a temporary anomaly susceptible to eventual elimination through reformist efforts. They insist that the process of Islamization,[4] understood as a tendency entailing a conscious rejection of syncretic elements that persist as remnants of pre-conversion orientations and ethos, would result in a gradual elimination of caste among Muslims in India. Islamization has not always been found to result in the spread of orthodox Islamic beliefs and practices at the cost of what is called the heterodox or syncretic complex. Satish C. Misra suggested some years ago that it was wrong to conceptualize the process of religious change in Indian Muslim society simply in terms of

4. There are two processes at work in Muslim society in India: Ashrafization and Islamization. Ashrafization denotes emulation by the lower castes of the lifestyle and manners of the upper castes in a bid to achieve social mobility. Islamization denotes shedding heterodox beliefs and practices in favour of those prescribed in scriptural sources. 'The typical mode of Islamization,' as Clifford Geertz had noted in the Indonesian context, was visualized as being painfully gradual. First comes the Confession of faith, then the other pillars of the faith, then a certain degree of observance of the law, and finally, perhaps, especially as a scholarly tradition develops and takes hold, a certain degree of assimilation of the law and the Qur an, and Hadith upon which it rests. The intricate norms, or at least of Sunni Islam, can be apprehended only step by step, as one masters, to a greater or lesser degree, the scriptural sources upon which it rests. For most people, such control never goes beyond accepting, at second hand, the interpretations of those who directly control those sources. That learning, however crude, and access to scholarship, however shabby, are central to becoming a Muslim in anything more than a formal sense, and is apparent everywhere in the Islamic world. . . Islamic conversion is not, as a rule, a sudden, total, overwhelming illumination but a slow turning toward a new light (1965: 96-7).

Islamization (Misra, 1964: 185–7). He distinguished two processes that had been, according to him, operating throughout the Medieval period, and he called them indigenization and Islamization. This enabled the elements of the heterodox religious complex to persist alongside the orthodox without any apparent indications of conflict or contradiction. This is as true of caste as other folk elements among Muslims in India.

Let me conclude by making two points. One, any consideration of caste among the Muslims at once raises the question whether the term caste can be applied to the system of social stratification of a community which professes a faith other than Hinduism. Leach (1960) has raised this question about whether caste is best considered as a cultural or structural phenomenon. There are two broad points of view on this question. On the one hand, there are some who, following Weber (1947: 396), take the position that caste is a fundamental institution of Hinduism and its use should be restricted to Hindus or at best to social groups which, though professing other faiths, live with or near Hindu communities, within what Dumont (1957) calls the 'Pan Indian civilization' (see, for this point of view, Leach, 1960, Srinivas et al., 1959, and Dumont, 1970). On the other hand, a second group of sociologists and social anthropologists defines caste in structural terms so as to be applicable also to the relationship between two or more groups in other religions and societies (see Bailey, 1963, Berreman, 1960, and Harper, 1968).

Caste first came to be identified as a principle of social stratification amongst Hindus and this has had a determining influence on the sociologists' orientation to the question of the application of the term caste to groups outside Hinduism. Even those who take a purely structural view of the institution recognize that there are limits beyond which a social system cannot differ and yet still merit the label 'caste.' Moreover, while analysing systems of social stratification in other religions and societies, they tend quite unconsciously to follow a culture-specific definition of the institution and base their discussion on the Hindu phenomenon. Obviously, then, a consideration of caste among Muslims would need to be based not on purely structural criteria but rather on the degree to which their social stratification displays principles and features characteristically associated with caste among Hindus.

There has been much fresh thinking on this subject in recent years. According to this, caste systems are defined as moral systems that differentiate and rank the entire population of a society in corporate units generally defined by descent, marriage, and occupation (see Marriot and Inden, 1974). It is contended that caste systems need not be thought of as being unique to South Asia or to its emigrants but may be more widely encountered. From this perspective, caste among Muslims in India can be seen as an independent system and not merely as an extension of the Hindu caste system.

The study of Muslims and Islam has traditionally been a province of the Islamicists and Muslim theologians. Sociologists and social anthropologists have paid comparatively little attention to the subject. The reason for this academic division of labour is easily understandable. The fundamental theological and philosophical principles that can be said to constitute the core of the Islamic faith are enshrined in a single scriptural source and are supposed to be universally adhered to by all those who call themselves Muslims. This reinforced the belief amongst sociologists and social anthropologists that the Islamicists' understanding of the religious faith of the Muslims could be viewed as being entirely accurate and valid, especially as the sociologist or social anthropologist could not, in any case, match the Islamicists' expertize in handling textual materials.

Undoubtedly the Islamicist's contribution to the study of Islam has been considerable. Through painstaking study of the textual sources and scriptural literature they have been successful in identifying and elucidating for us the fundamental Islamic precepts and rules to which every Muslim is universally expected to adhere. Unfortunately, however, the rigidly normative thrust of this approach has also prevented an appreciation of the bewildering diversity of beliefs, rituals, and religious practices that underlies the faith in different parts of the world. It has also inhibited a satisfactory analysis of the response of the Islamic religious tradition to different cultural situations and contexts, and the adaptations and adjustments that it had to make in the course of its journey from its West Asian heartland to distant parts of the world.

Sociology and social anthropology are committed, as academic disciplines, to the empirical investigation of the social phenomenon. Where religion in concerned, they are concerned not so much with the theological and philosophical tenets of a particular religion but rather with the concrete form that those tenets take in the actual life of the people. Sociological or social anthropological analysis of religion thus covers the entirety of a people's beliefs and practices towards the supernatural as well as the purpose to which they may put their faith in dealing with their daily concerns and hopes. Thus, the sociological or social anthropological understanding of religion is at once more comprehensive and more concrete. Further studies on Muslims in India by sociologists and social anthropologists are necessary for a more accurate picture to emerge.

REFERENCES

Ansari, Ghaus (1959), *Muslim Castes in Uttar Pradesh: A Study in Culture Contact,* Lucknow, Ethnographic and Folk Culture Society.

Bailey, F.G. (1963), 'Closed Social Stratification in India', *European Journal of Sociology,* 4: 107–24.

Benur, Fakruddin (2004), 'The Dynamics of Caste Problems of the Indian Muslims', Paper presented at a seminar on Dalit Muslims organized by Deshkal Society, New Delhi.

Berreman, G.D. (1960), 'Caste in India and the United States', *American Journal of Sociology,* 66: 120–7.

Dumont, L. (1957), 'For a Sociology of India', *Contribution to Indian Sociology,* 1: 7–22.

——— (1970), *Homo Hierarchicus: The Caste System and its Implications,* Delhi, Vikas Publishing House.

Falahi, Masood (2009), *Hindustan Mein Zaat Paat aur Musalman* (Urdu), Mumbai, Ideal Foundation.

Farooqui, Jalil (1989), 'Caste and Indian Muslims', *Journal of Objective Studies,* Vol. 1, nos. 1 & 2.

Gaborieau, Marc (1978), *Ni Brahamnes Ni Ancetres,* Paris, Maison de Sciences d'la *Hommes.*

Harper, E.B. (1968), 'A Comparative Analysis of Caste: The United States and India', in Milton Singer and B.S. Cohn (eds.), *Structure and Change in Indian Society,* Chicago, Aldine Publishing Company.

Hasnain, Nadeem (2005), 'Muslims in India: Caste Affinity and Social Boundaries of Backwardness', in H.S. Verma (ed.), *The OBCs and the Ruling Classes in India,* Jaipur, Rawat Publications.

Leach, E.R. (1960), 'Introduction', in E.R. Leach (ed.), *Aspects of Caste in South India, Ceylon and North-West Pakistan,* London, Cambridge University Press.

Lindholm, Charles (1965), 'Paradigms of Society: A Critique of Theories of Caste Among Indian Muslims', *European Journal of Sociology*, pp. 131–40.

Marriot, McKim, and Ronald E. Inden (1974), 'Caste Systems', *Encyclopaedia Britannica*, 15th ed., Macropaedia, Vol. 3, Chicago, Helen Hemingway Benton, pp. 982–91.

Misra, S.C. (1964), *Muslim Communities in Gujarat*, Bombay, Asia Publishing House.

Momin, A.R. (1989), 'Islamic Egalitarianism vs Social Hierarchy: Reflections on Caste Among Indian Muslims', *Journal of Objective Studies*, Vol. 1, nos. 1 & 2.

Nazir, Parvaiz (1993), 'Social Structure, Ideology and Language: Caste Among Muslims', *Economic and Political Weekly*, Vol. xxviii, no. 52, 25 Dec.

Sikand, Yoginder (2005), *Islam, Caste and Dalit-Muslim Relations in India*, Delhi, Global Media Publications.

Sorokin, Pitirim A. (1959), *Social and Cultural Mobility*, New York, The Free Press.

Srinivas, M.N. et al. (1959),'Caste: A Trend Report and Bibliograpy' *Current Sociology*, 8: 135–85.

Veblen, Thorstein (1999), *The Theory of the Leisure* Class, New York, Macmillan.

Weber, Max (1947), *From Max Weber: Essays in Sociology*, H.H. Gerth and C.W. Mills, eds. and trans., London, Routledge & Kegan Paul.

Introduction

Imtiaz Ahmad

There is a rich and voluminous sociological literature on caste in India. But the great bulk of this literature is confined to the study and analysis of caste as it functions among the Hindus. Caste as it exists and functions among the Muslims and other non-Hindu groups of Indian society has not been studied in equal detail by sociologists and social anthropologists although it has often been recognized that their social structures are also organized according to caste principles.[1] One of the obvious consequences of this almost total absence of sociological information on caste among non-Hindu groups has been that we know relatively little about the nature and form of their social stratification and about the extent to which caste among them is comparable to caste among the Hindus.

This collection of papers on caste and social stratification among the Muslims was planned with a view to bringing

[1]Ghaus Ansari's *Muslim Caste in Uttar Pradesh* (1960) has been the only reference on caste among the Muslims for over two decades. Ansari's source materials were censuses and reports of British administrative officials which were always superficial, and occasionally, not quite accurate. The kind of data which Ansari used led him to view castes as separate entities and he did not realize sufficiently that caste was a highly localized phenomenon and needed to be analyzed within the context of a local community. It must, nevertheless, be admitted that Ansari was the first sociologist to focus on the presence of caste among the Muslims.

together studies dealing with the structure and functioning of social stratification among Muslims in particular localities so that we could form some idea of the extent to which caste could be said to be in existence among them and to explore the degree of the similarity of their social stratification to caste among the Hindus. Although each contributor has written about these questions from a personal, individual point of view, certain interesting generalizations emerge from their joint discussions, and in this Introduction I shall try to set them out briefly. I should stress, however, that the conclusions suggested by these papers should still be taken as largely tentative. We would need a larger number of individual studies of particular communities in different parts of India than are included here before we can hope to reach anywhere close to a comprehensive and complete understanding of this complex social institution.

A consideration of caste among the Muslims at once raises the question whether the term caste can be applied to the system of social stratification of a community which professes a faith other than Hinduism. Leach (1960:2) has raised this question as to whether caste is best considered as a cultural or as a structural phenomenon. There are two broad points of view on this question. On the one hand, there are some who, following Weber (see Weber, 1947:396), take the position that caste is a fundamental institution of Hinduism and its use should be restricted to Hindus or at best to social groups which, though professing other faiths, live with or near Hindu communities, within what Dumont (1957) calls the 'Pan Indian civilization' (see, for this point of view, Leach, 1960, Srinivas, *et.al.*, 1959, and Dumont, 1970). On the other hand, a second group of sociologists and social anthropologists defines caste in structural terms so as to be applicable to the relationship between two or more groups in other religions and societies as well (see Bailey, 1963, Berreman, 1960, and Harper, 1968).

Caste first came to be identified as a principle of social stratification among the Hindus and this fact has had a determining influence on the sociologists' orientation to the question of the application of the term caste to groups outside Hinduism. Even those who take a purely structural view of the institution recognize that there are limits beyond which a social system cannot differ and yet still deserve the label 'caste'. Moreover, while analyzing systems of social stratification in other religions and societies, they tend quite unconsciously to follow a culture-specific definition of the institution and base their discussion on the Hindu phenomenon. Obviously, then, a consideration of caste among the Muslims would require to be based not on purely structural criteria but rather on the degree to which their social stratification displays principles and features characteristically associated with caste among the Hindus.

This is also the view taken by most of the contributors to this volume. The majority of them base their definition of caste on the Hindu phenomenon and then go on to examine the extent to which the social stratification of the communities studied by them corresponds to the Hindu model. Even Aggarwal, who begins his analysis of the Meos with a fairly broad structural definition of caste as 'a ranked social division in which membership is determined by birth' (p. 142), comes increasingly, as his analysis proceeds, to see the Meos in terms of the cultural characteristics of caste and finally employs the degree of correspondence between them and Hindu caste groups as a basis for characterizing them as a caste. But while there is this general agreement among them on the question of definition and on the basis of specific characteristics as a way of establishing degrees of comparableness with caste among the Hindus, they are clearly divided on whether the systems of social stratification described by them can be compared to the Hindu caste system.

Mines' view is that the system of social stratification among Tamil Muslims is not comparable in any respect to the Hindu caste system. He contends that the different Muslim subdivisions described by him are not ranked hierarchically and are regarded as approximately of equal status, though there is ranking of individuals in terms of age, wealth and religiousness, etc., (p. 162). Again, he argues that, though endogamy occurs, the overriding concern for endogamy is not on account of a 'desire to maintain purity of blood, as one would expect to find associated with the system of Hindu caste ranking', but rather arises from a tendency to match spouses who 'share the same economic background and the same cultural and, particularly, religious traditions' (p. 164). I am personally unable to accept Mines' explanation about the incidence of endogamy and I also suspect that the evidence presented by him does not completely rule out the presence of hierarchical ranking and caste considerations among the Tamil Muslims. He himself mentions at one place (p. 162) that the Kayalars are regarded as being of lower status since their occupation is considered undesirable by the members of the other Muslim groups, although unfortunately he does not elaborate his statement. On the whole, however, his contention is that the Tamil Muslim subdivisions in Pallavaram cannot be considered Muslim prototypes of Hindu castes.

All other contributors are of the view that the system of social stratification among the Muslim communities studied by them is certainly comparable to the Hindu caste system though an exact parallel between them cannot be said to exist. This is evident both from the manner in which they title their papers as well as their explicit statements and the logic of their arguments. For example, Bhattacharya designates the system of social stratification among the Muslims of rural West Bengal as a system of inter-ethnic stratification rather than as a caste system and justifies this usage on the ground that it 'shares certain features of the caste system but is not quite like it' (p. 270). Similarly, Dube suggests that the social groups she describes from the Laccadive Islands off the south-west coast of India are analogous to caste among the Hindus but do not correspond to it in every detail. Clearly, the hesitation on the part of our contributors to characterize the social stratification of the Muslims as a caste system arises from the fact that some of the characteristics of caste are missing in each situation.

Caste among the Hindus is usually defined in terms of a list of cultural characteristics or traits which are supposed to form a syndrome (Leach, 1960:2). While admitting a great range of detailed variation, the authorities have mostly maintained that the minimal set of primary characteristics which together constitute the real essence of caste among the Hindus are the following (see Hutton, 1946:49; and Ghurye, 1950):

(1) A caste is endogamous.
(2) It involves occupational specialization.
(3) Castes are hierarchically ordered.
(4) Caste has an ideological, religious basis involving restriction on social intercourse and commensality.

Exceptions and modification in some of these features can be found in various parts of India, particularly in the urban areas (Kapadia, 1958: 119ff.).

Let us now consider the evidence in the case of Muslims. The picture presented by our contributors is that Muslim groups are endogamous. Occasionally, marriages between two or more social divisions are allowed, especially at the higher levels, but the evidence presented clearly suggests that such marriages are greatly restricted and occur mostly between groups of more or less equal status. Bhattacharya claims that rules regarding inter-group marriages are in any case largely theoretical as 'there is no evidence to suggest that these rules have ever been put to a test' (p. 289fn). He concludes that local Muslim groups in rural West Bengal may conveniently be regarded as endogamous units. Endogamy among castes occurs even in the metropolitan situation described by Siddiqui. 'Inter-ethnic marriages, in spite of similarity in class status, are severely discouraged' (p. 258). Siddiqui shows that endogamy obtains even among the immigrant groups. These, he suggests, live in Calcutta detached from their places of origin and periodically go back to them for important life cycle rituals, including marriage. Consequently, their marriages are also arranged according to the norms that govern the local situation and are usually endogamous. Where intermarriages take place across groups, as is illustrated by the case of the marriage of a local girl to an Afghan man, the girl is excluded from her parental family and retains practically no contact with it. It would seem that in all such situations the child belongs to the caste of one parent and the separate caste populations are maintained by this ascription.

There is, however, some difference of opinion among the contributors about the reasons for the occurrence of endogamy. As indicated earlier, Mines claims that endogamy occurs among the Tamil Muslims studied by him because of a concern among the families for matching spouses in terms of economic background and cultural and religious traditions. He rules out the possibility that endogamy among the groups studied by him has anything to do with the desire to maintain purity of blood. On the contrary, Siddiqui and Ahmad suggest that the occurrence of endogamy is underscored by the notion of ritual purity of blood. Siddiqui says that 'some sort of sanctity is attached to the purity of descent as is evident from the use of such terms as *sudh* as against *bisser* or impure, *najib-ut-tarfain* as against *birre* or *birrahe* i.e., of mixed descent' (p. 258). Ahmad shows that a notion of ritual purity not only occurs among the Sheikh Siddiquis but that it also constitutes the main source of the split between the two marriage circles (p. 199). He also points out that family genealogy is frequently used as a means of asserting this ritual purity of blood and bone, and that each family maintains a fairly detailed account of its descent and marriages as proof of its purity of blood. Siddiqui and Ahmad also indicate that the notion of ritual purity of blood is accompanied by a belief in the possibility of its pollution through intermarriage.

The picture in respect of occupational specialization is similar to endogamy. A close link between caste and hereditary occupation not only exists but also serves as the basis for an economic interdependence of castes. Bhatty's account of Kasauli in Uttar Pradesh and Aggarwal's discussion of the Meo village in Rajasthan provide evidence of the existence of a full-fledged *jajmani* system with the locally dominant caste serving as the nucleus of the exchange of goods and services. Moreover, both contributors also show that each caste is not only associated with a traditional occupation but that there is also a close correspondence between the actual and traditional occupations pursued by the different groups. So also is the picture suggested by Bhattacharya and Dube. Bhattacharya shows that each of the main groups resident in rural West Bengal is traditionally associated with a particular occupation which is frequently implied in its name and is closely tied to the system of exchange of goods and services characteristic of Hindu India. Similarly, Dube also points out that the Koyas, the Malumis and the Melacheris have specific occupations associated with them and attempts by some groups to break away from their traditional occupations and to encroach upon those of others have resulted in social tensions and strife. Siddiqui does not provide data on the link between caste and occupation, but it would be fair to assume that a close correspondence between caste and occupation does not exist in his field situation on account of the pressures of an industrial and urban economy. Evidence from other places suggests that particular trades and industrial activities tend to be monopolized by particular groups even in urban centres. Siddiqui, however, does not provide any indication of the occurrence of such a pattern.

There is a difference in the degree of correspondence between caste and traditional occupation at the various levels of the social hierarchy. Such links seem to be stronger at the bottom of the social hierarchy than at higher levels. For example, Bhattacharya points out that the upper groups in rural West Bengal do not claim any hereditary occupation and live mainly by agriculture, and Ahmad suggests that the Sheikh Siddiquis are not engaged in any particular traditional occupation though they were originally land record keepers. I am inclined to think, however, that this pattern does not constitute a basic departure from the Hindu caste pattern. A correspondence between caste and occupation is strikingly greater at the lower levels even among the Hindus, and even Hindu high and intermediate castes usually follow a more diversified pattern in occupational specialization. Moreover, occupational association is important not so much in the literal sense of who is engaged in it nor in the structural sense that there is an organically interdependent series of ascribed occupations, but rather in the sense that an occupation is hierarchically graded and thereby affects the status of the people belonging to the group traditionally associated with it (Mayer, 1967: 6-7).

The discussion of endogamy and occupational specialization brings us to the third feature of the Hindu caste, that of the hierarchy of groups. It is clear from the contributions to this volume that there is a notion of hierarchy among the Muslims, though it is hard to say how far the criterion of ranking amongst them can be said to conform to the Hindu model. Caste hierarchy among the Hindus is based on the relation between pure and impure, which leads to a hierarchy of status based on pollution. Our contributors are divided on the question of how far the notion of ritual purity and pollution can be said to exist among the Muslim castes. D'Souza, while admitting that the different Muslim social divisions in Karnataka and Kerala are hierarchically ranked, does not associate considerations of ritual purity and pollution with the basis of caste ranking. Dube points out that the social disabilities attached to the lower castes on the Laccadive Islands were an integral part of the deference structure. She says, 'Their violation did not indicate any possibility of pollution through touch or shadow, or through the sharing of air. Nor has any idea of pollution been attached to food. The Melacheris, as the servants of the Koyas, have always cooked for the feasts of the latter, and on the *odams* while sailing. The Koyas could eat food cooked at the houses of the Malumis or the Melacheris; singers, priests and religious specialists, and carpenters and masons, who were from among the Koyas, expected to be fed by these people during their professional visits. If in the past there was insistence on special seating and eating arrangements for the Koyas, it was a part of the deference structure, emphasizing inequality of status, *and it was not related in any way to considerations of ritual purity and pollution*' (italics mine; p. 78).

On the other hand, Siddiqui and Bhattacharya are inclined to feel that considerations of ritual purity and pollution are present in the case of the Muslims. Siddiqui shows that the most common pattern of interdining is the one confined to one's kin group or known range within the kin group. 'The symbolic ritual quality of the members of an ethnic group is expressed in such terms as *tat* or *chatai* upon which members can sit, smoke and eat together' (p. 260). He, however, admits that the idea of pollution in matters of interdining is limited to 'clean' castes with regard to the 'unclean' ones. Thus, members of groups within the higher categories do not eat or drink with the Lal Begis, a caste of Muslim scavangers. The Dafalis, who work as priests for Lal Begis, or the Qalandars who sometimes live in their neighbourhood, refuse to accept food or water from Lal Begis. Bhattacharya does not find any direct evidence of the notion of ritual pollution but nevertheless feels that such a notion is present in the relations of Muslim groups. For example, he claims that the emphasis placed by the higher castes on cleanliness and sense of hygiene as reasons for refusing to eat with the Momins, Patuas and Shahs arises from ritual considerations. 'In reality', he says, 'they have a concept of ritual purity and pollution' (p. 291).

It is quite likely that the emphasis placed by Muslim groups on ritual considerations in West Bengal is a regional variation. Such regional variations are occasionally to be found in the case of the Hindus as well. For instance, Srinivas *et. al.* suggest that the ritual aspect of caste has received greater attention from students of South Indian communities than it has from those working in other parts of the country (see Srinivas *et.al.*, 1959: 147; also see Dumont, 1970:134-36), and I suspect that the ritual dimension is much more developed in South India than in other parts of India. But there is unmistakable evidence even in the data provided by Siddiqui and Bhattacharya themselves that the notion of ritual purity and pollution is not as elaborate among the Muslims as it is among the Hindus. As a matter of fact, it is considerably weak, so weak that it is not immediately obvious and must be inferred from indirect evidence.

Because the ritual dimension of caste is weak among the Muslims, ranking of castes is based quite frequently on a number of non-ritual criteria. D'Souza lists four principal criteria of social ranking among the Moplah Muslims. These are: (a) hypergamy; (b) the amount of dower payable by the husband to his wife in the event of a divorce; (c) use of special articles of distinction; and (d) segregation and restrictions on social intercourse (pp. 47-9). Bhattacharya mentions as criteria of ranking the seclusion of women (purdah), performance of ablutions after urination and the observance of daily prayers. Siddiqui suggests that ranking is based on the nature of occupation, the comparative numerical strength of the groups, and descent. Ahmad mentions descent, particularly the source from which it is traced and its distance from Muhammad, as well as the degree of Islamization of customs and ritual practices of the group. According to Dube, social ranking on the Laccadive Islands is based on hypergamy, the nature of occupation and the relative standing of the caste in the politico-economic structure. Such ranking criteria naturally allow for a greater interplay of wealth, prestige and status honour in the determination of the status of castes and individuals.

Several contributors note the occurrence of a pattern of hypergamy among Muslim groups. Ahmad provides detailed data on the pattern of hypergamous marriages and shows how hypergamy has been used by the socially mobile Sheikh Siddiquis as a means of social climbing in their search for a new status identity. Bhattacharya describes how Sayyad men are allowed to marry women of lower groups but Sayyad women cannot marry below their group. Dube points out that Koya men can marry Malumi women but the marriage of Koya women with Malumi or Melacheri men is severely discouraged. Such discouragement is also characteristic of the Moplah social divisions described by D'Souza. Unfortunately, the authors have not provided specific details on when such marriages can take place at all. Such details would have greatly illuminated the hierarchical principle. Also, one would have liked to have correlations of the various types of marriages with the non-caste attributes, such as wealth and education, of the partners as well as with the caste membership of off-springs. Such evidence as is available nevertheless clearly suggests that the pattern of hypergamous marriages issues largely from hierarchical caste considerations in matchmaking and hypergamy is a significant expression of hierarchy.

Caste among the Hindus is based on a religious philosophy which supports social divisions, and certain theological notions serve to reinforce them (see Dumont, 1970: 36-39). 'Certain Hindu theological notions like *karma* and *dharma*', writes Srinivas, 'have contributed very greatly to the strengthening of the idea of hierarchy which is inherent in the caste system. The idea of *karma* teaches a Hindu that he is born in a particular sub-caste because he deserved to be born there. The actions he performed in a previous incarnation deserved such a reward or punishment, as the case might be. If he had performed better actions in his previous incarnation he would have been born in a higher caste. Thus the caste hierarchy comes to be an index of the state of an individual's soul. It also represents certain milestones on the soul's journey to God' (Srinivas, 1952:25). 'The other important concept', Srinivas goes on, 'is *dharma* which has many meanings one of which is "that which is right or moral". The existing moral code is identified with *dharma*. A man who accepts the caste system and the rules of his particular sub-caste is living according to *dharma*, while a man who questions them is violating *dharma*. Living according to *dharma* is rewarded, while violation of *dharma* is punished both here and hereafter. If he observes the rules of *dharma* he will be born in his next incarnation in a high caste, rich, whole, and well-endowed. If he does not observe them he will be born in a low caste, poor, deformed, and ill-endowed. Worldly position and success indicate the kind of life a man led in his previous incarnation' (Srinivas, 1952:26). Indeed, the religious and philosophical basis of Hindu caste is so pronounced that Bergel feels that 'The caste system cannot be understood unless it is recognized as a religious institution' (1962:37), and Dumont sees the religious opposition of pure and impure as the fundamental structure which gives the social system its unique form (Dumont, 1970).

All the contributors to this volume are agreed that the Hindu ideological justification of the caste system does not exist in the case of Muslims. Aggarwal cites the Koranic verse which explicitly rejects gradation of groups and individuals in terms of birth and the ideology of pure and impure and suggests that the only criterion of social evaluation recognized in Islam is religious piety (p. 141). Bhattacharya notes that the formal religious values of Islam are opposed to any rigid system of ethnic and social stratification as the Islamic Great Tradition does not offer any sanction for it. Siddiqui also asserts that the existence of an hierarchical order generally receives overt denial from the great traditional values of the Muslims. But the evidence presented by these and other contributors clearly indicates that, while the formal religious ideology to which all Muslims claim adherence denies caste distinctions, there is another alternative ideology which recognizes such distinctions and according to which observable social inequalities are correlated to Islamic tenets. Bhattacharya thus points out: 'To my mind, inequalities in the social status of different Muslim ethnic groups, in contrast to their conscious Islamic model of an egalitarian society, make them mentally insecure. They try to overcome this mental dilemma caused by a sharp contrast between their ideology and practised pattern by rethinking the undeniable social fact of status inequality in terms of suitable idioms that can be successfully related to their traditions' (p. 294). Bhattacharya goes on to suggest that these idioms are often inadequate as explanations for the complex nature of Muslim social hierarchy and the presence of caste features in their social life, but the significant point is that such idioms nevertheless exist. It shows that, if the formal Islamic ideology rejects caste, the actual beliefs held by the Muslims not only recognize caste distinctions but also seek to rationalize them in religious terms.[2] Presumably, it is this

[2]Among all the writers on caste among the Muslims, Dumont alone

rationalization that has, as Siddiqui suggests towards the end of his paper, allowed caste distinctions among the Muslims to persist without much evidence of internal conflict (p. 267).

What conclusion can we, then, draw from the evidence presented in this volume about caste among the Muslims? It is clear that caste exists as a basis of social relations amongst them, but its form has been greatly weakened and modified and it differs from the Hindu caste model in certain details. The principal points of difference are four. Firstly, the acceptance of the caste principle among the Muslims is considerably weak and does not enjoy any sanction or justification in their great traditional religious ideology. Secondly, while both the Hindu and Muslim systems of social stratification resemble each other in the pattern of endogamy, a keen sense of pride in birth and descent and a notion of hierarchy, caste among the Muslims has not attained the degree of elaborateness characteristic of the Hindu model. Thirdly, caste status among the Muslims does not rest on an ideology of pure and impure so that Muslim castes observe social distance on the basis of deference, privileges and descent. This allows for a greater interplay of wealth and other secular factors in status determination. Lastly, among the Muslims there is no ritually pure caste like the Brahmins with dispensations and obligations which may be peculiar to them. The Sayyads, who enjoy a prominent place among the Muslims on account of their descent, lack the charisma which has given Brahmins their unique place in the Hindu social system (for a discussion of the position of the Brahmin in Hinduism, see Dumont, 1970:62-78).

Our conclusion that caste exists among the Muslims at once raises the question whether it owes itself directly to the acculturative influence of Hinduism, or are there some elements within Islam itself which support such distinctions. The common view in this connection seems to be that caste is directly attributable to the acculturative influence of Hinduism (see, for instance, Ansari, 1960:96; Srinivas *et. al.*, 1959:149; Misra, 1964; and Dumont, 1970:205-12). Srinivas *et. al.* suspect that 'It is likely

seems to be conscious of this dichotomy of values. He notes that 'lying beneath the ultimate or Islamic values are other values presupposed by actual behaviour' (Dumont, 1970:211).

that Hindus who were converted to Islam continued to regard themselves as castes, while foreign, conquering groups of Muslims, like Arabs and Pathans, fell into the position of upper castes' (1959:149). Dumont thinks that caste was consciously adopted by the Muslims in India as a compromise which they had to make in a predominantly Hindu environment. After tracing the conflicting nature of the two groups, he suggests that Hindus and Muslims in India entered a sort of tacit and reciprocal compromise. On the one hand, the Hindus adjusted themselves to political masters who did not recognize Brahmanic values and 'they did not treat even the most humble Muslim villagers as Untouchables' (1970:205-206). On the other hand, the influence of caste made itself felt among the Muslims. Dumont traces the acceptance of the caste principle by the Muslims to the proximity of the Hindu environment which predominates both generally and regionally (Dumont, 1970:270). Bhattacharya shows that the Muslims also view the existence of caste among them as resulting from Hindu influence (p. 293).

The large majority of the Muslims in India were originally recruited to Islam from the intermediate and lower rungs of Hindu society wherein status was rigidly defined in terms of birth and maintained by strong social sanctions. When these groups became incorporated into Muslim society through conversions either by peaceful persuasion or by threats of force or by offers of material and political advantages or by aspirations of social mobility, they must have imported their social system with them. Since much of the early conversion to Islam was a group process, this must have been easy. Some acculturative influence of Hinduism was thus inevitable. But if caste among the Muslims owed itself entirely to Hindu influence, then the Islamization of Muslim groups over the centuries should have resulted in the slow and gradual elimination of caste principles and ideology. However, such evidence as is available suggests that Islamization serves to reinforce rather than weaken or eliminate caste distinctions. Consequently, the question whether there are some elements in Islam which support caste distinctions becomes relevant.

Limitations of space preclude a detailed discussion of this question here, but a general point is worth noting briefly. Islam is claimed by its adherents to be an egalitarian religion and there is scarcely any doubt that an early Koranic verse denounced all distinctions based on birth and pride of ancestry (Levy, 1962:155). But the proclaimed egalitarianism of Islam remained largely an ideal. The system of local groups with emphasis upon birth and unity of blood (Smith, 1903:1), which had existed in Arab society before the coming of Islam, survived the egalitarian preaching of the Koran. Paradoxically, Muhammad himself became the basis of a status system wherein kinship with him came to be regarded 'as the touchstone of true nobility, and even the slight degree of relationship to him which was implied in fellow-membership of his tribe—that of the Quraysh—was regarded as a patent of high distinction' (Levy, 1962:56).

This emphasis upon birth and ancestry acquired acceptance in Islamic law as time went by. Muhammad, whose statement 'There are no genealogies in Islam' is widely cited as evidence of his belief in the equality of all believers, himself suggested that considerations of birth should receive special attention in the instance of marriage. According to a tradition, he is supposed to have taught, 'Take ye care, that none contract in marriage but their proper guardians, and that they be not so contracted except with equals' (Bukhari, 1862:436). Basing themselves on this very principle, Muslim jurists worked out an elaborate scheme of social grades of birth and descent. Thus, according to the Hanafiites, six elements were necessary to produce equality of status of which descent was the most important. These elements were used to elaborate rules which could be followed in establishing the precedence of groups. According to these rules (a) an Arab was superior to a non-Arab; (b) amongst Arabs, all Quraishites were of equal social standing in a class by themselves, and all other Arabs were equal irrespective of their tribes; (c) amongst non-Arabs, a man was by birth the equal of an Arab if both his father and grandfather had been Muslims before him, but only if he were sufficiently wealthy to provide an adequate *mahr* (marriage endowment); (d) a learned non-Arab was equal to an ignorant Arab, even if he was a descendant of Ali, 'for the worth of learning is greater than the worth of family'; and (e) a Muslim *kazi* or theologian ranked higher than a merchant and a merchant higher than a tradesman (see Levy, 1962:63; also see Karim, 1957:87). The Shafiites, who followed the Hanafiites, likewise admitted the significance of birth as a criterion of social precedence (see Dube, pp. 92-3). The Malikiites, a great many of whom were negroes and whom the Arabs definitely considered as of inferior social status, alone stood by the spirit of egalitarianism which rules in principle (Levy, 1962:63). Clearly, then, Islamic law as practised in India would seem to support caste distinctions based on birth and descent, and there is some evidence that it was used to justify a rigid social stratification in Indo-Muslim society from time to time (see, for instance, Ashraf, 1959:61-3; Nizami, 1961:105-6 and Misra, 1963:25-26, and 1964).

Khan has stated that 'even if there were no caste influence on Muslim peasantries in India and Pakistan, the social structure would still be as rigidly stratified as it is now, resulting from a strict adherence to precedent recognized by Islamic societies as well as Islamic jurisprudence' (Khan, 1968). This statement seems highly debatable. In order to establish its validity, it would be necessary to prove that social stratification in the Muslim countries which lie outside the so-called 'Pan Indian civilization' displays similar social rigidities as those found in the Indian situation. However, the available evidence shows that Muslim social stratification elsewhere does not approximate even remotely to the Indian model. It seems to me, therefore, that a more reasonable conclusion would be that caste among the Muslims in India owes itself directly to Hindu influences, but it has been reinforced by the justification offered for the idea of birth and descent as criteria of status in Islamic law.

Caste has been viewed by most contributors to this volume as a form of social stratification. Masselos has, however, dealt with caste as a principle of social identification. He shows how the Khojas, who were a caste earlier, came increasingly to see themselves as a sectarian group as a result of the Aga Khan's effort to gain control over the Khoja caste organization. Caste, sect, and religion are three main primordial identities in terms of which a Muslim may see himself in Indian society. It is a common assumption among the writers on Muslims in India that these identities are mutually exclusive and the identity of the highest level tends to supersede the ones below it. Mines, thus, writes, 'Given the contrasts between Muslim Tamil and Hindu Tamil ethos and social structures, one might expect the Muslims to identify themselves less with their Hindu neighbours than with their cohorts in religion, the greater Indian Muslim population' (p. 165). It is, however, possible that caste, sectarian and religious identities each exert pressure and categorize affiliations that vary from instance to instance, shaping the response of the individual Muslim according to differing situations. Perhaps, further research may delineate how and in what context each of these principles of social identity attains its real significance and meaning. This, however, was not the task to which the contributors to this volume had addressed themselves.

Bibliography

Ansari, G. (1960), *Muslim Caste in Uttar Pradesh: A Study in Culture Contact*, Lucknow, Ethnographic and Folk Culture Society.

Ashraf, K.M. (1959), *Life and Condition of the People of Hindustan*, New Delhi, Jiwan Prakashan.

Bailey, F.G. (1963), 'Closed Social Stratification in India', *European Journal of Sociology*, 4, pp. 107-124.

Bukhari (ed.), (1862), *Kitabul Munaqib*, Lyden, E.J. Brill.

Bergel, E.E. (1962), *Social Stratification*, New York, McGraw Hill.

Berreman, G.D. (1960), 'Caste in India and the United States', *American Journal of Sociology*, 66, pp. 120-27.

Dumont, L. (1957), 'For a Sociology of India', *Contribution to Indian Sociology*, No. 1, pp. 7-22.

———, (1970), *Homo Hierarchicus: The Caste System and its Implications*, Delhi, Vikas Publishing House.

Ghurye, G.S. (1950), *Caste and Class in India*, Bombay, Popular Prakashan.

Harper, E.B. (1968), 'A Comparative Analysis of Caste: The United States and India', in Milton Singer and B.S. Cohn (eds.), *Structure and Change in Indian Society*, Chicago, Aldine Publishing Company.

Hutton, J.H. (1946), *Caste in India: Its Nature, Function and Origin*, London, Cambridge University Press.

Kapadia, K.M. (1958), *Marriage and Family in India*, London, Oxford University Press.

Karim, Nazmul (1957), *Changing Society in India and Pakistan*, Dacca, Oxford University Press.

Khan, Zillur R. (1968), 'Caste and Muslim Peasantries of India and Pakistan', *Man in India*, 47, pp. 138-48.

Leach, E.R. (1960), 'Introduction', In E.R. Leach (ed.), *Aspects of Caste in South India, Ceylon and North-West Pakistan*, London, Cambridge University Press.

Levy, R. (1962), *Social Structure of Islam*, London, Cambridge University Press.

Mayer, Adrian C. (1967), 'Introduction', in B.M. Schwartz (ed.), *Caste in Overseas Indian Communities*, San Francisco, Chandler Publishing Company.

Misra, S.C. (1963), *The Rise of Muslim Power in Gujarat*, Bombay, Asia Publishing House.

———(1964), *Muslim Communities in Gujarat*, Bombay, Asia Publishing House.

Nizami, K.A. (1961), *Some Aspects of Religion and Politics in India during the Thirteenth Century*, Aligarh, Department of History, Aligarh Muslim University.

Smith, W. Robertson (1903), *Kinship and Marriage in Early Arabia*, London, A and C Black Ltd.

Srinivas, M.N. (1952), *Religion and Society among the Coorgs of South India*, Oxford, Oxford University Press.

Srinivas, M.N. *et. al.* (1959), 'Caste: A Trend Report and Bibliography', *Current Sociology*, 8, pp. 135-85.

Weber, Max (1947), *From Max Weber: Essays in Sociology*, H.H. Gerth and C.W. Mills (eds. and trans.), London, Routledge and Kegan Paul.

1

Elements of Caste among the Muslims in a District in Southern Bihar[1]

Hasan Ali

As a member of the Muslim society of Ranchi I was conscious of the fact that, while Islam envisaged perfect equality among its followers, the society I inhabited was organized on the basis of separate endogamous groups, known locally as *beradaris*,[2] which bore a resemblance to caste. The caste system, as we are aware, is supposed to be primarily a pan-Hindu phenomenon with Hindu society as the archetype 'model'. However, a few studies on Muslim society, such as those by Ghaus

[1]The research on which this paper is based was carried out in connection with a research project of the Anthropological Survey of India, Calcutta, entitled 'The Muslims of Rural and Urban Ranchi: A Study of a Minority Community'. I wish to express my gratitude to Dr. S.C. Sinha, Director, Anthropological Survey of India, for his guidance throughout my research and helpful suggestions in the preparation of this paper. I also express my thanks to Dr. M.K.A. Siddiqui from whose suggestions I have greatly benefited.

[2]*Beradari* is the local term used to denote endogamous Muslim descent groups having a common traditional occupational background and it is widely used among the Muslims, both in the rural and urban areas. This connotation is also extended to mean the entire ethnic group beyond the local context. The endogamous Muslim *beradari* groups have been referred to in this paper as ethnic groups.

Ansari (1960) and Raghuraj Gupta (1956) on Uttar Pardesh, Misra (1964) on Gujarat, Z. Khan (1968) on the Punjab and Bengal and very recently Imtiaz Ahmad (1973) on various parts of India, suggest the presence of caste-like features among the Muslims of various parts of the Indian subcontinent.

It had always intrigued me as to how far the Muslim '*beradari* system' was structurally and functionally comparable to the Hindu 'model' of the caste system. It was also of significance to see what were the idioms and bases of rationalization of such a hierarchy among the Muslims as observed by several scholars, given the fact that Islam continually asserts the basic equality of all Muslims. With a view to probing into this problem in an actual field situation I selected a Muslim-dominated village, named Itki, about twenty-five kilometres north-west of Ranchi city, and Hindpidi, a Muslim-dominated section of Ranchi city in southern Bihar, for my research.[3]

Ethnic Composition of Itki and Hindpidi

Itki is a multi-ethnic[4] village with a predominant Muslim[5] population—168 Muslim families as compared to 56 Hindu and

[3]The total duration of my fieldwork was about ten months, divided into three different phases spread over a period of three years from 1967 to 1969. The field methods employed were filling of household census schedules as well as observation and interview. My community identity and the presence of seven ethnic groups in the village which I studied intensively and the even larger number of ethnic groups living in the closely knit urban neighbourhood of Hindpidi provided me with a good opportunity for studying their patterns of social stratification. The presence of the Muslim Bhangis, locally known as Halalkhor, was yet another important factor that enabled me to observe the inter-ethnic relationships of the Bhangis *vis-a-vis* the other ethnic groups among the Muslims.

[4]The term ethnic group has been used here and elsewhere in this paper in the sense in which it has been used by Marriott who considers it to be 'a hereditary group within a society which is defined by its members and by others as a separate people, socially, biologically and culturally; it need not be distinguishable in objective fact by any unique complex of cultural and biological traits' (Marriott, 1960: 2).

[5]The Muslims of both Itki and Hindpidi belong to a single religious sect, i.e., the Sunni sect.

9 tribal Oraon families (see Table 1). The total population of Itki is 1,587, which is distributed in 251 households. In Tables 2 and 3, the households of the Muslims and the Hindus have been analyzed on the basis of their *beradari*/caste affiliations. Among the tribals there are only 9 Oraon families. The Hindus and the tribal groups (mainly Oraons) are the main inhabitants of the villages in the immediate neighbourhood of Itki, though some of them also have a considerable number of Muslims.

TABLE 1
Hindus, Muslims and Tribals in Itki

Communities	*No. of families*	*Population*	*Percentage to total Population*
Muslim	186	1224	77.13
Hindu	56	314	19.79
Tribal (Oraon)	251	1587	3.08

TABLE 2
Muslim Ethnic Groups in Itki

Muslim ethnic Group	*Occupation*		*No. of families*	*Population*
	Traditional	*Present*		
Iraqi (Kalal)	Liquor Distillation	Agriculture Business	87	613
Ansari (Momin)	Weaving	Agriculture Business Weaving	71	424
Dafali	Drum-making & *Mujawari*	Agriculture Business	23	161
Pathan	Not wedded to specific occupation	Agriculture Business	2	11
Sayyad	Not wedded to specific occupation	Service	1	5
Faqir (Shah)	Mendicancy	Mendicancy	1	9
Chudihar	Glass bangle-selling	Service	1	1

At Hindpidi, a centrally located zone in Ranchi city, Muslims are numerically preponderant. According to a rough estimate there are about 1,000 Muslim households in Hindpidi,

TABLE 3
Hindu Castes in Itki

Caste	*Occupation*		*No. of families*	*Population*
	Traditional	*Present*		
Baniya	Business	Business Agriculture	12	77
Gadra	Blanket-weaving	Blanket weaving	12	49
Gorait		Manual Labour	8	34
Ahir	Milk selling	Agriculture	6	33
Teli	Oil-pressing	Oil-pressing Agriculture	5	34
Lohar	Blacksmithy	Blacksmithy	4	22
Dhobi	Laundry	Laundry	3	13
Brahmin	Priesthood	Priesthood, Business, Agriculture	2	27
Rajput	Rulers and Warriors	Agriculture	2	17
Chamar	Leather work	Leather work	1	8
Nai	Hair cutting	Hair cutting	1	10

which are divided into twelve endogamous ethnic groups. Of these, the Idrisis or Darzis (tailors) predominate numerically. Next in order come the Ansaris. The other Muslim ethnic groups are the Iraqi or Kalal, Pathan, Sayyad, Rai or Kunjra, Gaddi, Dafali, Bhangi or Halalkhor, Nai, Hawari or Dhobi and the Chick.

Both in the village as well as in Ranchi town, a visitor's first impression is normally of a marked egalitarian mode of social interaction in contrast to the caste-ridden Hindu villages. The local Muslims also emphasized the egalitarian aspects in such a way that it tended to obscure the hierarchic aspects of inter-*beradari* interactions.

The obviously egalitarian nature of inter-*beradari* interaction during religious activities made me come to the conclusion in the early phase of my fieldwork that *masawat*, i.e., equality of all Muslims, was practised and not just preached. My respondents, while denying the presence of caste stratification, indicated the existence of a dichotomous division of their society in terms of *amir* (rich) and *garib* (poor). They maintained that rank was judged and determined among the Muslims at the level of the individual and according to whether an individual led his life in accordance with the Shariat or not. In support of the theme of ideal equality of all Muslims, a few of the informed respondents even quoted a Koranic verse reiterating the equality of all believers.[6]

Thus local Muslims in general tended to deny the existence of caste among them even to a Muslim investigator and insisted that the *beradari* groups did not constitute castes. They asserted that there was no caste in Islam and claimed that all Muslims, irrespective of their *beradari* affiliation, could say *namaz* together and that they did not observe commensal restrictions among them. My informants tended to gloss over the practice of endogamy and, whenever it was mentioned, they maintained that there was no formal restriction on inter-ethnic marriages and that, in fact, Islam encouraged it. The existence of an inter-*beradari* hierarchy was also, at first, denied. Thus, the local Muslims very frequently emphasized the 'ideal' egalitarian concept of society, conveniently overlooking the fact that a social hierarchy was, indeed, prevalent among them. Of course, it was also observed that their reiteration of the ideal concept of equality was not altogether baseless. In fact, it has a considerable functional value which is reflected in some of the socio-religious aspects of their life. Their ideal model is, of course, wholly true so far as the religious sphere is concerned but is not so to the same degree in the other spheres of social life. However, when the anomalies between the 'ideal' and the 'practice' were distinctly shown, they admitted the social fact of their 'operational model'—the practice of endogamy, considerations of high and low, and inter-*beradari* commensal distance maintained by some groups in relation to certain others.

Let us first of all define more elaborately the nature of *beradari* as it is operative in the field of our study.

[6]'O mankind, we created you from a single pair of a male and a female and made you into nations and tribes that you may know each other (not that you may despise each other). Verily the most honoured of you in the sight of God is the one who is the most God-fearing of you' (Koran: S.X. 11 x 2 13: 1407. Tr. Abdullah Yusuf Ali).

Beradari, Zat or Jati

The term *'zat'* or *'jati'* is used both among the local Muslims as well as the Hindus to denote an endogamous ethnic group. The Muslims, however, prefer to use the term *beradari* to denote both the ethnic component of their society and the local units of larger ethnic groups embracing a wider region. Among the Muslims another term, i.e., *'qaum'*, is also used to denote the entire Muslim community within and beyond the village.

Though the term *beradari* in its entire connotation is not exactly identical to what is meant by the term caste, yet in its inner structure it exhibits the fundamental characteristics of caste—membership is determined only by birth, the group boundaries are maintained through endogamy, and group councils and occupational specialization are present. However, violations of the rules of endogamy are not dealt with in an identical manner; they range from mere censorship to ostracism. The inter-*beradari*, inter-commensal distance maintained by the high *beradari* groups, who consider themselves socially superior in relation to certain other *beradari* groups, is significant enough to be taken into account. Distinct styles of life can also be seen to operate among high and low *beradari* groups. The notion of an inter-*beradari* hierarchy, though a highly controversial point, may also be said to exist.

Taking into consideration the basic attributes of the caste system, let us now in the light of our field situation examine in greater detail the *beradari* system and see to what extent it corresponds to as well as differs from the caste system. The Muslims of Itki village and of Hindpidi have been stratified into seven and twelve endogamous groups respectively.

Endogamy is one of the major attributes of the caste system. Endogamy, though contrary to the spirit of Islam, is strictly followed among the local Muslim ethnic groups both in the rural and urban settings and tends to approximate to the norm of caste endogamy. This, in my view, is the most important factor upholding *beradari* consciousness and maintaining the distinctiveness of groups among the various Muslim ethnic categories. Despite the commonly held views on the desirability of inter-ethnic marriages, inter-*beradari* marriages are discouraged despite similarity in class status. Among the Gaddis, for example, marriage even with a Sayyad is vehemently opposed. The Gaddis are invariably ostracized by their *beradari* panchayat for marrying outside and non-Gaddi Muslims are always distinguished and are known as *parwin*.

Instances of inter-*beradari* marriages have been remarkably few. Table 4 shows that of the 186 Muslim families in Itki consisting of 1224 individuals and comprising seven ethnic groups only three cases of inter-marriage were recorded.

TABLE 4

Cases of Inter-*beradari* Marriages at Itki

Beradari to which the groom belongs	*The Area the groom belongs to*	*Beradari to which the bride belongs*	*The Area the bride belongs to*	*Year of Marriage*
Ansari	Itki	Pathan	Delhi	1960
Dafali	Itki	Iraqi	Balsokra	1966
Ansari	Hazaribagh	Iraqi	Itki	1968

These cases of inter-*beradari* or inter-ethnic marriages were not arranged marriages but the result of personal choice. The prevailing notion among the local Muslims regarding hypergamy is that a Sayyad can marry a girl of any other ethnic group while the reverse is not possible. The only example of a hypogamous marriage involving an Ansari boy and a Pathan girl in the village was the result of the personal choice of the two. The marriage took place at Delhi where the girl comes from. The practice of hypergamy among the Ashrafs (Sayyad, Sheikh, Mughal, Pathan) has been considered by Levy to be a result of the influence of the Hindu caste system (Levy, 1962:72).

In Itki as well as in Hindpidi strict ethnic endogamy is seldom violated. A vague notion of superiority and the hypergamous rights of those enjoying superior status is discernible in attitudes but is very rarely illustrated by actual practice. This situation, however, is not explicable in terms of the notions of ritual purity and pollution as prevalent among the local Hindus. Occupational specialization leading to specialized training in specific economic pursuits is an important argument in favour of the practice of endogamy. Very often, they also justify the practice in terms of the differences in the styles of life.

Though among the Muslims the attitude towards intermarriage is not rigidly linked with the notions of purity and/or impurity of caste/*beradari*, it seems that the notion that inter-ethnic marriages result in the impurity of the caste holds good to some extent among the Muslims also.

Normally, a Hindu caste has its *jati* or caste panchayat. Similarly, *beradari* panchayats have been found to be one of the main attributes of the social system of various local Muslim ethnic groups. At Itki the Ansaris and the Iraqis have fairly strong *beradari* panchayats. Itki remains the headquarter for both of these organizations. They have representatives in each village within the jurisdiction of the *beradari* panchayat who have to present the cases from their villages during the periodic meetings. Similarly, the Dafalis have a *beradari* panchayat of their own. These panchayats play a decisive role and exert their influence over their members mostly in the field of marriage and divorce as well as in property distribution. The head of the panchayat is known as Sadar or Sardar. Being numerically small the Pathans (two families), Shahs (one family) and Chudihars (one male person only) have no formalized panchayat organization, though they maintain links with their *beradari* group in the surrounding villages and occasionally cooperate in resolving inter-personal matters within their respective *beradari* panchayats.

Similarly, at Hindpidi the various ethnic groups have their own traditional panchayats within the area or are linked with their *beradari* panchayats outside where their *beradari* members constitute a substantial population. The Sayyads, however, have no panchayat among them both at Itki and Hindpidi.

A broad distinction in the styles of life between those ethnic groups with a higher status and those with a lower one can be observed. This distinction was noticed particularly at Hindpidi where a relatively larger number of ethnic groups are present and it operates specially in relation to the observance of purdah and in the observance of religious duties. The norms of purdah are generally found to be strictly observed among the ethnic groups of higher status (Sayyads and Pathans). Though purdah is broadly observed by Muslim women of all ethnic groups in general, laxity in its observance can be observed among certain ethnic groups of middle and lower status. However, it is true that even the Muslim families of the traditionally higher status groups very often do not maintain purdah under the influence of modernization though this seldom affects their status. Certain ethnic groups of middle and lower status freely violate the norms of purdah. The women of the Rais (greengrocers) do not observe purdah and engage in fruit and vegetable selling in public. Similarly, among the Howaris or Dhobis (washermen) and Bhangis, women frequently violate the norms of purdah and freely carry on their traditional occupations. The educated and better off families, however, especially among the Dhobis and the Rais, tend to withdraw their womenfolk from their traditional occuptions. Observance of purdah is also largely related to one's economic condition.

A closer look reveals that a stricter observance of the rules of the Shariat as also purdah is positively correlated not only to ethnic groups of higher status but also to higher classes irrespective of their ethnic background. This is generally true both in the village and in the city.

The Hindu notion of inherent and permanent uncleanliness is foreign to Islamic ideology. There are, however, elaborate and fairly defined rules relating to *napaki* (uncleanliness) and its removal which apply to all Muslims equally. Contact with a defiling object or person causes impurity that can be removed through washing and sanitary methods. A woman's state of pollution is removed after the period is over. One is not supposed to recite the Koran or say *namaz* while in a state of uncleanliness.

But in practice certain rules regarding inter-commensal distance are found to be maintained by ethnic groups of a higher status in relation to certain lower ones. This is more obvious in the case of the Bhangis in the city against whom discrimination is maintained by the rest of the ethnic groups. This is often explained not in terms of ritual pollution but on the basis of a repulsion on account of their unclean occupation.

In the village, however, owing to the absence of Bhangis, no such commensal discrimination was noticed during communal feasts. Only the Shahs, the mendicant beggars, are not invited to social feasts. This again is rationalized not in terms of ritual pollution but in terms of avoidance of a 'class' of people with unclean habits. It may also be noted that begging as a profession is discouraged in Islam.

In Ranchi city also no elaborate rules of commensality, which might be comparable to those prevalent among the Hindus, were observed among the local Muslims. Even then, in their actual behaviour commensal distance was found to be maintained in some form or the other by certain ethnic groups *vis-a-vis* certain others.

The main reason for the commensal distance maintained against the Bhangis is stated to be their physically unclean job, i.e., scavenging. Along with this, certain other practices were also stated to be responsible for the discrimination against them, such as, unrestricted consumption of liquor and indulgence in gambling, which are *haram* (forbidden in Islam). The Bhangi womenfolk were also reported to have served as hired singers, specially at Hindu marriage ceremonies, thus violating the rules of purdah.

Despite the rationalization based on non-ritual criteria, it was noticed that the drummers, known as 'band party group', among the Bhangis who have abandoned scavenging are served food separately at social ceremonies sponsored by the other Muslim groups. Because these attributes are generalized in respect of the entire group, the Bhangis also accept these social stigmas and seem to suffer from a sense of inferiority on these counts.

It should, however, be noted that no discrimination is made against the Bhangis in the religious sphere. My finding in this regard is somewhat contrary to that of Ansari's (1960) report on their exclusion from the mosque congregation and also to Guha's (1965) findings on the basis of her study in the 24 Parganas in West Bengal with regard to restrictions on fishermen's entry into the mosque (see also Mandelbaum, 1970:549). In contrast, the Bhangis of Ranchi town have never been debarred from entering a mosque or a shrine nor discriminated against in the line formation for *namaz*. Even if they occupy the rear line during *namaz*, it is of their own accord. Muslims belonging to other ethnic groups were observed attending their funeral ceremonies though very few of them were seen attending socio-religious ceremonies held in their houses.

The situation in case of the Gaddis is somewhat contrary to what is observed in the case of the Bhangis. While the Bhangis are avoided by all the others, the Gaddis tend to avoid all the other Muslim groups in matters of commensality, irrespective of their status in the hierarchy. But it is interesting to note that this restriction is maintained by the Gaddis in their own places only, i.e., when a feast has been sponsored by a Gaddi and the members of other ethnic groups have been invited. On the other hand, the Gaddis are not discriminated against by others and they also on their part do not maintain any restrictions while being invited by others. Again, restriction on commensality is observed by them during ceremonial feasts only and not during daily life.

The Gaddis, as has been mentioned earlier, consider all the other Muslims as well as non-Muslims as *parwin*, meaning non-Gaddi. The Gaddi *beradari* panchayat has strict coercive rules regarding the restrictions on inter-*beradari* commensality as well as inter-*beradari* and/or community marriage, the violations of which lead to the imposition of a fine and ostracism.

The commensal scene in respect of the Iraqis varies from the village to the city. While liquor distillation is still being carried on by a few Iraqis in Ranchi city, in Itki they had abandoned this occupation long ago and hence no inter-commensal distance is maintained from them by the members of other ethnic groups. In Ranchi city the stigma attached to the liquor distillers' occupation is extended to the *beradari* as a whole. In this case also the discrimination is not rationalized in terms of ritual pollution but in terms of ethics and the discrimination against them is only partial and is a matter of an individual's conscience.

While considering the commensal relationship of the higher ethnic groups *vis-a-vis* the lower ones, namely, the Nais and the Dhobis, we find that the commensal distance is much less rigid as compared to the Bhangis who are assigned the lowest position in the local Muslim society.

Inter-Ethnic Hierarchy

One of the major characteristics of the caste system is its 'institutionalized inequality' or 'hierarchical gradations'. Within a caste society each caste is ranked in relation to the other (Dumont, 1970:65; Sinha, 1967:94; Berreman, 1967:48). Ranking is primarily a matter of general consensus, judged largely in terms of co-relative stratified interactions among the various castes. Marriott points out that ritual interaction, which greatly affects caste ranking, is mainly of two types—the ritual giving and receiving of food and services (Marriot, 1960:16).

The presence of twelve and seven ethnic groups at Hindpidi (city) and Itki (village) respectively offer us an appropriate opportunity to examine rank in terms of inter-group interaction. Firstly, we notice, both in the urban and rural settings, the absence of interaction in terms of ritualized giving and receiving of food and services as is usually present in Hindu society. No commensal distance exists among the various Muslim ethnic groups, except in the case of the Bhangis *vis-a-vis* the others, and even then the distance is not judged in terms of 'ritual pollution'. The giving and receiving of services are not limited to certain ethnic groups only. Any individual, irrespective of his ethnic affiliation, can become a religious specialist, and any one or any group can receive the former's religious services.

There are twelve endogamous ethnic groups locally known as *beradari* at Hindpidi. These include the Pathan, Sayyad, Idrisi or Darzi, Ansari, Rai, Iraqi or Kalal, Howari or Dhobi, Gaddi, Hashmi or Dafali, Bhangi or Halalkhor, Nai and Chick or Butcher (dealers in mutton only). Itki has seven *beradaris*, namely, Ansari, Iraqi, Sayyad, Pathan, Dafali, Chudihar and Shah.

In the regional context, both in the village and the city, the Muslims tend to classify the community into ethnic groups consisting of three broad hierarchical blocks—high, middle and low. This is done by taking into account the most overriding local factors of ranking, i.e., descent and traditional occupations rated either clean or unclean and thereby superior or inferior. Excluding the Sayyads and the Pathans, all others have a background of specific traditional occupations which they either practise in varying degrees or have abandoned altogether (see Table 5). The three ranked orders of high, middle and low have emerged on the basis of a broad consensus despite 'class' divisions cutting across the ethnic groups. The other important criteria relevant to ranking are education, wealth and observance of purdah. The numerical strength of a group and consequent local dominance also influence its status.

While the block position of each ethnic group is not disputed, the ranking of groups within each block is surrounded by a lot

TABLE 5
Ethnic Groups and their Traditional Occupations

	Ethnic Group	*Traditional Occupation*	*Traditional Occupation Followed/Subsidiarily Followed/Not Followed*
	Sayyads	Not wedded to specific occupation	
	Pathan	,,	
	Iraqi	Liquor distillation	Followed subsidiarily
	Ansari	Weaving	Not followed
	Idrisi	Tailoring	Followed
C	Gaddi	Milk-selling	,,
I	Rai	Vegetable and fruit selling	,,
T	Chick	Meat-selling (Mutton)	,,
Y	Dafali	Drumming and *mujawari*	Not followed
	Dhobi	Laundry	Followed
	Nai	Barbering	Followed
	Bhangi	Scavenging	Followed subsidiarily
	Sayyad	Not wedded to specific	
V		occupation	
I	Pathan	,,	
L	Ansari	Weaving	Followed subsidiarily
L	Iraqi	Liquor distillation	Not followed
A	Dafali	Drumming and *mujawari*	,,
G	Faqir (Shah)	Mendicancy	Followed
E	Chudihar	Bangle-selling	Not followed

of controversy as is evident from Tables 6 and 7. This is more so the case with the relative ranking of the groups in the second block. In fact, no one was willing to give an elaborate relative rank order for all the ethnic groups.

TABLE 6
Inter-Ethnic Hierarchy at Hindpidi

Number of Block of stratum	*Block Position and Relative Position within the Block*
I High	Sayyad, Pathan
II Middle	Iraqi, Ansari, Idrisi, Rai, Gaddi, Chick, Dafali
III Low	Nai, Dhobi, Bhangi

TABLE 7
Inter-Ethnic Hierarchy at Itki

Number of Block of Stratum	*Block Position and Relative Position within the Block*
I High	Sayyad, Pathan
II Middle	Iraqi, Ansari, Dafali, Chudihar,
III Medium	Shah

The Sayyads, almost by common consensus, are assigned the highest position in the ranking strata by virtue of their descent from Prophet Muhammad through his daughter Fatima and her husband Ali. The Bhangis are similarly assigned the lowest rank at Hindpidi due to the 'unclean' or lowly nature of their occupation. In the village, where Bhangis are absent, the Shahs, religious mendicants, are assigned the lowest position in the hierarchy due to their occupation of begging. Thus, the highest and lowest positions of the Sayyads and the Bhangis or Shahs respectively are generally agreed upon. The Pathans, with their ruling and fighting background, claim and are assigned the position immediately after the Sayyads.

It should be noted, however, that though there is no priestly caste in Islam and anybody with the required qualifications may act as a leader or specialist in the religious spheres, the *pirs* (spiritual leaders), who are esteemed very highly in Muslim society, are drawn mostly from amongst the Sayyads. However, all Sayyads are not *pirs*.

Let us now consider the ranking order of the ethnic groups within the second or middle block. The largest number of ethnic groups are placed within this block, and a comparatively greater amount of controversy surrounds the relative ranking among them within this block. At the first instance the respondents of all ethnic groups seemed very prone to attribute an equal middle position to all the groups within this block. But while probing further into the matter, some sort of hierarchy emerged, though the specific rank order of each group still remained somewhat vague and uncertain. Thus, the groups within the second block are further divided into three sub-blocks consisting of Iraqis and Ansaris in the first, Idrisis, Rais and Gaddis in the second and Chicks and Dafalis in the third. Similarly, at Itki the Iraqis and

Ansaris were placed in the first and the Dafalis and Chudihars in the second sub-block. Each group within the sub-block jostles for a superior position over the others.

Apart from attributing various positions to a specific ethnic group, the members of the ethnic groups often claim various ranking positions for their own group. This tendency was observed both at Hindpidi and at Itki. The nature of occupation, wealth and education and the observance of purdah are the main factors taken into account for determining the relative ranking.

At Hindpidi we find that the third position is claimed by both the Ansaris and the Iraqis while the members of the other ethnic groups were not certain about the relative ranking of these two. The Ansaris in this area have long since abandoned their traditional occupation of weaving and have made considerable material and educational advancement. The other regional ethnic groups today do not seem to be very conscious about the Ansaris' traditional occupation and consider their educational and material achievements while assessing their relative rank. In Itki village, unlike in the city, the Iraqis have completely abandoned their traditional and degrading occupation of liquor distillation and have made economic and educational advancements comparable to the Ansaris. As such, each claims precedence over the other in the hierarchy. In the case of the Iraqis, the members of the other ethnic groups are still very conscious of their traditional occupation and they are often assigned a lower status despite their material prosperity.

There is again a lot of dispute regarding the fifth, sixth and seventh positions which are contested by the Darzis, the Rais and the Gaddis in the city. The same is true for the eighth and ninth positions which are disputed by the Dafalis and the Chicks.

In the village also there is controversy and confusion for the fifth and sixth rank order between the Dafalis and the Chudihars. It is said that the Dafalis, with a view to raising their social status, have adopted an Arab surname and call themselves Hashmi. But their claim to an Arab ancestry is not fully supported by the other ethnic groups. The elderly people of the other ethnic groups at Itki are found to be well-informed about the Dafali's traditional occupation of drum-making and *mujawari*, and on this basis the Dafalis are assigned a lower rank than the Chudihars.

However, as the Dafalis in this village as well as in Ranchi city have abandoned their traditional[7] occupation and have largely adopted the business of selling stationery articles, their status has been raised in the eyes of the local Muslims and they are ascribed a rank higher than the Chudihars. But this is not supported by those who place the Chudihars over the Dafalis on the ground that the former had been engaged in a clean occupation of bangle-selling from the very beginning. In the village, the Dafalis have adopted the hide and skin trade besides their stationery business. A few Muslims ascribe the Dafalis a lower status than the Chudihars for they consider the hide and skin business of the former as also unclean. At the same time, the Chudihar womenfolk are accused of violating the rules of purdah and are hence assigned a lower status.

The Shahs in the village have, by common consensus, been assigned the lowest rank in the hierarchy. The Shahs there are considered to be ordinary beggars and not religious mendicants. There is, however, only one Shah family in the village, and its relative isolation as well as poverty partly accounts for the position assigned to the group.

Within the third or lower block at Hindpidi the main controversy is between the Nais and the Dhobis who are jostling for a higher status among themselves. The members of the other ethnic groups were also not fully agreed on the relative positions of the Nais and the Dhobis. The Bhangis, however, are assigned the lowest position in the ranking structure by general agreement.

The claim of status supremacy over others is often made on the basis of an occupation which is generally considered respectable. The Darzis claim superior status over the Rais because they consider their occupation of tailoring as comparatively more respectable and skilful and because they have more personal contacts with the higher classes in the society, both Muslims and Hindus.

The local Rais are fruit and vegetable-sellers. Though their occupation is also considered to be 'clean', they do not command

[7]Though neither in Itki nor in Ranchi city were members of the Dafali *beradari* observed to be carrying on their traditional occupation, they were reported to be pursuing it elsewhere. I was informed that the traditional occupation of singing and *mujawari* were still carried on by some members of their *beradari* at Arrah district in North Bihar.

as much respect as the Darzis. One of the important reasons for attributing a lower status to the Rais over the Darzis and some others is the fact that their womenfolk also violate the rules of purdah. The Gaddis, on the other hand, though their occupation was not considered very respectable in the local society, are very often attributed a status higher than the Rais on the ground that their womenfolk observed purdah very strictly. However, the Rais claim superiority in ranking over both the Gaddis and the Darzis. Thus, observance of purdah also influences inter-ethnic ranking as a higher value is attached to it in Muslim society.

It is important to note that the ethnic groups such as the Rais, Dhobis, and Bhangis, who enjoy a lower status in the hierarchy are also found to have a lower standard of education. They also display a comparatively lower style of life in relation to the groups in the upper strata, specially in regard to fervour and punctuality in the discharge of religious obligations, observance of purdah and involvement of womenfolk in their traditional occupation.

The Hindus in general, both in the village and in the city, have some knowledge about the existence of endogamous ethnic groups among the Muslims. However, they have no clear conception about the hierarchy among the Muslims. Of course, they assign the lowest position to the Shahs (at Itki) and the Bhangis (at Hindpidi), because of their begging and scavenging activities, which are obviously lowly and unclean occupations. But they fail to assign any hierarchical ordering to the other groups. Though a few Hindus accord the highest social status to the Sayyads, they seem unable to say why they do so.

Obviously, the influence of the Islamic Great Tradition and thereby the overt egalitarian mode of interaction among the Muslims restrict the Hindus' ability to conceptualize the stratification aspect of Muslim society. The right of any Muslim, irrespective of his ethnic affiliation, to become a religious specialist and the consequent absence of a priestly caste as well as the relatively free inter-dining relations among the various Muslim ethnic groups also inhibit the Hindus' understanding of this phenomenon. The Muslims have no classifications in terms of 'vegetarian' and 'non-vegetarian' groups among them nor do they have *pukka* and *kaccha* categories of food as among the local Hindus. The *haram* (tabooed) items of food apply uniformly to all the Muslims irrespective of their ethnic background. These factors also seem to have hampered the Hindus' understanding of the stratification aspect of Muslim society.

The Community

Despite the obvious existence of ranked groups, the concept of the brotherhood of all Muslims remains an ideal among the local Muslims and displays a significant functional value. Moreover, the existence of a hierarchy of ethnic groups and of consideration of 'high' and 'low' ethnic status in various spheres notwithstanding, certain religious functions or duties are of such a nature that they constantly obliterate the notion of high and low and promote 'equality'. For example, during *namaz*, *qurankhani*, *milad* and funerals no discrimination is normally practised on group basis. No discrimination is observed in the line formation during *namaz* and any able Muslim, irrespective of his ethnic status, may become the Pesh Imam and lead the congregation in prayer.

We do not find any elaborate rules of commensality among the Muslims. No commensal distance exists among the various Muslim ethnic groups on the basis of ritual purity and/or impurity. The discrimination maintained against the Bhangis is also not rationalized in terms of ritual pollution. But we also find that in certain social spheres the operational model is not fully consonant with the ideal model of Islamic brotherhood. The Muslim ethnic groups, in terms of functional endogamous groups, approximate in fact to the Hindu model of castes.

Conclusion

Our analysis of the local Muslim 'caste system' leads us to conclude that, though both structurally and functionally the Muslims of rural and urban Ranchi are organized broadly in a hierarchic pattern of endogamous, occupationally specific, descent groups which fall within the general structural pattern of the Hindu/Indian caste system, the cultural nexus of the regional

Muslim *beradari* system remains somewhat distinct.

Unlike the Hindu caste system which is essentially based on the traditional *varna* system, the Muslim caste system lacks both a comparable ideological frame and a tendency towards rigid elaborateness. The Muslim *beradari* system is more a structural approximation to the regional caste system lacking the cultural prop of Islamic Great Tradition. The *beradari* system of endogamy and hierarchy is only partially rationalized and that, too, with difficulty, in terms of Islamic tenets. As has been observed by Barth, an elaborate hierarcoy of ritual rank has no meaning in an Islamic framework (Barth, 1960:139).

The Muslim and Hindu world-views also vary from one another in this regard. The Muslims cherish an ideal of equality, while inequality remains the basis of social organization among the Hindus. At the regional level, the Muslims visualize themselves as a small local unit related to a larger pan-Islamic world.

Again, ranking among them is determined not on the basis of ritual criteria but is rationalized in non-ritual terms. It lacks elaborateness in terms of ritualized giving and receiving of food and services. The overriding determining factors are descent and the nature of occupation rated as high and low in social esteem. Other important factors influencing their ranking order are wealth, education and the observance of such practices as purdah. While the block position of each ethnic or *beradari* group is evident, the relative positions within each block remains highly disputed.

In spite of some overriding similarities in both the Hindu and Muslim caste systems, inter-caste relations among the local Muslims reflect the egalitarian influence. This is mostly noticeable in inter-group commensality, communal prayer and the right of the members of apparently lowly *beradari* groups or castes to become religious specialists. But at the same time Muslim inter-ethnic stratification approximates to the Hindu model in terms of the practice of endogamy, the maintenance of commensal distance in a very broad sense, a notion of hierarchy, and the factor of birth being the only criterion for caste membership. The various Muslim ethnic groups (excepting the Sayyad) are associated, at present or in the past, with certain specialized hereditary caste occupations. The presence of such Hindu caste features, though in a modified form, in its certain aspects is understood in terms of the model of the Hindu society and is suggestive of the presence of caste-like features among the local Muslims also.

Summing up, we may therefore note that the *beradari* system, or inter-ethnic stratification, of the local Muslims is comparable to the Hindu caste system though the two are not exactly similar. The egalitarian influence of the Islamic Great Tradition has considerably modified and simplified its form which marks a departure in certain details from the Hindu caste system. It approximates the Hindu caste system most in the sphere of endogamous functional groupings. It deviates farthest from the Hindu model in its relatively diffused hierarchy, general lack of the concept of pollution, absence of a priestly caste and lack of ideological support for an elaborate hierarchy. The *beradari* or caste system of the local Muslims may be regarded as a structural variant of and analogous to the Hindu caste model.

Bibliography

Ahmad, Imtiaz (ed.) (1973), *Caste and Social Stratification among the Muslims,* Delhi, Manohar Book Service.

Ali, Abdullah Y. (n.d.), *The Holy Quran: Text, Translation and Commentary*, Lahore, Firozesons.

Ansari, Ghaus (1960), *Muslim Caste in Uttar Pradesh: A Study in Culture Contact*, Lucknow, Ethnographic and Folk Culture Society.

Barth, Fredrik (1960), 'The System of Social Stratification in Swat, North-west Pakistan', in E.R. Leach (ed.), *Aspects of Caste in South India, Ceylon and North-west Pakistan*, Cambridge, Cambridge University Press.

Berreman, Gerald D. (1967), 'Comparative Analysis of Caste', in Anthony de Reuck and Julie Knight (eds.), *Caste and Race· Comparative Approaches*, London, Ciba Foundation.

Dumont, Louis (1970), *Homo Hierarchicus: The Caste System and its Implications*, Delhi, Vikas Publishing House.

Guha, Uma (1965), 'Caste among Rural Bengali Muslims', *Man in India*, 45, pp. 167-69.

Gupta, Raghuraj (1956), 'Caste Ranking and Inter-caste Relations among the Muslims of a village in North-Western U.P.', *Eastern Anthropologist*, 10, pp. 30-42.

Khan, Zillur (1968), 'Caste and Muslim Peasantry in India and Pakistan', *Man in India*, 47, pp. 133-48.

Levy, Reuben (1962), *The Social Structure of Islam*, Cambridge, Cambridge University Press.

Marriott, McKim (1960), *Caste Ranking and Community Structure in Five Regions of India and Pakistan*, Deccan College Monograph Series No. 23, Poona, Deccan College Post Graduate and Research Institute.
Mandelbaum, David G. (1970), *Society in India: Continuity and Change*, vol. 1, Berkeley and Los Angeles, University of California Press.
Misra, S.C. (1964), *Muslim Communities in Gujarat*, Bombay, Asia Publishing House.
Sinha, Surajit (1967), 'Caste in India: Its Essential Pattern of Socio-cultural Integration', in Anthony de Reuck and Julie Knight (eds.), *Caste and Race: Comparative Approaches*, London, Ciba Foundation.

2

Status Groups among the Moplahs on the South-west Coast of India

Victor S. D'Souza

The long-standing Arab contact with the coast of India has left its permanent impress in the form of several Muslim communities. These communities came into existence through the marriage of local women to Arab sailors and traders and grew through local conversions to Islam by Arab missionaries. Since the women the Arabs consorted with and the people whom they converted in different regions of India belonged to different cultures, the Muslims of Arab influence developed into different communities. These communities, however, have certain common features resulting from their similar origin. One such characteristic is that all of them are the followers of the Shafi school of the Sunni sect. In India only the Muslims with Arab influence are of this persuasion. On the west coast of India there are three main distinguishable sections of Shafi Muslims, the Moplahs being one of them. The other two sections are the Konkani Muslims of the coast of Konkan and the Navayats of Kanara.[1]

The Moplahs are spread along the west coast of India in a contiguous tract from Cape Comorin in the south to about Mangalore in the north. The major portion of this tract is

[1]For details regarding the Navayats of Kanara see D'Souza (1955a). This work also contains a brief discussion on the origin and growth of Muslim Communities on the West Coast of India.

included in the State of Kerala and the remainder in the district of South Kanara which is in Karnataka State. In Kerala, however, it is in the district of Malabar[2] that they abound in numbers, accounting for about one-third of the total population of the district. Incidentally, it is in this district that these people are called Moplahs or Mopillas and for practical purposes this name is applied to the entire community. They are also found in the Laccadive Islands off the coast of Malabar where the entire population consists of Moplahs alone. In the interior of South India they are also found in some parts of the Karnataka State, particularly Coorg, but their number there is not appreciable as compared with the non-Moplah population. All Moplahs speak Malayalam but with variations in their dialects from place to place.

Regional Variations

Despite their similar origin and many common characteristics, such as religious persuasion, language and dress, the Moplahs do not constitute a homogeneous group for certain ethnological and political reasons.

It is true that the foundation of the Moplah section was laid by the early Arab settlements resulting mainly from the unions of Arab sailors and traders with the Hindu women of the coast of Kerala. But the large increase in the population of the community was due mainly to conversions. Thus, among the Moplahs we find both descendants of Arabs through local women and converts from among the local people. Again, the women the Arabs associated with and the people they converted belonged to different Hindu castes. Although the cementing bond of Islam created a new sense of fellow feeling among all Moplahs, it has not eliminated the old differences.

The indigenous society of Kerala may be divided into two broad sections, one following father-right and the other mother-right social systems. Of course, the groups following these

[2]Geographically, the entire coast of Kerala is sometimes called the Malabar coast. But here the name Malabar is used to refer to the political district which is the northern most coastal division of Kerala State.

systems manifest them in different degrees. One of the prominent cultural elements of the mother-right section is a type of visiting marriage in which the wife does not leave her parental house and the husband has to visit her at her own place. Incidentally, this type of visiting marriage is also found in almost all Muslim communities generated by the Arab sailors. It was prevalent in the past on the coast of South Arabia, especially Yemen (Smith, 1903:158,199), which was the region from whence the Arab sailors came, and is found in varying degrees in the Muslim communities of Arab descent on the West and East coasts of India, in Ceylon and Sumatra.[3] This type of marriage was particularly suited to the peculiar mode of life of the Arab sailors, and the Arabs made full use of this institution which was locally prevalent in Kerala. With only a few exceptions, the Moplahs of Arab descent have still retained many of the mother-right traits. Moreover, among the converts there are people belonging to both the mother-right and father-right culture complexes. Thus, the culture of the Moplahs contains both father-right and mother-right characteristics, some sections being predominantly father-right, some predominantly mother-right, and the others showing different degrees of variation between these two extreme positions.

With the reorganization of Indian States in 1956, the Malayalam-speaking people in general and the Moplahs in particular were brought under one political and administrative unit of the State of Kerala for the first time in centuries.[4] Before the advent of the British, Kerala was divided into a number of principalities under the Indian princes. Even during British rule the former States of Travancore and Cochin were under two different Indian princes. All these different political divisions have fostered regional peculiarities which are also reflected in the culture of the Moplahs.

When studying the regional peculiarities of a people spread in a contiguous area the demarcation of different regions becomes

[3]The prevalence of visiting marriage among the Navayats of Kanara and the Konkani Muslims of the coast of Konkan has been discussed in D'Souza (1953).

[4]A considerable number of Moplahs are, however, still outside this political unit, particularly in Karnataka State, being found in places like Mangalore, Coorg, etc.

arbitrary to some extent. Moreover, this field study was restricted only to the districts of South Kanara and Malabar which, between them, accommodate the majority of the Moplahs. At any rate, the purpose of this paper is not to present an exhaustive picture of the social organization of the Moplahs but mainly to highlight its salient features. With these considerations in view the area of the Moplahs covered by this study is divided into four broad regions.

The following are the regions and the representative places in which the field study was conducted: (1) The coastal area of North Malabar represented by the towns of Cannanore, Tellicherry and Quilandy. (2) The coastal area of South Malabar represented by the towns of Calicut (Kozhikode) and Ponnani. (3) The interior of South Malabar represented by the towns of Manjeri and Tirur and the neighbouring villages. All these three regions belong to Malabar district which is the stronghold of the Moplahs. In the coastal area of Malabar the Moplahs are concentrated primarily in the towns. In the interior of South Malabar they are densely spread also in the villages. There are, however, very few Moplahs in the interior of North Malabar. (4) Mangalore taluk represented by the town of Mangalore and some neighbouring villages. This area is from the South Kanara district of Karnataka State. Besides Mangalore taluk the Moplahs are also commonly found in Kasargod taluk which was formerly a part of South Kanara district but is now amalgamated with Kerala owing to the reorganization of States. The Moplahs of the area were scattered in places like Kasargod and Manjeshwar.

It is therefore clear that the social organization of the Moplahs has to be studied from the regional perspective, noting the differences between the regions. The Moplahs of a region are in intimate contact with one another and so display a meaningful pattern of social behaviour, while between regions there are noticeable cleavages in their social organization. However, even among the Moplahs of the same region there are various dividing lines. One is the presence of father-right and mother-right elements in different sections. The father-right and mother-right Moplahs usually form two different compartments. While these sections cut across the regional boundaries each functions as a group more effectively in the same region.

Within the father-right or mother-right sections there are further groupings generated by a host of other factors.

Social Divisions

Cutting across both regional boundaries and distinctions of father-right and mother-right culture complexes, there are certain sections which are clearly distinguishable from the large general body of the Moplahs. Among the Moplahs in Malabar itself, the main body of the Moplahs is termed Malbaris or Malabaris and the other sections are called the Thangals, the Arabis, the Pusalars and the Ossans. These distinctions, however, are not familiar to the non-Moplahs.

The Thangals are a small section among the Moplahs which traces its ancestry through the progeny of the Prophet's daughter, Fatima. In the Muslim world such people are known as Sayyads and among the Moplahs they are called by the respectable term of Thangals. Among the Hindus of Kerala the term Thangal is reserved only for the Nambudiri Brahmins. Although the Thangals are confined mainly to South Malabar, their sphere of influence extends to other regions as well. By virtue of their descent from the revered family of the Prophet, the Thangals are held in the highest esteem by all Moplahs.

The so-called Arabis or Arabs are also a small group concentrated mainly in Quilandy, which is a coastal town north of Calicut. They are descended from the union of Arab men and local women but have retained their Arab lineage. Among the Malbaris also there are a large number of people of similar origin but they have lost the identity of their Arab origin by their adoption of mother-right cultural traits. Next to the Thangals, the Arabis occupy a position of high status in Moplah society by virtue of the fact that they trace their lineage from Arabia, the hallowed country in the Muslim world.

Probably in contradistinction to the prominent sections of Thangals and Arabis who trace their descent from Arabia, the main body of the Moplahs are called Malbaris (i.e., people of Malabar). But in this sense the Pusalars and Ossans, who are of local origin, should be termed Malbari also. But they are not called so because they form distinct sections. The term

Pusalars literally means 'new Muslims', that is, Muslims who are later converts. Whether it be among Muslims or Christians the new converts in India as a rule do not have the same status as the people who have been in the faith for an unknown number of generations. This is because Indian society is made up of innumerable endogamous groups and it is the endogamous group which is an effective unit of social life. By and large a person is a member of some endogamous group or another irrespective of his religious affiliation. While it is true that the members of an endogamous group follow the same religion, any religious category will have a number of different endogamous groups. Now, when a person is converted to Islam or Christianity he automatically loses his membership of the old endogamous group following a different religion while, on the other hand, not becoming a member of any one of the endogamous groups of the new religion. Thus, he comes to acquire a distinct status after conversion and is usually referred to by his new co-religionists as a 'new Christian' or a 'new Muslim' implying thereby a slightly inferior status.

The so-called Pusalars are converts from among the Hindu fishermen called Mukkuvans. Their conversion took place relatively late and, because of this and their low occupation of fishing, they are allotted a low status in Moplah society. The Pusalars are spread all along the coastline of Kerala and they still continue their traditional occupation of fishing.

The Ossans are a group of barbers among the Moplahs and, by virtue of their very low occupation, are ranked the lowest. Their womenfolk act as hired singers on social occasions like weddings.

Thus the five distinct sections of Thangals, Arabis, Malbaris, Pusalars and Ossans form a social hierarchy in which the Thangals are the highest and Ossans the lowest. In numbers the Malbaris preponderate and the Pusalars form the second largest section. The Thangals, Arabis and Ossans are fewer in numbers when compared with these two groups. The Malbaris and Pusalars are characterized by further subdivisions of varying social status.

The coastal regions of North and South Malabar and Mangalore are the strongholds of the mother-right Moplahs, the interior of South Malabar is the stronghold of the father-right

Moplahs, while in each area there are also some Moplahs belonging to the culture complex of the other area. It is a well authenticated fact that the Moplahs belonging to the interior of South Malabar are mostly converts from among low castes Hindus, such as the Cherumars who have the father-right social organization. On the other hand, almost all Moplahs of Arab descent are found in the coastal regions of Malabar and Mangalore. In addition to these Moplahs, these regions also have a large number of converts from among the Hindu castes of the coastal areas, like Nairs, Thiyars and Mukkuvans, who have mostly mother-right characteristics. The Moplahs of the coastal line in general are economically and socially superior to those in the interior of South Malabar.

Status Criteria

The working of the status system of a society can best be understood when viewed in a regional perspective for it is in a region that the different groups and sections are in direct, face to face relations with one another. It is therefore proposed to discuss the social stratification of the Moplahs within the framework of the different regions. But before that it would be useful to point out certain marks of distinction on the basis of which the relative status of groups can be established. The following are some of the distinctive features of status which are more or less common to all regions.

(a) *Hypergamy*: While the Moplahs form themselves into several endogamous groups, in rare cases intermarriages do take place among the various groups which are normally endogamous. But such marriages are strictly of a hypergamous nature in which only the male of a superior group can marry the female of an inferior group and not *vice versa*. For instance, Thangal males can marry women from any other group of Moplahs but Thangal women cannot marry any man other than a Thangal. An Arabi male can marry any Moplah woman other than a Thangal, but an Arabi woman can marry, besides an Arabi male, only a Thangal male, and so on. If a woman belonging to a higher group marries a man from a lower group, she and her children automatically lose their group membership.

On the other hand, when a man from a higher group marries a woman from a lower group his group status remains unaltered.

(b) *Custom of fixed mahr*: *Mahr* is the amount which a Muslim husband is required to pay his wife as a formal nuptial gift. It is one of the most important conditions of the Islamic marriage, so much so that even if it were not mentioned in the marriage contract a husband would still be liable to pay it whenever his wife demands it. There is, however, no limit to the amount of *mahr* and it usually depends upon the rank, special beauty or accomplishments of the wife and on the conditions which the parties agree upon when the marriage is contracted. But among the Moplahs, in common with some other Shafi' Muslim communities on the west coast of India, the amount of *mahr* is determined and fixed by custom.[5] Among the Moplahs the fixed amount of *mahr* is different for different sections and usually varies from 3 to 31 *mithquals*. In some sections the *mahr* is calculated in terms of rupees or *varaha*. As has already been pointed out, *mahr* is seldom paid among the Moplahs. But the fixed amount of *mahr* has come to acquire a significance of social status. When the entire Moplah society is taken into consideration, the differing fixed amounts of *mahr* prevalent in different sections and regions may not make much sense, just as the relative social status of groups taken at random is difficult to evaluate. But in any given locality the amount of *mahr* of a group is correlated with its social status—the higher the amount of *mahr* the higher is the group's social status.[6]

Since the fixed amount of *mahr* of a group is associated with its social status, if persons belonging to a section with a lower fixed amount of *mahr* mention in their marriage contract a higher amount which is proper to a different section, their action would be construed as an insult by the other section and such a situation is fraught with the possibilities of a conflict.

(c) *Deferential treatment*: People belonging to higher groups

[5]For a detailed discussion of this particular custom see D'Souza (1955b).

[6]However, while the *mahr* of the Thangals is also fixed it does not necessarily bear any relation to their social status, for in some places some sections of the Malbaris have a higher fixed amount of *mahr* than the Thangals and Arabis.

do not mix with those from the lower groups on an equal footing. When they are invited to social functions, the Thangals and Arabis have to be provided with separate seating arrangements and they have to be served separately. This segregation, however, does not bear any implication of pollution as in the case of the Hindus, but it is purely a mark of distinction. The *karnavar* of the household celebrating the function or persons of special status like the bridegroom may sit with the distinguished company. The people of higher status categories have to be invited personally by the host while the others may be invited through hired persons or printed cards. In their presence the others cannot sit down. Their women too have to be treated with special consideration by the other women. They have always to be addressed as *bibi* (lady) and this title must not be used for other women in their presence. Further, the other women have to remove their footwear and sit down.[7]

(d) *Use of special articles of distinction*: On ceremonial occasions only people of higher ranks are entitled to carry specially decorated umbrellas. They alone can make use of carpets during the *nikah* (nuptial) ceremony and so on.

(e) *Segregation*: When the social distance between sections is very great, not only are hypergamous marriages excluded but all social and even religious intercourse is curtailed. In such cases the sections even have separate mosques, separate religious organizations and separate burial grounds.

The salient features of Moplah social stratification may now be briefly examined with reference to the social relations among groups in different places.

Stratification Patterns

In Tellicherry, the main sections of the Moplahs are the Malbaris and the Pusalars. These sections form water-tight compartments. The Pusalars live in segregated residential quarters where they have their own religious organization. It is

[7]It is interesting to note that while in the presence of men of high status the other men cannot sit down, in the presence of women of high rank the other women cannot stand up.

a recognized practice among the Muslims for members of a residential quarter to meet for their daily prayers at the mosque of their locality. But it is enjoined by Islam that for Friday prayers the Muslims of a town should meet in a common mosque. In Tellicherry and in many places where Moplahs reside, the Malbaris and the Pusalars not only have different mosques for their daily prayers, which is understandable in view of their separate residential areas, but also have separate *jami* mosques for their *juma* (Friday) prayers. Their *kazis*[8] and burial grounds are also different. This fact highlights the existence of a huge social gap between the Malbaris and the Pusalars. Almost all Moplahs of Tellicherry, including the Pusalars, have the matrilineal kinship organization.

The Malbaris and Pusalars have further endogamous subdivisions. Each endogamous division consists of several groups of inter-related *tharavads*. The Pusalars of Tellicherry have two main endogamous divisions, one having 24 *mithquals* and the other 17 *mithquals* for *mahr*. The division having the higher amount for *mahr* is considered superior. In the past, intermarriages between these two divisions were not possible. At present there are a few instances of such marriages, but they are mostly of the hypergamous type.

Among the Malbaris the exogamous section called Keyis are accorded the highest status. In the past the men of these *tharavads* were big merchants and bankers. They have the highest amount of fixed *mahr*—21 *mithquals*—in Tellicherry. The Keyis have a unique position in Tellicherry. Although for their Friday prayers the Keyis attend the local *jami* mosque, they have a separate mosque for their daily prayers. They also have a separate burial ground and a separate *kazi*. When they are invited by other Moplahs to their social functions, they have to be given deferential treatment and are provided with separate seating and eating arrangements.

The various other sections among the Malbaris follow the regulations of endogamy and hypergamy, but in their ordinary inter-group social relations one does not notice such striking

[8]In Muslim countries a judge is called a *kazi*. But in India the *kazi* has no judicial functions these days and his main function is the solemnization of Muslim marriages.

differences as found in the social relations between the Keyis and the rest or between the Pusalars and the rest.

Just as the Keyi *tharavads* have the highest status in Tellicherry, the Arakkal *tharavad* occupies pride of place in Cannanore. Before the advent of the British, the *karnavar* of the Arakkal *tharavad* was the ruler of the territory round about Cannanore. The *tharavad* is still in possession of the town of Cannanore, but is deprived of all powers. Many of the customs of this *tharavad* are peculiar to itself. Of all Moplah *tharavads* this *tharavad* alone is excluded from the act of partition whereby individual members of the *tharavad* can claim their separate shares. The *karnavar* of this *tharavad* is known as Sultan Ali Rajah and the rest of the members have the title of Adi Rajah. Whereas in other matrilineal *tharavads*, whether those of Moplahs or Hindus, only the senior-most male member is entitled to the position of *karnavar*, in the Arakkal *tharavad* the senior-most member, whether male or female, becomes the head of the family. During my visit to the *tharavad*, the head of the family was a female, Sultan Ali Rajah Mariumma Bibi.

The women of the Arakkal *tharavad* do not marry men from Cannanore, however respectable they may be, as the latter are regarded as their subjects. So they marry men from places like Tellicherry and Calicut and who belong to the highest sections in society in those places. Without exception, these men have to reside in the wife's house. Among other Moplahs the husband addresses his wife in the singular as *ni* (thou), but the Arakkal ladies have to be addressed in the plural, as *ningal*, by their consorts. It is reported that their husbands have to adopt a rather subservient attitude towards them.

There is, however, no objection to the Arakkal males marrying women of the locality,[9] but they do not live in the *tharavads* of their wives. They cannot live with their wives in their own *tharavad* house either. So they have separate houses at Cannanore and live with their wives separately. Since the Arakkal *tharavad* has considerable income, each member of the *tharavad* receives a tidy sum sufficient for an independent and comfortable living. The house in which the man and his wife

[9]This practice is in keeping with the rule of hypergamy.

live is presented to the wife so that after the death of the husband it does not revert to his maternal *tharavad* but becomes the property of his wife and children. Normally, after the death of the husband the wife and children have to go to the *tharavad* of the wife. The dislocation of life that this situation would entail is minimized by the fact that the wife and children need not leave the dead man's house, while they can claim their share of income from their maternal *tharavad*. Moreover, the daughters of the Arakkal males are, as a rule, married to the sons of their father's sister who are members of the Arakkal *tharavad*. This ensures that they will enjoy the same comforts as they were accustomed to in their father's house.

The members of the Arakkal *tharavad* have a separate mosque, a separate *kazi* and a separate burial ground. The women have to be paid a *mahr* of 34 *mithquals* which is the highest among the mother-right Moplahs, the next higher figure being 21 *mithquals*.

Incidentally, the type of marriage in which the husband settles down permanently in the house of his wife, which is peculiar only to Tellicherry and Cannanore, becomes explicable if we take into account the special features of the social stratification there. Both in Tellicherry and Cannanore the highest strata of the Moplah society, namely, the Keyi *tharavads* and the Arakkal *tharavad* respectively, are exogamous. The visiting type of marriage, which is common among the mother-right Moplahs, becomes convenient if the two partners belong to the same locality. But the Keyi and Arakkal Moplahs do not like to marry their women to local Moplahs because they regard them as inferior in social status and so they have to seek husbands from other localities. Under such circumstances, when it is not possible for the wife to settle down in the *tharavad* of her husband, it is incumbent upon the husband to live in his wife's *tharavad*, for visiting marriage becomes impossible when the *tharavads* of the partners are separated by long distances. When such marriages are adopted by the highest stratum of society, it is but natural for those who aspire for a higher status to imitate this custom. In these places, apart from the Keyi and Arakkal *tharavads*, only the richer sections have this peculiar type of marriage. In the other localities of mother-right Moplahs, such as Quilandy, Calicut, Ponnani and Mangalore, the Moplahs of each stratum form an endogamous group of *tharavads*, so that marriages within the local group become possible and hence visiting marriages are convenient. It may, however, be pointed out that this is only a plausible explanation and the Moplahs themselves are unable to trace the genesis of this peculiar custom.

Among the Moplahs of South Kanara there are three main divisions. One of them is the section of Pusalars who, as everywhere else, lead a separate social life and have a separate social and religious organization. The other two divisions are found among the main body of the Moplahs who correspond to the Malbaris of Malabar but are locally known as Byaris.[10] The Moplahs of four matrilineal clans called Sultan, Chamukka, Akka and Kaisarekutakar, which comprise among them a large number of exogamous *tharavads*, form a distinct endogamous group. This group is considered to be superior to the other Moplahs who belong to both the father-right and mother-right systems. Their superiority is formally recognized by the others in that on all social and ceremonial occasions the representatives of the four clans are consulted. For instance, if the date for a wedding has to be fixed, the other Moplahs have first to obtain permission from the representatives of this group.

The Moplahs of the four clans are also called Talakars which name is derived from their peculiar custom of dining in public (*tala*). *Tala* literally means a dinner plate, but in practice sixteen persons eating from the same plate are said to constitute a *tala*. Among these people no person other than those belonging to the four clans is allowed to sit in a *tala*. If per chance an outsider sits along with the group members, the latter may regard it as an insult and stage a walk-out. The *tala* regulations are more rigorously enforced among the women, among whom the sixteen participant women should not only be Talakars but also of impeccable character.[11] In case persons of

[10]The Pusalars usually keep the group name of Marakkan after their personal name. It was reported to me at Manjeshwar in the Kasargod taluk that when, a few years back, a local Pusalar wrote Byari instead of Marakkan after his personal name, there was a quarrel between the Byaris and Pusalars. The dispute was settled by a local Hindu leader who asked the Pusalars to withdraw the new group name.

[11]It is noteworthy that women of dubious character are treated on par with outsiders.

the necessary qualifications fall short of sixteen, any other person may be invited to join the *tala* by common consent. Regarding the requirement that sixteen persons should dine from the same plate, there is a tradition that the four clans initially consisted of sixteen households and that all these households had to be represented in any public function. This peculiar custom is also practised by the other Moplahs, but they are not called Talakars. At any rate, the Moplahs cannot dine with the Talakars on certain occasions although they can take food from the same house.

In Mangalore the Talakars have the highest amount of *mahr*—24 *mithquals*. The other Moplahs pay 11 *varaha* and the Pusalars 4 *varaha*. The management of the chief *jami* mosque of the Moplahs in Mangalore is entirely in the hands of the Talakars. So, in every respect, the pre-eminent position of the Talakars among the Moplahs of Mangalore is only too evident. At the top there are the Talakars, at the bottom the Pusalars and in between are the large body of Moplahs who, while they accept the higher status of the Talakars and command respect from the Pusalars, do not among themselves observe any striking social distance between the various sections which are usually endogamous.

Since the Talakars belong to the highest social stratum of the Moplahs in Mangalore, their women cannot marry outside the group. If a woman marries outside the group, she and her children will lose their group membership. On the other hand, there is no objection to a man taking a wife from outside. While his position in the group will remain unaltered, his wife and children, who are not members of the group, will have no privileges, such as sitting in a *tala*, which accrue to the members only.

In every locality some section or other among the Malbaris assumes the dominant position. The same position as that held by Keyis, Arakkals, and Talakars in Tellicherry, Cannanore and Mangalore respectively, is occupied by the section called Koyas in Calicut. Social stratification among the father-right Moplahs is similar to that among the mother-right Moplahs. For instance, at Manjeri the *tharavads* called Kurikkal, Naha, Mooppan, etc., form an endogamous group of the highest status. The group composed of the *tharavads* of Koorimannin,

Valiamannin, Palath, Kodithodi, etc., comes next, and that formed by the *tharavads* of Avunhipurath, Puzhikuth, Athimannin, etc., comes third. The highest section everywhere manages the community affairs such as looking after the mosques, arranging religious and ceremonial functions, settling disputes and so on.

While it is true that the Thangals and the Arabis are accorded a higher status than that given to even the highest sections among the Malbaris, the social status of the former sections is mainly of a spiritual nature, while social differences among the Malbaris are based upon more tangible considerations like wealth, occupation, family connections and so on. The higher sections among the Malbaris may be regarded as the elite of the Moplah community, although, purely as a matter of etiquette, the Thangals and the Arabis are given greater respect. It is noteworthy that while the Thangals and Arabis do not give their women in marriage to men of lower sections, the men themselves do not mind taking their wives from any of the lower sections, even including the Pusalars and the Ossans. But in the case of the Malbaris who observe hypergamy, a man may marry a woman only from a section which is just one or two steps below his own group in social status. He does not marry a woman who belongs to a section which is very much below his section in social status and the Pusalars and the Ossans are ruled out from any such connections. The higher sections among the Malbaris may give their girls in marriage to the Thangals or Arabis not merely because of their higher status but only if the bridegroom comes of a rich and well-connected family, although in a mother-right system there is no financial gain to the bride's party from such unions. Most of the Arabis are comparatively poor and so the higher sections among the Malbaris do not give their girls in marriage to the Arabis at all.

Bibliography

D'Souza, Victor S. (1953), 'Mother-right in Transition', *Sociological Bulletin*, 2, pp. 135-42.

———(1955a), *The Navayats of Kanara: A Study in Culture Contact*, Dharwar, Kannada Research Institute.

———(1955b), 'A Unique Custom regarding *Mahr* (Dowry) observed by certain Indian Muslims of South India', *Islamic Culture*, 29, pp. 267-74.

Smith, W. Robertson (1903), *Kinship and Marriage in Early Arabia*, London, A & C Black Ltd.

3

Caste Analogues among the Laccadive (Lakshadweep) Muslims

Leela Dube

This paper examines the system of interdependent, hierarchically graded, and exclusive and exhaustive groups that has existed, under Islam, for centuries in two groups of coral islands off the south-west coast of India.[1] The Laccadive group has four inhabited islands and the Amindivi group has five. Together, they are popularly known as the Laccadives (now renamed Lakshadweep). The inhabitants of these islands are Sunni Muslims whose Hindu ancestry, through settlers from the Kerala coast, is beyond dispute. The distant island of Minicoy, which is also a part of the Union Territory of Lakshadweep, is excluded from this study because, ethnically and culturally, it forms a part of the Maldive islands.

[1]In writing this paper, I have drawn heavily on the data collected for the islands of Kalpeni by Dr. A.R. Kutty and myself, and for the islands of Amini by Dr. K.P. Ittaman. Kutty's account of Kalpeni was published in 1972; Ittaman's doctoral work was completed in 1973 and has now been published (1976). Both worked on their respective islands during the early sixties; I visited Kalpeni in 1969. I am thankful to Dr. Ittaman for letting me have access to his data. I thank Dr. Roy Burman, then Deputy Registrar-General of India, for his help. I am also thankful to Dr. Lokhandwalla, Fellow, Institute of Advanced Studies, Simla, for stimulating discussions and, particularly, for drawing my attention to the importance of ancestry in Islam and to the distinction between menial and non-menial occupations.

The islands produce only coconut, fish, some fruits, coarse grain, and vegetables. Coir-making has been their principal industry, and coconut has been the basis of their economy. All along, the islands have sustained themselves through trade with the mainland, from where they get those necessities of life that they do not produce themselves.[2]

The social system of the island communities has several uncommon features.

The system of descent is matrilineal, residence being predominantly duolocal or natolocal. Female links alone are recognized for the sharing and transmission of the property of the matrilineal groups known as *tharavads*; where individual property is concerned, however, Islamic law operates. On some islands *tharavad* property is divided on a stirpital basis; on others the division is per capital. The management of property is in male hands who also hold positions and offices of responsibility and authority. Succession to these, however, follows the matrilineal principle. The traditional pattern of residence after marriage is duolocal, in which neither the husband nor the wife is required to leave his/her natal home; the husband is only a nightly visitor and a child lives with its mother and her matrilineal relatives.[3]

During the regime of the Arakkal Muslim rulers, these islands were being administered by *karyakars*, or agents of the ruler, assisted by a few *mokhyastans*, or important people from the islands. For this, the Amindivi group was treated as one unit. This group passed into the hands of the British from Tippu Sultan of Mysore at the end of the eighteenth century. The *karyakars* were replaced by *monegars* but the *mokhyastans* continued. The Amindivi group was attached to South Canara district, while the Laccadive group, still with the Arakkal ruler, was under the control of the British only intermittently. From 1875 it remained in the hands of the British and was finally taken over by them in 1905. From 1877 each island of the

[2]These islands are situated between 123 and 210 miles off the south-west coast of India. The inhabitants of these islands are treated as Scheduled Tribes by the Government of India. In 1961, the population of the Union Territory (excluding Minicoy) was 19,970; in 1971, according to provisional census figures, it was 26,456.

[3]There are, however, slight inter-island variations in these patterns (see Dube, 1969; Kutty, 1972).

Laccadive group had an *amin*, appointed by the Government from among the *karnavars* or elders; other *karnavars* assisted him in the administration of justice. This group was attached to the district of Malabar. The appellate jurisdiction for both groups of islands lay with appropriate courts on the mainland. The Inspecting Officers of the Government heard and decided cases with the help of the elders during their visits to these islands. There was no codified law—it was the customary law of the islands (with local variations and some influence of Islamic law) which provided guidance to the administrators.

Coir monopoly, introduced in 1764-65 during Arakkal rule, has been the main source of revenue for the Government. Tree tax is levied on *pandaram* or Government land. The coir depots established on the islands around 1922 have made provision for supplying rice in exchange for coir at exchange rates fixed by the Government from time to time.

With the reorganization of States in 1956, the Laccadive, Minicoy, and Amindivi Islands were formed into a Union Territory and were placed under an Administrator. He operated first from Calicut, but his office is now on the island of Kavaratti. There is an Advisory Council consisting of members from the islands. Over the years, the pattern of administration, including that of justice, has undergone several changes. The islands have been grouped into tehsils. Several committees have been formed to increase public participation in governmental activities. Medical facilities, opportunities for secondary education, and a degree college have been made available on the islands. Students from the islands get stipends for higher education and technical training on the mainland. Encouragement is being given to cottage industries, and a Department of Fisheries has been set up. The cooperative societies help the people to sell copra, and make available to the people rice and other consumer goods at reasonable prices. A scheme to electrify the islands is in progress. The Public Works Department is putting up new buildings and is laying roads. The islands now have better facilities for communication with the mainland.[4]

[4]Regular steamer as well as postal and telegraph services are the important measures that have been introduced to increase communication.

Early History

The first settlers of these islands, according to their oral history, were a shipwrecked group travelling from the Malabar coast to Mecca to bring back Cheraman Perumal, the last of the Perumals, who had mysteriously disappeared after dividing his kingdom. The coastal Muslims believe that Perumal's conversion to Islam took place during the lifetime of the Prophet.[5] These traditions, thus, point towards the seventh century A.D. as the period when these islands were first settled.[6] However, in the light of recent historical knowledge about the second Chera Empire, it is clear that Cheraman Perumal was not the name of a particular king—it was the name by which all kings of the Chera dynasty or country were known. It has been established that the last Chera king reigned in the late eleventh and early twelfth centuries (Narayanan, 1972a), and as for Perumal's conversion to Islam, although both Hindu and Muslim chronicles speak of it the evidence is not conclusive (A.S. Menon, 1967: 136-37). Thus, the tradition that the islands were first settled in the seventh century is probably apocryphal.

A Musaka king, Valabha II, is stated to have conquered several islands in the Indian ocean[7] which are identified by historians as the Laccadives. The reign of Valabha II is placed somewhere around A.D. 1000 (Narayanan, 1972a:293-95; A.S. Menon, 1967:170). Perhaps this conquest can be connected with significant migrations to the islands. On the basis of linguistic evidence also, the most plausible period of major migrations from the coast to the island appears to have been around the ninth and tenth centuries A.D. The spoken language

Many development schemes are in operation. The land survey has been followed by radical land reforms. Special regulations made in 1965 have introduced many changes in the system of law and in the set-up and procedure for the administration of justice; but the customary law of inheritance largely continues to be effective.

[5]Shaykh Zaynuddin, writing in the sixteen century, mentions this tradition but disputes its accuracy (Nainar, 1942:53-6).

[6]It was on this evidence that I mentioned the seventh century as the most probable period of migrations from the Indian coast to the islands in *Matriliny and Islam* (1969).

[7]*Musakvansa,* composed in Sanskrit by Atula, narrates the history of the Musaka kingdom of north Kerala.

of the people of these islands is corrupted and archaic Malayalam, with local variations, which contains many Tamil as also Arabic words. Old records preserved on the islands tell us that long after its disappearance in Kerala, Vattelutu, the script of early old Malayalam period, was being used on the islands. From the ninth century onwards, inscriptions in Kerala were generally written in Vattelutu characters. It is only from this time that speech forms which could be described as Malayalam began to appear in inscriptions. This means that, till then, the Malayalam dialectal forms developed on the west coast had not become acceptable in writing. Broadly, the tenth century is regarded as the earliest stage in the development of Malayalam as an independent language (Shekhar, 1953:5-13).

The question of the period of major migrations to these islands is tied up with the probable composition of the migrating people and the kind of social organization they brought with them. The island tradition says that the early settlers were the Nambudiri Brahmins, the Nayars, and the Tiyyars. These represent three important levels in the caste hierarchy of Kerala and may be viewed historically.

The Nambudiris had come to acquire a position at the apex of Hindu society in Kerala, being ritual and scholastic leaders, landlords, and managers of temples enjoying royal patronage. According to a tradition in Malabar, the Nambudiris received their land as a gift from Parsurama, the mythological hero who exterminated the Kshatriya race. This is indicative also of their high position in secular spheres. Opinions vary regarding the period of their entry into Malabar. The Nambudiri Brahmins perhaps represent the later elements among the Brahmin immigrants (A.S. Menon, 1967:52). According to M.G.S. Narayanan the 'so-called Parasurama Brahmins' probably established their settlements in Kerala between the third and the eighth centuries of the Christian era (1972b:2).

It is generally accepted that the matrilineal Nayars entered into the caste society of Kerala from a tribal position, but it is not definitely known when this happened. According to Panikkar (1960:3), they occupied the country before the Nambudiri Brahmins entered it. Gough states that there is no mention of any matrilineal caste like the Nayars having existed in the early Chera kingdom and supports the view that they must have descended to the Kerala plains in about the fourth century A.D. (1962a:303). The Syrian Christian copper-plates I and II of the ninth century contain an indirect reference to the Nayars. From the Tiruvalla copper-plates assigned to about the eleventh or twelfth centuries it is clear that the Nayars were matrilineal. While giving an elaborate account of the social and economic conditions of Kerala between A.D. 800 to 1124, M.G.S. Narayanan (1972a) makes it quite clear that by the ninth century the distinctions of birth, status groups, with Brahmins at the top, and the pattern of their inter-relationship had become crystallized in Kerala.

The Nayars have been chieftains, feudals, soldiers, landlords, village headmen, and non-cultivating tenants with superior rights (*kanam* tenure). In her account of Nayar lineages and kinship in the period between the mid-fourteenth and the end of the eighteenth centuries, Gough mentions high-caste Nayars consisting of royal matrilineages, chiefly lineages, village headmen, and retainer Nayars of various sub-castes; matrilineal castes of temple servants similar to the Nayars; and Nayar servant castes of funeral priests, washermen, and barbers who served only higher castes. She has also described the pattern of hypergamous marriages starting from the Nambudiris, who formed alliances with high caste Nayar women (1962a:306-14).[8] At another place Gough has mentioned the feudal system which existed among the small kingdoms of the Malabar coast: it consisted of 'a pyramidal political structure in which different orders provided service and tribute to those above them in return for rights in land. There, the king granted lands to hereditary chiefs, the chiefs to village headmen, and the village headmen to Nayar retainers, in return for tribute and military service, and within each village, lower castes had cultivation rights in certain plots in return for services to the Nayars' (1960:21). About the growth of the feudal structure in Kerala, Panikkar writes, 'in the period between the ninth and twelfth centuries a feudal Kerala grew up' (1960:6). But there is also a view that there existed kingdoms

[8]K. Gough (1962a:306-14) presents the most elaborate account of the Nayars and takes note of important previous writings on the Nayars.

much before the ninth century which were feudatories paying allegiance to the Perumals.[9] In any case, we can safely assume that the migrants to the islands went from a system in which different castes had developed different types of interest in land and were bound together in a functional hierarchy.

The Tiyyars, the third important caste which provided early settlers for the islands, were associated with the growing and plucking of coconuts and were toy-tappers. They are also regarded as the first tillers of the soil in Kerala (Aiyappan, 1965:116). Tradition has it that they were immigrants from Ceylon who brought the coconut tree with them. They probably came to Kerala not later than the beginning of the Christian era. In a copper-plate inscription of the ninth century, their privileges in regard to the tapping of coconut trees and the collection of pepper find an indirect mention. In the caste hierarchy of Kerala, the Tiyyars were below the line of pollution, i.e., they were regarded as being outside the society of caste Hindus and hence polluting (Gough, 1962b:412-13; Aiyappan, 1965:84). In North Kerala and parts of central Kerala, the Tiyyars have been matrilineal. Most commonly, they have been cultivating tenants of the Nayars or other higher castes and of those from other religious groups. They have also been free labourers and manufacturers of palm wine.

Thus it appears certain that, in the period of principal migrations to the islands, all these three castes or levels had assumed their respective roles and places in Malabar society. Judging by the location of the islands, it seems reasonable to assume that migrations to them must have occurred from the Malabar coast. The island tradition—that the Raja of Kolattiri, the northernmost kingdom of feudal Kerala, sent a party in search of Cheraman Perumal which was shipwrecked on these islands—corroborates this. And it is not any less significant that the system of strong matrilineal descent groups and duolocal marriage that flourished on these islands was characteristic of the Nayars of central Kerala (Gough, 1962a:298-384). As regards the conversion of the islanders to Islam, which is attributed by tradition to the efforts and the miraculous deeds

[9]Logan (1887) mentions this in reference to the early history of Kerala.

of an Arab missionary, it is probable that this took place as a result of contact with Muslim Arab traders who were a common phenomenon in the Arabian Sea. A mixed community had also sprung up in Kerala. The period of conversion is again a matter of controversy, but the most plausible period appears to be somewhere between the thirteenth and fourteenth centuries (Logan, 1887: Appendix xxi).[10]

We may say, thus, that for a few centuries the Hindu settlers maintained their earlier style of life and followed their original customs and beliefs, modifying them in response to the new surroundings. There is enough evidence of this on the islands. There are relics of large tanks such as those commonly attached to Hindu temples in Kerala. Idols of Hindu gods have been excavated while references to snake worship and praise of Rama have been found in some old songs. *Ficus Religiosa*, the sacred tree of the Hindus, which is located at a central place on the island of Amini, probably served a functional purpose for the Hindu inhabitants of pre-Islamic days.

The notions of ritual purity and pollution which govern the Hindu caste system lost their hold under the new religion, and this transformation perhaps led to the amalgamation and blending of many small caste groups to form only three (or four) groups. However, the caste-like character of these groups—endogamy, hierarchical gradation and participation in a common system of rights and privileges and corresponding disabilities—and the pattern of social distance and the deference structure that were maintained even under egalitarian Islam, leave hardly any doubt that, at the time of their conversion, the islanders had become fully entrenched in the socio-economic system which had evolved from what had been brought from the mainland.

The Groups

From the middle of the nineteenth century we find explicit

[10]R.H. Ellis has based his conclusion on the fact that the Kazi of the *Juma* mosque in Androth, who died in 1920, was regarded as the twenty-fourth in direct descent from Ubaidulla, the Arab missionary who converted the islanders to Islam (1924: 15-16).

reference to the presence of caste-like groups on these islands in the reports of the officers of the East Indian Company and of the British Government. Although we cannot accept as authentic all that has been said in these reports about the customs and behaviour patterns of the people on these islands, we do get some idea of the nature of social groupings that obtained there in the last century and at the beginning of the present one.

Robinson, in his reports (1846 and 1848) noted that it was remarkable that Hindu caste prejudices had survived through 600 years. He mentioned that the inhabitants could still point out the high-caste families of their respective islands and that they retained some of the general distinctions of caste. On Amindivi there were four castes said to correspond to the castes in Malabar.

In a short account of the Laccadive islands which Logan provided in Appendix xxi of his *Malabar Manual*, first published in 1887, we find the following: 'The people, . . . are organized after the Hindu fashion into three simple classes or castes:

(1) Karnavar (doers, agents) consisting of the families of principal people who monopolize boat-owning;
(2) Malumis sub-divided into (a) Malumis proper (pilots or sailors), and (b) Urukars (boat people) employed formerly as common sailors, but now in various occupations; and
(3) Melacheris (climbers) who are the tree climbers and toddy-drawers and universally dependent on the higher classes.'

Logan adds that some of the principal inhabitants claim descent from the Nayars and even the Nambudiris of Malabar, and that the Melacheris are apparently the descendants of the Tiyyars and the Mukkuvans (fishermen) of the coast.

For Kavaratti[11] and Androth Logan mentions the following main classes:

[11]The names of the Islands are spelt differently in different books and reports. The spellings standardized by the Government of India are used here.

(1) Karnavars sub-divided into Karnavars proper and Thanakapirantha Kudiyans (less wealthy cultivators).
(2) Malumis (pilots and sailors) sub-divided into (a) Malumis proper and (b) Urukars.
(3) Melacheris (tree-climbers).

'The first class of Karnavars is composed of the rich odam (vessel) owners and panchayatkars (arbitrators). The male members of this class are also distinguished by the title of Koya—a religious dignitary. The island Karnavars, Amin and Kazi, all belong to this class. The Thanakapirantha Kudiyans are less wealthy and cultivators. The second class or the Malumis are, as the name implies, sailors. They are generally Patta Kudiyans, i.e., partly independent and partly dependent on the higher classes. The only difference between the Malumis proper and the Urukars appears to be in the names. The third class, Melacheris, are servants and toddy-drawers (the name signifies one who works aloft) (Logan, 1887: ccxci).

The account of the Laccadive islands in the *Imperial Gazetteer of India* (1908) states that '. . . they are divided into three main castes: Karnavars or Koyas, the aristocracy, who claim descent from Nambudiris and Nayars, and originally monopolized land and boat owning; Malumis or Urukars, the sailor caste, who sailed the Karnavar's boats, and were allowed small holding of land on various conditions of service on their lords' lands and in their boats; and Melacheris or climbers, the serfs, whose duty was to pluck coconuts, till their lords' lands, row the boats, and so forth.'

In *A Short Account of the Laccadive Islands and Minicoy*, published in 1924, R.H. Ellis mentioned that in the three Malabar islands (viz., Kalpeni, Kavaratti, and Androth) the people were divided into three classes—the Koyas, the Malumis, and the Melacheris. Intermarriage between the three classes was almost unknown. The fourth island, Agatti, was known as a Melacheri island. But about Amini, he says that the people were divided into four classes: Tharavad, Tanakampranavar, Kudiyati, and Melacheri. He estimates that about 5 per cent of the population belonged to the first, 35 to 40 per cent to the second, 5 per cent to the third, and the remainder 50 to 55 per cent to the Melacheri class. According to him, these distinctions were based originally upon status relating to property. In the early days of the settlement the Tharavad class alone had tenants; the Tanakampranavar possessed property of their own but had no tenants; the Kudiyatis were originally the tenant class, while the Melacheris were the landless climbers. Ellis further mentions that the first two classes could intermarry, and refers to one matrilineage of the highest group which would not give its women to Tanakampranavar men, but whose men could marry Tanakampranavar women. According to his information, marriage between the first two classes and the Kudiyatis was also allowed but had taken place very seldom; intermarriage between the first two classes and the Melacheris was strictly prohibited, while intermarriage between the third and the fourth classes was allowed (1924:69-71).

Occupations and Hierarchy

The islanders generally believe that the original migrants to these islands were the Nambudiris,[12] the Nayars, and the Tiyyars. Another caste which is mentioned as having been part of the island population are the Mukkuvans, or fishermen, who stand lower than the Tiyyars in the mainland coastal

[12]Most Nambudiris were landlords of substance, but they included a number of ranked occupational subcastes of varying wealth. As Thurston (1909:152) says, they formed the socio-spiritual aristocracy of Malabar. The Nambudiris have been patrilineal, with impartible estates, and have followed a custom by which only the eldest son could marry and beget children for the *illam* (house), while the younger sons of the Nambudiris contracted unions (*sambandham*) with matrilineal Nayar women, the children born of such unions becoming Nayars. Only the Nambudiris of Payyanur have followed the *marumakkatayam* (matrilineal) system (Thurston, 1909:153). It is not possible to say whether the Nambudiris that migrated to the islands were patrilineal or matrilineal. But even if all the migrant groups who were thrown together did not practise matriliny, the islands seem to have provided a congenial setting for all of them to adopt this system along with a duolocal residence pattern (see Dube, 1969: 77-78).

hierarchy.[13] The upper group in Amini, Kalpeni, Androth, and Kavaratti claims to have descended from the Nambudiris and the Nayars. There are many Koya *tharavad* names which can be identified with the names of Nambudiri *illams* (family names) or high class Nayar *tharavads* (matrilineage or clan) on the mainland. A close scrutiny of *tharavad* names on the islands can be very useful in identifying the original caste group of some of the present inhabitants. The Malumis, also known as Malis or Malmis, and the Melacheris are regarded as being of low origin in the context of the caste hierarchy of Kerala. The Melacheris, who are more numerous than the Malumis and who do all the coconut plucking and toddy tapping on the islands, are specially associated with the Tiyyars as having descended largely from them and as continuing their tradition of coconut cultivation and toddy tapping on the islands. They are also associated with the Mukkuvans. No particular caste from the west coast seems to be associated with the Malumis.

The four islands of Amini, Kavaratti, Androth, and Kalpeni are known as Tharavad islands and the four islands of the Amindivi group are known as Melacheri islands for, with negligible exceptions, their inhabitants have belonged to the lowest group. The three-fold distinction is found on Agatti of the Laccadive group but it is not known when it came into existence. It was obviously an imitation of what was operative on the high class islands. However, the disputes between the higher and the lower groups have been very acute on Agatti during this century. The islands of Kadamat, Chetlat, and

[13]Quoting Buchanan, Thurston (1909) writes that the Mukkuvans live near the sea coast of Malabar. Their proper business is that of fishermen; they are palanquin bearers for persons of low birth or of no caste, and they serve also as boatmen. He also quotes the *Gazetteer of Malabar* (1905): 'A caste, which according to a probably erroneous tradition came originally from Ceylon, is that of the Mukkuvans, a caste of fishermen following Marumakkatayam (inheritance through the female line) in the north. . . . Their traditional occupations also include *chunam* (lime) making and *mancheel*-bearing (a *mancheel* is a kind of hammock slung on a pole, and carried by four men, two at each end) . . . . The Mukkuvans rank below the Tiyans and the artisan classes . . . .' (1909, 106-7). There have been large-scale conversion to Islam among the Mukkuvans. These Muslim fishermen are known as Pusalars (new Muslims).

Kiltan are supposed to have been populated by Melacheri migrants from Amini. Bitra was populated, in 1928, by migrants from Chetlat. On these islands also, there are some people who call themselves Koya; they are the people who do not practise tree climbing, who conduct religious classes, and who also trace some connections with the Koya *tharavads* of the Laccadive group; but, in regard to these islands, hardly any kind of inter-group relations within the island need to be considered. The really significant thing to be noted here is the extent of control —and the devices used for maintaining it—exercised by the Koyas of Amini over the people of Chetlat, Kadamat, and Kiltan because of the latter's lowly origin having come from Amini.

For a long time these islands remained under the economic, religious, and political control of the Koyas of Amini. This aspect of intergroup relations will be discussed more fully later. In the discussion of the caste-like groups living in interaction with each other, we shall take into consideration mainly the situation on those islands which have all three groups—the Koyas, the Malumis and the Melacheris—resident on them.

The name Koya, by which the highest group is known, is derived from Khoja, an Arabic word which means 'the respected'. Evey male member of this group adds the suffix Koya after his name. Similarly, women and girls belonging to this group have the suffix *Bi* (which also signifies respect) added to their names.[14] Traditionally, they have been landlords, and have had members of the other two groups work for them as sailors, tenants, labourers, and menials. Much of the land on the islands was the freehold property of the Koyas. The fact that most of the *jenmom* or fee-simple properties were associated

[14]It is difficult to say when and how the term Koya came into vogue on these islands. In the earlier reports of Inspecting Officers and in the Records of the Court, we do not find this suffix attached to the names of Jurors or other persons belonging to the upper groups. The term appears to have gained popularity towards the latter part of the nineteenth century. On the Melacheri islands those who acquired superiority over their brethren in terms of wealth or religious functions and by discontinuing demeaning activities like toddy tapping and coconut plucking, styled themselves as Koya, although on the high class islands they were not given the treatment due to a real Koya. In the changing circumstances we find that the terms Bibi and Koya stand the risk of losing their group significance and exclusive use.

with paticular Koya *tharavads* can be discerned through their history, while the original names of plots still in use, though ownership may now have changed, indicates that the Koyas must have been landlords. On Kalpeni, a cursory look at groupwise ownership of trees on fee-simple land (as of 1962) tells us that the average number of such trees (in round figures) owned by Koya households was 100, by Malumi households 49, while Melacheri households owned only 14 trees. It appears that the pattern of land control has changed through a number of factors: through gifts of land or of trees to the lower groups by Koyas giving them the right to plant trees on certain land; through permission to build houses, to make soaking pits and so on; and also in some cases—as found on Amini—through the extinction of Koya *tharavads*, as a result of which their tenants who had tenancy rights over certain trees came into absolute possession of the land on which the trees stood. One significant factor responsible for undermining the traditional landlord status of the Koyas in the Laccadive group has been the introduction by the Government of *cowle*, i.e., leasing of *pandaram* or Government land for coconut cultivation to anyone, irrespective of group distinctions, who entered into an agreement with them and fulfilled its conditions.[15] A large number of Malumis and Melacheris have been able to take advantage of this arrangement and acquire land. Formerly the Koyas were exclusive owners of sailing craft, but now this privilege has been taken away. As a result, trade with the mainland and also shopkeeping are now open to the Malumis and the Melacheris. Through this means some of them are in a position to take trees on lease or mortgage from the Koyas. Some businessmen from the mainland settled on Amini, married Melacheri women, and flourished through this kind of activity.

Within the Koya group, such *tharavads* as sent their representatives to the administrative body, and thus had political

[15]The proportion of *jenmom* and *pandaram* or Government land (which is given on lease by the Government which realizes tax for the fruit-bearing trees on it) varies on different islands. In the Amindivi group, excepting a few minor leases in Kadamat and Chetlat, all land is tax-free. There are interesting historical accounts of how particular areas on different islands and some small islets became entirely *pandaram* land during Arakkal rule.

power and certain special privileges, enjoyed greater prestige. On Kalpeni this is true to a certain extent even today. On Amini there is clear evidence of the presence of two groups among the Koyas: the Tharavattukar and the Thanakkanpirannavar. The Tharavattukar group had two *kootams*, each consisting of some *kudumbams*, and each *kudumbam* consisting of a few *tharavads* or matrilineages. Actually a *kootam* is a group of matrilineally related *tharavads* and the rule of *tharavad* exogamy should be applicable even up to the *kootam* level. The other group, the Thanakkanpirannavar, had five *kootams*. Intermarriage between the two groups appears to have started in the last century. On all the islands the Kazi's *tharavad* has been held in high esteem.

The term Malumi or Malmi is derived from a Maallim, an Arabic word for the leader of a crew. The traditional occupation of the Malumis was to sail the craft of the Koyas and to transport goods between the mainland and the islands. On some islands this group appears to have been divided into captains and boatmen, which perhaps means that the *tharavads* that provided captains enjoyed greater prestige. The Malumis are consulted about auspicious times for fishing, for sailing, for conducting socio-religious ceremonies connected with the crises of life, and so on, the calculations for which are astronomical. Compared to the other two, the Malumis have always constituted a small group. On some islands they possessed some land and trees of their own even in the nineteenth century, but they were also tenants of the Koyas and did the work that went with this relationship. Gradually, most Malumis have freed themselves from such relationships and, particularly with the lifting of the ban on the owning of *odams* and carrying on maritime trade, their condition has altered; they are no longer dependent on the Koyas. Nor are the Koyas dependent on the Malumis, for they have taken to sailing crafts themselves. The Malumis rank higher than the Melacheris and have always refrained from coconut plucking, tree climbing, and toddy tapping, which they consider demeaning.

The Melacheris perhaps acquired their name from their activity of climbing trees, and from the area of their habitation which is generally in the west or south-west of the island—west is known as *melacheri* on these islands. This group has borne the principal brunt of work on the islands. They pluck coconuts, tap toddy, carry loads, work as crew-hands, thatch the roof of houses and do much of the hard and sustained labour involved in house building. They are also adept at fishing. Depending on the type of agreement, they help their masters in husking the coconuts, in wetting and beating the husk, and in making copra and jaggery. In the traditional system the dependence of the Melacheris for subsistence on their landlords and masters was complete. In their turn, the Koyas were also fully dependent on the Melacheris for productive, transactional, and menial work.

Certain occupational services and crafts have been confined to the lowest group. Thus, the barbers, blacksmiths, and servants of the mosques are drawn from this group. On Amini, the goldsmith belongs to this group. It is said that one of the goldsmiths, who was brought from the mainland to make ornaments, embraced Islam, married a Melacheri woman, and settled down on the island. No one other than the Melacheris acquired the special skill of sucking the impure blood from a boil or wound. On Kalpeni the sawers used to be from the Melacheri group, but now some Koyas and Malumis have also taken to this work. Besides their routine work, barbers are required for certain ritual occasions like birth and circumcision. They do not form a closed endogamous group and their profession is not hereditary.

Endogamy has been the rule for these three groups. In Logan's account, published at the end of the last century, it is mentioned that perhaps the right of intermarriage with the Koyas had been accorded to the Malumis. However this statement was probably based on the existence of a few stray cases. Moreover, the exact nature of such intermarriages (hypergamous or hypogamous) and the reaction of the people to them cannot be ascertained. However, although endogamy is still observed, it appears that there is less resistance to hypergamous unions between the Koyas and the Malumis than there is to such unions between the Koyas and the Melacheris. On Kalpeni, out of the ten intergroup unions recorded in 1962, nine were between the Koyas and the Malumis and, in the majority of cases, the husband was staying in his wife's house. In 1969, the incidence of such marriages increased.[16] The children born of such unions naturally belong to their mother's *tharavad*. It should be pointed out that such marriages are not arranged marriages; and, because of easy divorce, such unions are often short-lived.

It appears that, once in a while, mainland Muslims visiting the islands married island girls and either divorced them while leaving or instead settled down on the island. It has been the Melacheri group which has, by and large, accommodated such people. In a sample survey of marriage and divorce on the island of Kalpeni conducted by me in 1969, a few cases were recorded where the man or some relative in the ascending generation was still recognized as a mainlander. Such instances have been recorded on Amini also. There is evidence of Hindu artisans and Mappillas having migrated to the islands and having been absorbed into the island population. In cases where the person was clearly identified as having a high group status from among the Muslims, such as Thangal and high class Mappilla, his absorption into the higher group was possible. It may be noted, however, that in the matrilineal setting of the islands, such males did not become lineage ancestors, but could only be husbands and fathers. In inter-island marriages the group association of a person was easy to ascertain.

Marriages between the Koyas and the Melacheris are strongly disapproved of even today. In 1969, a very pretty Melacheri girl from a well-to-do *tharavad* of Kalpeni, who had married a Koya boy from Kavaratti while he was posted at Kalpeni, was divorced by her husband who merely sent a telegram to the Kazi of Kalpeni. The girl was almost out of her mind during the period of my stay on the island. The islanders said that the boy's people must have disapproved strongly of this marriage and prevailed upon him to divorce the girl. The father of the girl, who was an important person on the island, was angry with her and felt that she had tried to go too far.

It may be noted that, in the few hypergamous unions that

[16]These data on intergroup marriages in Kalpeni should not be taken as being applicable to other islands as well. On Amini, for instance, not a single such marriage was reported in the survey of population made in 1963-64 by K.P. Ittaman.

took place, there was no problem regarding the placement of the children. No instances of hypogamous marriages have been reported. Group distinctions were so sharply maintained that it does not appear to have been possible for a girl to retain her group membership even after marrying a person from a lower group though she could then perhaps join the husband's group. We may then say that, given the unilineal descent system, the few breaches of endogamy that did occur did not blur group boundaries. Another significant point is that, since marriages have taken place according to Islamic forms, even where a marital union met with societal disapproval, it used to be, and is, legally valid. An individual's rights in property remained unaffected for, theoretically, these rights were inalienable and property was indivisible. There does not appear to have been any mechanism like a caste panchayat to enforce endogamy, but the authority and control of the Koyas have been effective.

Power and Deference Structures

As mentioned earlier, the Koyas were in possession of land and trees and the lower groups depended on them for their livelihood. Through landlord-tenant or master-servant relationships, the Koyas controlled the lower groups, particularly the Melacheris. Along with control over land, they had a monopoly over the ownership of *odams*. This gave the Koyas their economic supremacy. The significance of this prerogative has to be assessed in relation to the fact that, all along, the Islands have been dependent on the mainland—their economy is based on the carrying of copra, coir, and some minor products to the mainland and the bringing in return of rice—their staple food—cloth, and most of the articles of consumption. The Malumis were captains and sailors but had no right to carry on maritime trade by themselves. The Melacheris carried the loads, loaded the *odams* with the help of small boats, and served as crew. They also did the cooking while at sea. Those Koyas who did not own *odams* could hire them from the owners. Thus, the disposal of all the coir and copra of the island was in the hands of the Koyas and it was up to them to give or not to give the full value of these goods to their producers, and to get the necessities of life for them at fair prices. The tenants and labourers were obliged to send their goods in their masters' *odams* or along with their masters' goods. Even access to the mainland, thus, depended on the Koyas, for there was no steamer service in those days.

It is little wonder, therefore, that political power was also in the hands of the Koyas. Not much is known about the period when the islands were independent or under the Chirakkal rule, but a few legends popular among the people indicate that some persons from the highest group were chieftains or headmen, each in charge of a particular area on the islands. Thus, there were four such chieftains on Amini, all from the highest group. It is said that there may have been panchayats to assist them. The Chirakkal Raja made these chieftains his administrative representatives. When, during the regime of the Arakkal Raja of Cannanore, jurors were appointed from among the islanders to assist the *karyakar* (the agent of the ruler), Rs. 300 to 400 used to be charged as fee for the position of juror. All these jurors were Koyas and their positions were hereditary, running in the matrilineal line.

When the British changed the system in the Laccadive group of islands and appointed an Amin and his council of elders (*karnavar*) in place of a *karyakar*, political authority remained in the hands of the highest group. Thus on Kalpeni, till 1954, there were sixteen Koya matrilineages who sent elders to the council. The genealogies of some of them mention the ancestor who paid Rs. 300 to 400 and became a juror. In 1904, the *mokhayastans* numbered twenty-one. On Amini, those who enjoyed administrative and jural authority belonged to particular Koya *tharavads*. Thus, this group was able to suppress the lower groups and maintain the *status quo*.

The religion of the Prophet not only makes the Koran accessible to all followers, but enjoins upon them to read it. On the islands, children are required to complete one reading of the Koran in Arabic. All the male devotees of Allah are entitled to offer their prayers in congregation. Formerly, however, all religious positions were the prerogative of the Koyas. The Kazi, chief priest of the *juma* mosque and the religious head of the island, had to be a Koya; and these positions were hereditary in a particular Koya *tharavad* on each island. On Kalpeni it is still so; on Amini it is not a rigid rule although, so far, the Kazi there has always been from among the Koyas. The actual choice of a Kazi was made, however, on the basis of his religious learning. The Thangals (spiritual leaders) of Androth are regarded as the descendants of Ubaidullah, the proselytizer of the islands, and the Thangals of Kavaratti regard themselves as descendants of Sayyad Mohammed Kasim who, along with his descendants, introduced the mystic cult of Raffai and Qadiria. In the case of the Thangals, patrilineal, and not matrilineal, descent is relevant, and they are believed to be connected with the Prophet.

The priests of the mosque were Koyas while the servants required to do the menial work were Melacheris. Only the Koyas could specialize in the recitation of verses from the Koran or the names of the Saints and participate in the *mauloods* conducted on various socio-religious occasions. The Koya specialists had to be invited on such occasions by all. Similarly, it was the exclusive privilege of the Koyas to chant verses to fill in the intervals during a preacher's religious discourse (*baal*) (Kutty, 1972:26). The chanting of verses was considered necessary during various socio-religious and economic activities and the Koyas thus enjoyed a special privilege.

These distinctions in the economic, religious, and political spheres were emphasized, and thus maintained, through the expression of distance and differentiation in social life. The idom chosen for this was the one brought over from Kerala,[17]

[17] 'A Nayar should not come nearer than six paces to a Nambudiri, a man of the barber caste nearer than twelve paces, a Tiyan than thirty-six, a Malayan than sixty-four, and a Pulaiyan than ninety-six. Malabar is, indeed, the most conservative part of Southern India. The man of high caste shouts occasionally as he goes along, so that the low caste man may go off the road, and allow him to pass unpolluted. And those of the lowest castes shout as they go, to give notice of their pollution bearing presence, and, learning the command of the man of high caste, move away from the road. It is common to see people of the inferior castes travelling parallel to the road, but not daring to go along it' (Thurston, 1909, Vol. V:196). Regarding the spatial distance to be maintained between different castes we find some variations in the reports of different authorities. Hutton (1946:79-80) quotes a number of them, starting from 1807, and mentions that there may have been changes over

though shorn of its basis in the notions of ritual purity and pollution. Only a Koya was privileged to wear a shirt, shoes, and silk garments, or to use an umbrella. All this was denied to the lower groups, who were required to take the upper cloth off their shoulders and move aside if they encountered a Koya on the road. They were also expected to keep their lips covered with their fingers when talking to a Koya.

Dancing and singing in public, fireworks, and boisterous processions to celebrate marriages, circumcision, or other festive occasions were forbidden to the lower groups. If they wanted any music on such occasions, they had to invite Koya singers;

the hundred years which have been covered by the reports. The possibility of local variations in the observance of distance pollution too cannot be ruled out.

Prohibitions on wearing anything above the waist and on the use of gold ornaments and of items of luxury were widespread in Tamilnadu and Kerala (Hutton, 1946:85; 204-5). Sherring, in his *Hindu Tribes and Castes* (quoted by Bhattacharya, 1968:206), says about the Shanars, the counterparts of the Iruvas and the Tiyans of Kerala in the southern part of the present Tamilnadu: 'Their women were until recently not permitted to wear clothing above the waist. They were not allowed to carry umbrellas, to wear shoes or golden ornaments, to built houses above one storey in height. . . .' In writing about the *illam*, or exogamous descent groups of the Tiyyars, Thurston (1909, Vol. VII:43) refers to some of these disabilities by implication. He writes: 'Members of some of the Illams were allowed certain privileges and dignities. Thus, the men of the Varakat Illam (Varaka Tiyans) were in the old days permitted to travel in a *mancheel* (a hammock-cot slung on a pole). They were allowed this privilege of higher caste people, which was prohibited to the Tiyans of other Illams. . . . The Varaka Tiyans were further allowed to wear gold jewels on the neck, to don silken clothes, to fasten a sword round the waist, and to carry a shield.'

As essential parts of the traditional pattern of behaviour of the lower castes towards the higher castes in Kerala, Aiyappan (1965:86) mentions the following: (i) Keeping the prescribed distance in order not to pollute the superior person; (ii) removing the cloth, if any, covering the shoulders and/or head; (iii) using, in conversation, self-demeaning forms of speech with the special standardized servile expressions; and (iv) assuming bodily poses which have been culturally standardized. Gilbert Slater (1936:196) reports: 'Uptill 1916 no man . . . other than the. . . jenmis was allowed to tile his house, to build an upstair building or a gateway even now it is rash for a ryot to ask for such permission. . .' No man should approach him with more than a single cloth around his waist, which should not fall below his knees.

it was, however, not necessary for the Koyas to invite Melacheri singers. Members of the lower groups were not supposed to build houses better than those of the Koyas.

These disabilities were an integral part of the deference structure. Their violation did not indicate any possibility of pollution through touch or shadow, or through the sharing of air. Nor has any idea of pollution been attached to food. The Melacheris, as the servants of the Koyas, have always cooked for the feasts of the latter, and on the *odams* while sailing. The Koyas could eat food cooked at the houses of the Malumis or the Melacheris; singers, priests and religious specialists, and carpenters and masons who were from among the Koyas, expected to be fed by these people during their professional visits. If in the past there was insistence on special seating and eating arrangements for the Koyas, it was a part of the deference structure, emphasizing inequality of status.

Changing Inter-Group Relations

As a result of their struggle stretching over almost half a century, the lower groups were able to free themselves from most of these disabilities. Revolts, defiance, sustained effort to better their conditions, and appeals to the government—which lay largely beyond the political and administrative orbit of the Koyas—all have gone into achieving these changes. Some extracts from Kutty's account of events on Kalpeni will be useful in giving an idea of the turmoil in the Laccadives since the close of the last century. We shall also look into some events on Amini and the minor islands.

Kutty writes:

> The beginning of the twentieth century witnessed a mental stir among the lower groups; the Melacheris taking a lead. In 1913, at a wedding in the house of a Melacheri, the people of his group engaged themselves in singing. On hearing this a furious mob of the Koyas surrounded the house and destroyed most of its material possessions. In the same year some Melacheris filed a petition before the Malabar Collector for granting them the right to wear shirts

and sandals, to use umbrellas, and to sing on festive occasions. The verdict of the Inspecting Officer on the petition was interesting. He allowed the use of umbrellas only for protection from rain and sun and not with the specific intention of displaying it before the Koyas. Songs could be sung inside the houses, but not in a procession. And it was only during voyages that they were allowed to wear shirts. He, however, granted them the use of shirts on the island when the heat could become unbearable. Later a Melacheri succeeded in getting permission from the Collector to wear a shirt all the time on the island, but, after reaching the island mosque for Friday prayer clad in a shirt, he was assaulted by the Koyas and lost his shirt. The struggle of the lower group found a few supporters among the Koyas also. Some of the Malis who were becoming economically better off also supported the Melacheris, though indirectly. Towards 1931, owing to the strict warnings to the Koyas from various officers, the lower groups were able to assert their rights of wearing shirts and sandals, holding umbrellas, and singing in the processions. When some of the Malis and the Melacheris began to amass money and became economically secure, the Koyas found it difficult to prevent them from building taller and more beautiful houses. The two lower groups also started constructing mosques on government lands. The rights to own an Odam (big sailing craft) and to have a share in administration were yet to be achieved.

About a quarter of a century ago, a rich Mali started taking Odams on rent and sailing them to the mainland for trade. The Koya owners of Odams were only too glad to give their sailing craft on rent which was fairly attractive. This amounted to the tacit acceptance by the Koyas of the right of a member of a lower group to engage in maritime trade. Induced by the success of this man, in 1949 twelve Melacheris jointly purchased an Odam and applied for its registration in the court of the Amin. The majority of the Karnavars who formed the Council of Elders objected to this and the matter was referred to the Collector. The next day an outraged mob of the Koyas set fire to the coconut shed of those who had purchased the Odam and began assaulting the Melacheris. Unable to maintain law and order, the Amin

> requested the Collector for the help of the police. The Melacheris, on the other hand, decided to sail their Odam to the mainland with the remaining cargo. But the Odam and the whole cargo were sunk and destroyed by the Koyas. The next Visiting Officer convicted those Koyas who were found guilty, and gave the lower groups the right to own and run the big sailing crafts. At present, the Melacheris own two big sailing crafts. In 1952 the administration succeeded in persuading the Koyas to include two Karnavars from the Mali and four from the Melacheri group in the Council of Elders, thus fulfilling a desire which the lower groups had been cherishing for years (1972:23-4).

On Amini, the Koyas have been far less in numbers than the Melacheris. Ellis' estimate, which must have been for the beginning of the present century, has already been cited. According to the figures collected by Ittaman in 1962 (excluding Government employees and recent migrants, who accounted for 3.22 per cent of the total population of Amini) the Koyas formed 31 per cent of the population, the Melacheris 53.68 per cent, and the Malumis 12.10 per cent. All available accounts of intergroup strife—disputes over property and over landlord-tenant relations, assertions of religious rights, and revolts against social disabilities—present the Koyas and the Melacheris as the two groups confronting each other. It appears that on this island, as on other Tharavad islands, the Malumis (also known as Kudiyathis in Amini), who were never as servile to the Koyas as the Melacheris, did not work as a group against the Koyas, but tried to improve their economic condition and get closer to the Koyas. Since they did not tap toddy or pluck coconuts this was easier for them than it was for the Melacheris. They perhaps supported the Melacheris only where necessary, and that too indirectly. It is difficult to say if the social disabilities were enforced on them with equal rigour, and whether they continued to suffer from these disabilities as long as the Melacheris. There are indications that the Malumis' condition improved much earlier on some islands. The official reports also referred only to the dissatisfaction of the Melacheris. Ellis wrote about the occupational and social disabilities of the Melacheris alone. About the Malumis he said, 'some of the Malumis also are Jenmies but usually on a smaller scale than the Koyas. Most of them are tenants' (1924:70-2). The *Malabar Gazetteer* of 1908 mentioned that many of the *karnavars* (elders) on Kavaratti belonged to the Malumi group (Chapter XVI, pp. 508-31). Logan described the Malumis of Androth as *Patta Kudians*, i.e., only partly dependent on the higher classes. He mentioned that they were regarded as interlopers and rebels by the Koyas for they had some small *odams* in their possession (1887: ccxii).

It appears that, in the last decades of the nineteenth century, the Melacheris of Amini were developing a feeling of being oppressed. D. Cowrie, Acting Head Assistant Collector of South Canara, wrote in his report in 1891: 'There are no Moktessors to represent the lowest Melacheri caste. Some people of this caste hinted to me that they would like some to be appointed, but the Monegar's opinion is that the Moktessors of higher castes would strongly object to the innovation. . . .'

In those days Government officers did not encourage departures from customary practices, and worked with the advice of the Koya elders; but the struggle of the Melacheris gained momentum gradually and they pressed hard for action on the part of the Government. At the beginning of the present century the Melacheris proposed to the Inspecting Officers visiting the island that, since the Government activities carried out on the island were for the benefit of all, every group should be asked to participate in all the work including manual work. A favourable order was issued, but it was not implemented properly. In 1909, the Melacheris put their case before the Inspecting Officers again, saying that the services of the various classes should be defined. The *moktessors* and the people were consulted, and duties were defined in an Order. In this Order, group distinctions and the work customarily associated with each group were taken into consideration. Thus, all the groups were supposed to cooperate in activities such as the repairing of paths, rat-killing drives, and the launching of *odams*. Work on the roofs was to be done exclusively by the Melacheris, and menial work such as bringing firewood for Government officials and carrying water and heavy luggage, was assigned to them and to the Malumis.

We find a number of *jenmi-kudian* (tenant-landlord) disputes coming to the courts during this period. They are indicative of the consciousness of oppression that was developing among the Melacheris. Even after the end of Arakkal rule, all the land on Amini remained *jenmom* land, which was the property of the upper groups by whose will the lower classes lived and worked on it.[18] The traditional *pazhaya kudian* tenancy (which continued with modifications till the recent land reforms) was a kind of service tenure. Under it the tenants were given barren land for improvement and a certain number of trees (30 to 50) to harvest. They lived and worked on the landlords' plantations, and gave a part of the produce (one-fifth to one-tenth) as lease payment. The Melacheri tenants were obliged to do the work of cultivation, coconut plucking, and toddy tapping for the landlord in return for customarily defined payments, and had no right to work for others without his permission. They were also obliged to entrust their produce—coir and copra—to the landlord for sale on the mainland, and had to forgo one-tenth of the total produce by way of freightage. The customary services involved in this type of tenancy included acting as crew on the landlords' boats and sailing one or two trips to the mainland; oiling and painting the *odam* and thatching the *odam* shed; helping in fishing and in the loading and unloading of *odams*;

[18]The system of land control and use has not been uniform on all the islands. On Kavaratti, trees and cultivable land were given to the tenants by landlords on a share-cropping basis; as a part of the obligations of tenancy, tenant households were required to perform a number of services for the landlord's households and to send their produce in the landlord's *odams*. Different kinds of menial services and assistance in the tasks of production, as well as in festivals and crises of life, the obligation to make a certain number of trips to the mainland in the landlord's *odam*, and to send his own goods in it, have been the prominent features of tenancy on the islands. Thus it has had a feudal character involving customary services by the tenants to the landlords in return for occupational rights in land and the right to cultivate the trees on it. On Kalpeni the principal economic relationship has been the one between master and servant. The Melacheris did not take land or trees on service tenure but were attached as servants and did the coconut plucking and toddy tapping on the master's trees, receiving from a fourth to a third part of the produce. The other obligations which servants had towards their masters' households were almost the same as in the traditional landlord-tenant relationship. With some modifications, these arrangements have continued on Kalpeni (Dube, 1969:15-6).

and doing menial work for the landlord's household, particularly during ceremonies and at other festive occasions. It was a special privilege of the *jenmi* to receive the head of the animal slaughtered in the *kudian's* house. The relationship involved many such formalities, and also ritual obligations. A Melacheri tenant, for instance, was required to carry a notice on his shoulder on the day prior to circumcision; he also had to hold an umbrella over the bridegroom at weddings.

The tenancy rights of a *pazhaya kudian* were more or less permanent. The landlord could not evict the *kudian* whenever he wished. He could only enforce the customary services by bringing suits against the defaulting *kudians*. In the rare cases where this proved to be impossible and the *kudian* had to be ordered by the court to relinquish his tenancy rights, he was entitled to compensation according to island custom. Here, too, the Koyas must have been in an advantageous position, being able to get favourable decisions out of the *moktessors* who were mostly Koyas.

The *pazhaya kudian* properties, or tenancy rights, however, were somewhat permanent and were worked, shared, and inherited in the same manner as the *jenmom* properties. And when the *jenmom* properties were divided among the various branches of a matrilineal group, the *kudians* were divided correspondingly.

On Amini, at the beginning of this century, besides *pazhaya kudians* there were also *puthiya kudians*—tenants who could be evicted and for whom customary services were not defined—and labourers working on wage payments. But it was mainly the *pazhaya kudians*, with their long association with particular properties and particular landlords in a system of rights and obligations, whom we find involved in court cases and asserting their rights. Often they would refuse to sail to the mainland more than the prescribed number of times. The *jenmis* then took such measures as taking possession of the *kudian's* trees, refusing him entry to the land improved by him, and stopping him from using soaking pits standing on the *jenmom* land of the landlord or of his associates.

As mentioned earlier, the Malumis and some Melacheris came to acquire *jenmom* rights in some properties through a number of factors. Gradually, the Melacheri tenants started refusing to hand over their produce to their landlords. The establishment of a Government Coir Depot, which accepted coir and gave rice in exchange, must have contributed to the process of emancipation of the Melacheris.

Caste Disputes and the Struggle of Minor Islands

After 1933, we find a number of disputes over social disabilities between the Koyas and the Melacheris, for the latter started defying those customary practices that were indicative of their low status, and made representations and appeals to the Inspecting Officers. By wearing sandals and by walking on public paths, they were trying to assert their human dignity; but such behaviour was infuriating to the Koyas.

This pent-up anger burst out in 1933 when fireworks were used at a Melacheri wedding. The Koyas were furious, and there was physical violence resulting in serious injuries on both sides. Many were arrested. As a retaliatory measure the landlords withdrew all the privileges given to the Melacheri tenants and servants. They restrained the Melacheris from drawing water from their wells and destroyed many tanks and wells used by the Melacheris. Ditches prepared by the Melacheris to soak coconut husks were taken away from them, and many *kudians* were evicted. The *monegar* called the leaders of both sides and asked them to try to arrive at an amicable settlement among themselves, but no heed was paid to this suggestion. Many Melacheris were beaten by the Koyas for wearing shoes. The situation was brought under control with the Collector's Order in April 1934, which said that the government could not support such distinctions in social customs as would put one class at a disadvantage; it also emphasized the interdependence of landlords and tenants, and advised them to make matters smooth for each other. By this Order, two *moktessors* were appointed from among the Melacheris for the first time to look into matters concerning the Melacheris.

In 1950, the Melacheris put up a resistance against the religious disabilities which they had been suffering all along. They were not allowed to participate in *baitha*, the recitation of devotional songs sung in connection with *rathib* (*dhikr*), which used to be conducted in the Mohiddin and Ujra mosques. The two Kavaratti Thangals or Sheikhs who owned these mosques were supposed to be against caste distinctions and, when approached, agreed to teach *baitha* to some Melacheri young men. During Ramadan these young men, who were trained by them, forcibly took the *daffs* (tambourines) from the hands of the Koyas and joined the *rathib*. The Koyas were extremely angry with the Melacheris for going against the established custom. They lodged a protest with the Thangal, who refused to allow any such distinctions which, according to him, were against the principles of their religion. The Koyas split up: some joined the Melacheris for *rathib*; others established two separate mosques for the purpose. The Deputy Collector had to stop the custom of the *rathib* party going round the island on festive occasions, for the Koyas and the Melacheris had formed two parties which had clashed frequently.

In 1957, the Melacheris of Amini took a daring step. At the death of a Melacheri, they brought the corpse to the graveyard attached to the Jam'iyyat mosque and, ignoring the Kazi of the island whose duty it was to conduct the necessary prayer, brought one Kariachetta Mohammed, a Melacheri, whom they described as their own Kazi, for conducting the prayer and tried to proceed with the funeral. Kariachetta Mohammed was the man who, many years earlier, had applied and tried to push his case for the Kaziship of Amini when the position fell vacant. He had been rejected in favour of a Koya applicant belonging to a *tharavad* related to the original but now extinct *tharavad* that provided the Kazis for Amini. The Melacheris kept quiet, waiting for their chance to break away. They got this chance in 1957, when all kinds of changes were being made in the economic system and the administrative set-up.

The Koyas were furious and felt insulted by the insolent behaviour of the Melacheris. The Koyas did not allow the Melacheris to bury the corpse in the graveyard of the Jam'iyyat mosque. When this matter was represented to the Government, the Deputy Tehsildar issued orders forbidding both parties to have any kind of religious performance in the Jam'iyyat mosque. This stopped even the Friday community prayers. After a few days, the two parties reached a compromise and put in a request to allow them to hold these community prayers. This was granted. Many Melacheris took to inviting their own Kazi for different social and religious occasions. In 1963, they expressed their determination to fight for the Kaziship of the island when it should fall vacant after the death of the incumbent who was a Koya.

The extent of control that the upper groups of Amini (who gradually came to be called the Koyas) exercised over the Melacheris can be more clearly understood through the pattern of control—economic, political, and religious—evolved by them over the minor islands of the Amindivi group. The inhabitants of these islands—Chetlat, Kiltan, and Kadamat—were all Melacheris and were regarded by the landlords of Amini as their tenants. Amini was the seat of administration since the days of Arakkal rule. The *karyakar*, and later the *monegar*, was stationed on Amini and visited and administered these minor islands also. The *mokhyastans* or *moktessors* (jurors) were all from Amini and also had their say in matters concerning these islands. To facilitate their administration, the minor islands also had elders who acted as jurors in the absence of the *moktessors* of Amini. But they were known as *moopans* (elders) and not as *mokhyastans* (important people or chiefs) or as *moktessors* (ruling persons or chiefs). As A.F.G. Moscardi wrote in his report in 1899, 'the Mupans . . . must, originally, have been quite subordinate to the Mokhtessors who even now retain the right of sitting in the Kutchery while the Mupans stand up; and not only in Amini, but in any island which a Mokhtessor may have to visit.'

It was somewhere in the nineteenth century that the people of Chetlat and Kiltan started owning *odams*. But, as late as 1889, it used to be necessary for a *moktessor* from Amini to preside at the launching of a trading boat from these islands. This practice had been discontinued by 1904 as is apparent from the reports of Inspecting Officers. On Kadamat, before 1860, no islander had trees of his own. All were tenants of the landlords from Amini and had to ship their produce in the *odams* of these landlords. By 1869, the people of Kadamat had built three small coast-going boats. In 1886 Mir Shujaat Ali, the Inspecting Officer, wrote that after a prolonged struggle with the boat-owning residents of Amini, who claimed that the Kadamatians were their serfs, the latter had begun to build their own boats.

These minor islands did not have independent Kazis, but each had a Naib Kazi regarded as subservient to the Kazi of Amini who had his jurisdiction over the entire Amindivi group of islands. The Naib Kazis were supposed to perform the duties of the Kazi in his absence. Like the Kazi, they were also appointed by the District Collector of Canara after securing the approval of the Kazi of Amini. This was so even at the beginning of the present century.

Due to distance, Chetlat (35 miles away from Amini) and Kiltan (32 miles away from Amini) found it easier to wriggle out of the hold of Amini than did Kadamat, which is only 16 miles away from Amini. The distance made it impracticable for the Kazi of Amini to be present on Chetlat or on Kiltan too often and, therefore, these islands were left to themselves most of the time and could thus attain independence without much strife. The people of Kadamat, however, had to fight against the interference of the Kazi of Amini. Between 1886 and 1900, they appealed to the Government on five different occasions to make the Naib Kazi of Kadamat independent of the Amini Kazi; the Amini Kazi claimed in his appeal that he had a right to appoint, dismiss, and direct the Kadamat Naib Kazi, and that he was entitled to perquisites on the minor islands. The people of Kadamat launched a prolonged struggle to assert thier freedom from the control of the Kazi of Amini, in which they leant upon Islamic values and practices such as the role of the congregation in the selection of the Kazi and of the place to hold the community prayers.

Conclusion

In this paper an attempt has been made to present a picture of the evolution, nature, and functioning of the caste-like groups which form the social system of the Laccadive and Amindivi groups of islands. In the absence of an authentic social and cultural history of Kerala—covering the early centuries of the Christian era—and because of our lack of knowledge about the past of the islands, this account is necessarily sketchy. The pedigrees and genealogies of the islanders, and official and other records, could possibly provide valuable information, but so far these sources have not been tapped properly. The paucity of evidence notwithstanding, we can say with reasonable certainty that, when the major migrations to these islands occurred, Kerala had already developed a rigid caste system operating within a feudal structure; and that, before the coming of Islam to the islands, a socio-economic system closely approximating to the one operating in the original setting had adapted itself to the new ecological and demographic situation.

The islands were never self-sufficient and had to develop a pattern of regular trade with the mainland. It would appear that many craftsmen castes were not present on the islands, but service castes like barbers and washermen—the removers of ritual pollution—must have been there. It can hardly be doubted that, in the new setting, control over land devolved to the two highest castes (or caste categories): the Nambudiri Brahmins, traditionally priests and scholars, landlords and law-givers; and the Nayars, with their tradition of being rulers, leaders, landlords, and non-cultivating tenants (with superior rights) who leased land to others or employed sharecroppers. It is likely that the lineages of the chieftains and the headmen enjoyed high caste status as they did in Malabar. These higher castes could not have survived without the people who worked for them. If we go by the island tradition, the Tiyyars, with their tradition of coconut cultivation, farm service, and toddy tapping, must have provided the labour needed for cultivation and other activities. The Mukkuvans (or fishermen) were also likely to have been used by the upper groups for manual work. It is difficult to say if the untouchable agricultural labourers or any other castes had ever settled on the islands, but it can safely be assumed that these islands were not like a group of villages forming a region, and that each lived largely its own life, perpetuating itself from within. Inter-island migrations and marriages were sporadic. There were only a few grades of rights and interests in land; certainly not as many as had developed in Kerala.[19] The proliferation of occupational groups was not

[19]In the last few decades we have had many accounts of the caste structure of Kerala and its relation to the land tenure system with

possible in this setting. It is certain that the basic economic structure persisted even after the coming of Islam to the islands.

Some significant features of the social system of these island communities may be recapitulated. Instead of many castes, we find three (or four) major groups: the landowners, boat owners, and traders; the sailors of the masters' craft and tenants doing menial work; and the tree-climbers, toddy tappers, tenants, labourers, and menials. For some islands we have evidence of two groups at the level of landowners, for, the lineages of the important people, administrator, and religious heads form a distinct group. But, with the data that we have, it is not possible to say whether the original caste links of the two groups differed, or if there has been a pattern of hypergamy among the lineages belonging to them. The process of the gradual merging of the two groups needs to be studied.

There are no artisan or service and occupational castes on the islands, but the crafts and occupations associated with castes below the line of pollution in Kerala have been restricted mostly to the lowest group.

Religious learning, priestly functions, and the handling of religious lore on special occasions were the exclusive prerogative of the upper groups. This was not in keeping with Islamic values, but a carry-over from the past. Robinson (1846) mentioned that the lineage of the Kazi of Amini was originally of the highest status, tracing its origin to a Nambudiri house of pre-conversion days, and that the lineages of the Kazis of Kavaratti and Kalpeni were also related to this lineage. The legend relating to the islanders' conversion to Islam says that the first person to take to Islam was a woman from this *tharavad*. She was married by Ubaidulla, the saint who converted all the islands to the new faith. Ubaidulla is believed to have been an Arab tracing his ancestry to the Prophet. As charters of the rights and privileges, these stated genealogical connections are significant.

Thus, the essential distinction was between those who did manual labour and menial work and those who did not. This distinction between the working people and the leisure class

graded interests in land. See, for instance, Aiyappan (1942), Gough (1960), Mayer (1952), Miller (1960), Oomen (1971), and Rao (1957).

corresponded with the one between the landowners and the non-landowners, and with the one between those who were privileged to own sailing craft and to trade and those who were not so privileged. Of the two unprivileged groups, the one which refrained from tree-climbing and toddy-tapping could claim a somewhat higher status.

The group distinctions were maintained through the use of those social diacritical marks and devices expressing social distance between the higher and the lower groups that must have been in vogue before conversion. In the final analysis, the economic system, in which the Koyas controlled the utilization of resources and were the principal beneficiaries in material terms, was sustained through this system of social grouping which made for differential access to political, religious, and economic power and privileges. The disabilities were the idiom in which the differences of rank were expressed and, even without the notion of pollution, were effective devices to prevent the lower groups from acquiring higher status and more power. The lower groups did not have their own panchayats: the dominant groups—with their economic, administrative, and religious power—exercised control over all the groups.

The coming of Islam to the islands led to a kind of evaporation of the Hindu notions of ritual purity and pollution. As is well known, Islamic concern with the removal of impurity and the attainment of a state of purity is in reference to prayer or communion with God and to religious activities like fasting. This impurity derives mainly from body processes and applies equally to all devotees. Not being inherent, it is not used as a basis for group differentiation. As devout Muslims, the islanders follow the Islamic injunctions about maintaining a state of purity while approaching God; but the Hindu notions of vulnerability, of the purity of food, of pollution incurred at death, and of the pollution of menstrual blood are absent. Death does not cause pollution to others in the Hindu way. The corpse is washed to purity after the departure of the soul, which was until then its purifier. This is in accordance with the tenets of the Shafi school of Islam to which all the islanders belong. But the people who participate in the funeral do not seem to incur pollution; at the house of the deceased they are offered tea, cigarettes, and betels to chew. I came across a custom on Kalpeni known as *chavarikyam*—literally, 'sitting at death'—according to which the matrilineal kin of the deceased are supposed to abstain from productive work for a stipulated number of days. This custom seems to have been retained from earlier days, for it has been prevalent among the coastal Nayars. Now, however, it is an expression of common bereavement and does not indicate pollution and is functional in that it emphasizes the unity of the *tharavad.* In point of fact, the claims to property, particularly those of reversionary heirs, are closely related to this custom.

Menstruation also involves pollution, mainly in the context of prayer and fasting as enjoined in Islam. It is reported that, till a few decades ago, the first menstruation of a girl used to be celebrated; nowadays she only receives some presents of food from close relatives (Kutty, 1972:41). In the matrilineal context, giving importance to the first menstruation is easily understandable, for it announces the fecundity of a perpetuator of the line; this is not necessarily associated with the danger of pollution.[20]

The possible amalgamation of many small caste groups, resulting in a limited number of endogamous groups, can be partly attributed to this freedom from the Hindu ideas of ritual purity and pollution. Perhaps the fact that there was no horizontal spread of caste groups, with facilities for continuous interaction and give-and-take in marriage, may also have contributed to this amalgamation. And it is also important to remember that the island communities evolved their own unique system of groups under Islam away from the Hindu environment. The pattern of hypergamy in Kerala, which started from the Nambudiris and stopped at the lower groups of Nayars, had perhaps been carried by the immigrants to the islands; this also must have facilitated amalgamation at the higher levels.

It is evident that this system of groups—characterised by endogamy, interdependence, and hierarchy—has persisted without the operation of the dichotomy between ritual purity and pollution. It appears to have derived its justification from the

[20]Among the Nayars around Cochin, the practice of announcing the first menstruation of a girl by *korava* (shouts of joy by females) was in vogue till recently (Chandrika, 1971). For the puberty ceremony among the Nayars see Thurston (1909, Vol. V: 336-37).

principle of high and low ancestry and the distinction between menial and non-menial occupations. Beliefs about the past have provided a basis for the present scheme of differentiation. The Brahmins and the Nayars, from whom the Koyas are believed to have descended, represented those who had power, authority, and economic resources, and who refrained from hard manual labour and menial work. The Brahmin also represented piety and was the repository of religious knowledge. On the other hand, the supposed ancestors of the Melacheris, the Tiyyars and the Mukkuvans, and also those of the various occupational and artisan castes of the lower levels, subsisted on manual labour and menial work. In the pre-conversion scheme they were at a far lower level than the Brahmins and the Nayars.

This association of high or low birth could be perpetuated through matrilineal kinship groups which formed the structural base of the social system. Descent alone has been the basis of membership in these caste-like groups; a person's affiliation to his matrilineage gave him his rights and privileges, and economic relationships were between matrilineages or matrilineal segments. There was little possibility of shaking off this affiliation. *Tharavads*, *kudumbams* consisting of matrilineally related *tharavads*, and *kootams* consisting of related *kudumbams* and *tharavads*, all emphasized the ancestry of a person.

This brings us to the crucial question: Does the presence of caste-like groups on the Laccadive Islands indicate mainly the resilience of the Hindu caste system which manifests itself even under the egalitarian values of Islam, or is there something in Islam itself which could be utilized for supporting such distinctions? Are distinctions of birth repugnant to Islam? There is enough evidence in Islamic literature to show that, besides indicating a favourable attitude towards good custom (*urf*), that religion also places emphasis on ancestry. Two instances may be cited here. Tradition says, 'you will find people like mines (i.e., gold will come only from a gold mine and so on). The best of them in Jahiliya (i.e., before Islam) are the best of them in Islam when they learn the faith.'[21] Can this not be interpreted as favouring the retention of pre-Islamic distinctions of birth? This is what the Laccadive people have done. The following

[21]Taken from *Sahih*, Bukhari; Kitabu'l-Manaqib.

aspect of Shafi Law, which elaborates on the implications of the appropriate status of the parties to marriage, gives clear indication of the presence of graded distinctions between different types of ancestry and between different occupations:

> . . . Regarding ancestry, a non-Arab cannot be considered an equal of an Arab woman or a non-Qurashite (Prophet's tribe) that of a Qurashite woman, or a non-Hashimi and Muttalibi equal to any of the above. The similar ancestry could also exist amongst the non-Arabs. . . . About the professionals, a person having a menial profession is not an equal of a person having a higher profession. A sweeper, a barber, a watchman, a shepherd and conductor of baths are not equals of a daughter of a tailor, nor is a tailor an equal of a daughter of a trader and retailer, agriculturist or a dairyman, and they in turn are not equals of a daughter of a scholar or a judge.[22]

It may be noted that a person doing menial work is regarded as distinctly lower in status than one who is engaged in non-menial work and, again, that those who are engaged in learned professions are higher in status than those who work with their hands.

[22]Taken from an authoritative Shafi text: *Minhaju't-Taliban* of Yahya b. Sharaf an-Nawawi. Egyptian edition printed in 1318 *A.H.*: 83.

Bibliography

Aiyappan, A. (1942), *Iruvas and Culture Change*, Madras, Madras Government.

———(1965), *Social Revolution in a Kerala Village: A Study in Culture Change*, Bombay, Asia Publishing House.

Bhattacharya, J.N. (1968), *Hindu Castes aud Sects*, Reprint of the 1896 ed., Calcutta, Editions Indian.

Chandrika, M.D. (1971), *Nayar Taravads Through Generations*, Unpublished M.A. Dissertation, Department of Anthropology and Sociology, University of Saugar.

Dube, Leela (1969), *Matriliny and Islam*, Delhi, National Publishing House.

Ellis, R.H. (1924), *A Short Account of the Laccadive Islands and Minicoy*, Madras, Government Press.

Gough, E. Kathleen (1960), 'Caste in a Tanjore Village', in E.R. Leach (ed.), *Aspects of Caste in South India, Ceylon and North-west Pakistan*, Cambridge, Cambridge University Press.

———(1962a), 'Nayars: Central Kerala', in E.K. Gough and D.M. Schneider (eds.) *Matrilineal Kinship*, Berkeley, University of California Press.

———(1962b), 'Tiyyars: North Kerala', in E.K. Gough and D.M. Schneider (eds.) *Matrilineal Kinship*, Berkeley, University of California Press.

Hutton, John H. (1946), *Caste in India: Its Nature, Function and Origins*, Cambridge, Cambridge University Press.

Ittaman, K.P. (1976), *Amini Islanders: Social Structure and Change*, New Delhi, Abhinav Publications.

Kutty, A.R. (1972), *Marriage and Kinship in an Island Society*, Delhi, National Publishing House.

Logan, William (1887), *Malabar*, 2 vols., Madras, Government Press.

Mayer, Adrian C. (1952), *Land and Society in Malabar*, London, Oxford University Press.

Menon, A Sreedhara (1967), *A Survey of Kerala History*, Kottayam, Sahitya Pravarthaka Co-operative Society Ltd.

Miller, E. (1960), 'Village Structure in North Kerala', in M.N. Srinivas ed.), *India's Villages*, 2nd ed., Bombay, Asia Publishing House.

Nainar S. Muhammad Hysayan (1942), *Arab Geographers' Knowledge of Southern India*, Madras, Madras University.

Narayanan, M.G.S. (1972a), *Political and Social Conditions of Kerala Under the Kulasekhara Empire* (c. 800 A.D. to 1124 A.D.), Unpublished Ph.D. Thesis, University of Kerala.

———(1972b), *Cultural Symbiosis in Kerala*, Trivandrum, Kerala Historical Society.

Oomen, M.A. (1971), *Land Reforms and Socio-Economic Change in Kerala*, Madras, Christian Literature Society.

Panikkar, K.M. (1960), *A History of Kerala, 1498-1801*, Annamalainagar, Annamalai University.

Rao, M.S.A. (1957), *Social Change in Malabar*, Bombay, Popular Book Depot.

Shekhar, A.C. (1953), *Evolution of Malayalam*, Poona, Deccan College Post-Graduate and Research Institute.

Slater, Gilbert (1936), *Southern India: Its Social and Economic Problems*, London, George Allen and Unwin.

Thurston, E. & Rangachari, K. (1909), *Castes and Tribes of Southern India*, 7 vols., Madras, Government Press.

The following official documents and publications were also consulted:

Robinson's Report, (1846, 1848).

Inspecting Officers' Reports.

Malabar Gazetteer (1905).

Imperial Gazetteer (1908).

Laccadive Island and Minicoy Regulations, 1912, 1965.

Annual Administration Reports of the Union Territory of Laccadive, Minicoy and Amindivi.

4

The Khojas of Bombay: The Defining of Formal Membership Criteria During the Nineteenth Century

J.C. Masselos

The Khojas of Bombay are particularly well known (see, for example, Dumasia, 1939; Hollister, 1953; Picklay, 1940; Lokhandwalla, 1967). The strong personalities and the flamboyance of their religious leaders, the Aga Khans, as well as their successes in the worlds of finance, trade and politics in Western India during the nineteenth and twentieth centuries have attracted considerable attention. They are today a fairly prosperous, tightly knit and well organized body, despite their dispersion outside the subcontinent. This was, however, not always so. At the beginning of the nineteenth century, the Khojas were far more amorphous and considerably less affluent. It was only during the subsequent century that they moved from petty retailing and hawking into trade and thereby into prosperity. At the same time, the informal and implicit basis of membership that had hitherto existed amongst them came to be replaced by formal and rigid criteria which had the effect of excluding some members and appreciably altering the actual structure of internal power. This was achieved not without dispute and dissension, but, in the process, the self-view of the Khojas became clarified and their sense of identity, albeit at the cost of schism, was promoted.

Why and how did this occur? What were the social and historical forces at work that induced these changes and what was the effect of their impact? Preliminary and tentative answers to these questions are suggested in this paper. They have been derived from information contained in the archival records of the former Government of Bombay which found itself somewhat more involved in Khoja affairs than it perhaps desired. In addition, there were a number of celebrated law suits throughout the century that provide a wealth of information. It seems that the learned judges of the Supreme and then the High Court welcomed the diversion from the usual, somewhat dreary, cases of fraud and chicanery and delivered inspired and detailed judgements on law suits instituted by the Khojas. Moreover, the evidence given in these suits by various leading Khojas of the day furnishes information that, despite its bias, prejudice and inaccuracy, is otherwise not obtainable now.

The descendants of Lohanas and, possibly to a lesser extent, of other Hindu trading castes, the Khojas had been converted to Islam in the fifteenth century. From that time they seem to have been particularly mobile, both occupationally and geographically. They were originally agriculturists and petty farmers, but gradually moved into hawking and other kinds of small-scale retail activity until, eventually, a few of them began to achieve success in the larger spheres of trade and commerce in the 1830s and 1840s. By the end of the century, the number of such Khojas had grown considerably.

Concurrently, over the centuries, the Khojas had spread out of Sind to Kutch and Kathiawar, and thence, from the late eighteenth century, down to Bombay Town and Island, as well as across to Zanzibar, Muscat and other overseas centres of trade. They were not numerous: it was claimed that there were perhaps 150 or 200 families in Bombay by the end of the 1830s.[1] By 1847 this figure had grown to about 600 houses or families.[2]

[1]Evidence of Hassoon Syed in the 'Khojas and Memon's Case' [hereafter *KC*], *The Telegraph and Courier* [hereafter *T & C*], 24 June 1847.

[2]Evidence of Cassum Natha and statement of E. Perry in *KC*, ibid.

It further rose to 730 in 1950[3] and to 1400 in 1866.[4] The figures may well be inaccurate but they do give some indication of the fluidity of the Khojas and of their movement into Bombay and suggest, at least initially, a lack of close identification with that city. Of the leading Khojas, there were comparatively few who, like Habib Ibrahim, could maintain in 1847 that they had been born in Bombay and had never gone farther than Salsette and Thana on Bombay's outskirts.[5] Far more typical was Allarukia Soomar, Khoja Mukhi or treasurer from the fifties to the seventies, who had migrated from Sind at an early age and had then established himself successfully in Bombay in the sugar, piecegoods and commission business.[6] Equally typical was the succeeding Mukhi, Hassanbhoy Goolam Hoossein, who had lived in Bhavnagar till he was fourteen, had then gone to Muscat for two or three years, had returned to India (to Bombay) for three years and then went to Zanzibar for nineteen years before finally settling down in Bombay in the mid-sixties. In the process he established himself as a major shipowner and trader.[7]

[3]*The Bombay Times and Journal of Commerce* [hereafter *BT*], 21 July 1851; *The Times of India* [hereafter *TI*], 24 April 1866.

[4]Arnould's judgement in 'the Aga Khan Case' (or The Advocate General *ex relatione* Daya Muhammad, Muhammed Sayad and others *v*. Muhammad Husen Huseni (otherwise called Aga Khan and others) [hereafter *AKC*] in W.E. Hart (ed.), *Reports of Cases Decided in the High Court of Bombay* (Rajkot, reprint, 1907), p. 347. [Hereafter the usual legal method of citing law cases and judgements will be followed with volume number, abbreviated reference to the Report Series and page or pages given in that order. Thus the above reference would be 12 *BHC* 347].

[5]Evidence of 'Hubah Ebraim', i.e., Habib Ibrahim, in *KC*, *T&C*, 24 June 1847.

[6]Evidence of Allarukia Soomar in *AKC*, *TI*, 14 June 1866 and in *the High Court of Judicature at Bambay. On appeal from the Ecclesiastical Side of that Court. In Goods, Chattels, Rights, and Credits of Rahimbhoy Alloobhoy, late of Bombay, Khojah Mahomedan, deceased. Heerbaee, Widow of the said deceased. Applicant. Gorebaee Rahimutbaee, Caveatrixes* (n.d., n.d.). Hereafter this printed pamphlet based on the Judge's notes of the evidence will be referred to as *H. vs G.* bound in Bombay Secretariat Record Office [hereafter *SRO*] *Judicial Dept.* [hereafter *JD*], 1880, Vol. 31, p. 93.

[7]Evidence of Hassanbhoy Goolam Hoossein in *AKC*, the *Bombay Gazette* [hereafter *BG*], 22 June 1866 and in *H. vs. G.*, pp. 87-89.

In such circumstances of mobility, the customs and beliefs of the Khojas were preserved by one major collective institution, the *jamaat* and the *jamaatkhana*. The *jamaat* was the congregation of the adult males of the town or district, while the *jamaatkhana* was the council hall in which they met. They elected from amongst themselves a Mukhi or treasurer and a Kamaria or accountant. The posts were filled on an honorary basis by the leading and usually the wealthiest men of the community and seem, at least in the early part of the nineteenth century, to have rotated with some frequency, perhaps, as was later claimed, even annually.[8] By the mid-century, for reasons to be discussed below, these positions had become virtually permanent. Allarukia Soomar was the Mukhi for over twenty years, and was followed by Hassanbhoy Goolam Hoossein who retained the post until he was murdered in 1878. Wherever the Khojas went, it was not long before a *jamaat* was formally established, a *jamaatkhana* built and office-bearers elected. It was these that collectively provided the backbone of the caste, that provided it with its organization, and maintained its values.

How did the *jamaat* operate and what precisely did it attempt to preserve? The *jamaat* in Bombay dates back to the 1740s and its records and account books to 1806.[9] It met regularly, about four times a month, the members being summoned by a crier who went through the streets inhabited by Khojas. All adult males were entitled to attend, vote on, and accept or reject the matters put before them.[10] In practice, it would seem that in the first half of the century effective decisions were taken by ten or twenty leading men in consultation with the Mukhi and the Kamaria and the results of their deliberations were subsequently ratified by the assembled body.

[8] *BT*, 21 July 1851; evidence of Habib Ibrahim in *KC*, *T & C*, 24 June 1847; evidence of Rahimbhoy Hemjah in *AKC*, *TI*, 25 April 1866 and evidence of Dhurrumsey Kakoo and Ibrahim Soomar in *H. vs. G.*, pp. 62, 69.

[9] Shia Khoja Petition, 24 September 1878 in *SRO*, *JD*, 1878. Vol. 36, n.p.; Evidence of Hassum Cassum and Allarukia Soomar in *AKC*, *BG*, 19 June 1866.

[10] Evidence of Mhandjee Mahomed in *KC*, *T & K*, 24 June 1847 and evidence of Jairaz Peerbhoy in *H. vs. G.*, pp. 75-75A.

These leaders were either men of respectability, intelligence or, more commonly, of wealth.[11] But wealth alone was not entirely sufficient; a youthful son of a Shetia or wealthy magnate, for example, would not necessarily succeed by right to his father's position on the latter's death.[12] Nevertheless, whatever the internal mechanism of decision-making and the deployment of power, the *jamaat* as a whole tended to function, at least before the 1840s, virtually autonomously. Its decisions did not require, nor was it ever sought, any outside sanction, even over such a major matter as excommunication.[13] This was to change later as indeed was the frequency with which the *jamaat* as a whole was assembled.

In its activities, the *jamaat* was 'nothing but a caste meeting, like a caste meeting of the various Hindoo castes'.[14] One of its major tasks was to settle such disputes as were brought before it. In particular, it arbitrated over quarrels between husbands and wives, considered requests for divorce and ensured that a husband supported his wife adequately. In such disputes, it sought to find solutions acceptable to both sides and in keeping with established customs. It did not try to apply any rigidly consistent principle of abstract justice. If needed, the *jamaat* could alter specific customs of a minor nature but could not interfere with practices that had the force of law, such as inheritance or succession.[15] Essentially its role was a wide one, that of a watchdog over the identity of the caste. Concretely, no Khoja marriage was valid unless it had been approved by the *jamaat* beforehand. And the *jamaat* on no account ever sanctioned the marriage of a Khoja woman to a non-Khoja man. However, a man might marry outside the caste, although the *jamaat* was entitled to state whether such a marriage was advisable or not. Such marriages were nevertheless also rare. There was no available instance during the nineteenth century of a Khoja male marrying into even the very similar Memon caste.

[11] *BT*, 21 July 1851; evidence of Rahimbhoy Hemjah in *AKC*, *TI*, 25 April 1866 and of Jairaz Peerbhoy in *H. vs. G.*, pp. 76, 79.

[12] Evidence of Cassum Natha in *KC*, *T&C*, 24 June 1847.

[13] Evidence of Allarukia Soomar in *AKC*, *TI*, 16 June 1866.

[14] Evidence of Jairaz Peerbhoy in *H. vs. G.*, p. 79.

[15] Evidence of Rahimbhoy Dhurrumsey, Dhurrumsey Kakoo and Jairaz Peerbhoy in *H. vs. G.*, pp. 59, 60, 62, 75A-76.

The only instances of exogamy that could be cited were with African and Georgian female slaves. In such cases, the offending male seems to have been excommunicated and certainly the offsprings were denied caste privileges and were prohibited from inheriting property from their father.[16] By such means, the *jamaat* maintained the exclusives and closed character of the caste and preserved it from attrition in the new areas in which the Khojas come to settle, in Bombay as well as elsewhere.

There were other things that were also preserved. Over the years, through contributions from its members, the *jamaat* in Bombay came to control sizeable amounts of property. These ranged from cooking utensils (valued at over Rs. 20,000 in 1851) needed for caste dinners, to a burial ground where Khojas strongly felt they must be buried. The *jamaatkhana* served as a regular meeting place both for socializing as well as for religious ceremonies. There was, in addition, a mosque in the burial grounds which was presided over, until the 1860s, by a Sunni *mulla*.[17] For a Khoja to be denied access to these properties and places was a major hardship, and particularly so in regard to the burial ground. Control of the *jamaat* and hence of caste affairs and caste properties was thus no small matter, while excommunication, combined as it was with social ostracization and loss of intermarriage privileges, could be a potent weapon that only the bravest and most powerful might hope to withstand.

The Khojas had a distinctive identity, one that was a unique blend of Hindu and Muslim, as well as of Shia and Sunni, customs and beliefs. They retained, for example, the joint or undivided family although of course some brothers did divide and live apart. Property followed the male line in matters of succession and inheritance and women had minimal rights over even distant male relatives of the husband. On the other hand, women were not kept in purdah and were allowed to move about freely and served in their husbands' shops whenever

[16]Evidence of Allarukia Soomar in ibid., p. 94; Evidence of Rahim Hemjah in *AKC*, *TI*, 24 April 1866 and of Habib Ibrahim in *KC*, *T&C*, 24 June 1847; M. Melvill to Sec. to Govt., *JD*, 23 December 1879 in *SRO*, *JD*, 1880, Vol. 31. pp. 7 *et seq.*

[17]See, *inter alia*, *BT*, 21 July 1851.

necessary. All these were Hindu customs that had survived the Khoja adoption of Islam. The same pattern was repeated in their dress and appearance as well as in a number of ceremonies, such as that performed six days after the birth of a child.[18]

Despite the pervading Hindu influence on social practices, the Khojas were of course Muslims. Whether they were Shia or Sunni was a different matter, one which was to be the subject of heated controversy during much of the nineteenth century. Certainly, during the first part of the century, their particular religious forms drew upon those of both sects. In their Bombay masjid in the burial grounds, the Khojas followed Sunni forms of worship and that portion of the funeral ceremony that was performed there was also along Sunni lines. These were conducted, until the 1860s, by a Sunni *mulla.* Marriage ceremonies were also performed, again until the 1860s by a Sunni, the Kazi of Bombay or his deputies. Within the *jamaathkana* the position was reversed: prayer and worship were along Shia lines as was another portion of the funeral ceremony. Moreover, the reverence the Khojas paid to Ali, the son-in-law of the Prophet, placed them amongst the Shias. This was also evident in their holy books. Apart from the Koran, they gave equal, if not more, reverence to a work composed by the *pir* who had first converted them to Islam. This was the *Dasavatar*, the story of the ten *avatars* of Vishnu. It accepted the first nine conventional *avatars* but departed from orthodox Hindu theology in the final section where it maintained that the tenth was Ali. This was the most sacred portion: when it was read in the *jamaatkhana* the congregation would rise as a token of respect.[19]

'Some say we are Soonees, some, Sheas. Our religion is a separate religion' maintained Habib Ibrahim with some parti-

[18]Evidence of Cassum Natha, Hassoon Syed, Hassum Cassum and Habib Ibrahim in *KC, T & C*, 24 June 1847. For an easily accessible, detailed discussion of Khoja customs see either *Gazetteer of the Bombay Presidency*, Vol IX. Part II. *Gujarat Population: Musalmans and Parsees* (Bombay, 1899) pp. 36-51; or R.E. Enthoven, *Tribes and Castes of Bombay* (Bombay, 1922), II, pp. 217-30.

[19]See, *Inter alia*, the references cited above as well as *BT*, 21 July, 1851.

zanship in 1847.[20] Although there may have been some truth in this view at the time, it did not long continue to be so. The situation changed and the sectarian identity of the Khojas became clarified after the arrival in Bombay of the first Aga Khan in 1845. It was his ancestors whose emissaries had converted the Khojas to Islam and had in return been reverenced by them. The Khojas went on pilgrimage to wherever in Persia the current descendants resided, and from time to time they sent gifts of money that had been raised by donations from within the caste. In the first decade of the nineteenth century, Bombay's Khojas had even mortgaged their *jamaatkhana* for seventeen thousand rupees in order to meet a requisition from Shah Mullick, the father of the first Aga Khan[21]. Though these Persian noblemen were revered, they seem to have exerted little influence or control over the body of their adherents in India and particularly over their internal affairs. The Khojas functioned virtually autonomously, but held the ancestors of the Aga Khan in due spiritual regard.

At the end of the twenties, the Aga, then in Teheran, attempted to remedy this situation and tighten his control over the Khojas of Bombay. In 1828-29, he sent his agent, Mirza Abdul Kassim, and his maternal grandmother, Marie Bibi, to Bombay to enforce his claims to regular financial contributions from the Bombay *jamaat*. The contributions, he stated, were to support pilgrims in his palace at Teheran and to enable him to engage in perpetual prayer and other religious activities. Marie Bibi harangued the assembled *jamaat* but was able to obtain only twenty thousand of the one hundred thousand rupees required. In opposition to these demands were the caste's most wealthy men, Shetias like Habib Ibrahim and Datoobhoy Soomar. They were prepared to pay due regard to the Aga as a holy man, but were not prepared to concede that he had any right to receive any regular contributions from them.

In 1829, the agents of the Aga Khan took the matter to the Supreme Court and filed a suit against the twelve leading opponents. As their 'pier, or principal saint', the Khojas, it was claimed, had agreed to pay the Aga 12.5 per cent of the

[20]Evidence of Habib Ibrahim, *KC*, *T & C*, 24 June 1847.
[21]*BT*, 21 July 1851.

profits from their merchandise but some had not done so. The suit was, however, dropped in July 1830, and the recusants were instead directed to appear before the *jamaat*. When they still refused, all twelve of the defendants were excommunicated by the *jamaat*. There the Barbhai (or 'twelve brethren') remained outside the caste, until the Aga Khan sent another agent, Mahomed Kurreem, to Bombay to effect a reconciliation. A compromise was reached in 1835; the Barbhai agreed to pay contributions in the future and gave six thousand rupees in payment of arrears and a total of twenty-eight thousand rupees was remitted to the Aga. What had been achieved was a compromise—the demands of the Aga Khan had not been fully met but he had gained a foothold amongst the Bombay Khojas and his direct influence over them had been demonstrated. Thereafter, regular, if not the extremely large contributions that had been desired, were remitted to him in Persia. In addition, his agent, Mahomed Kurreem, remained in Bombay to look after his interests and, as his representative, to maintain and extend his influence.[22]

This trend towards increasing influence and interference by the Aga Khan was hastened by the course of internal affairs in Persia. In 1838, the Aga Khan rose in rebellion against the Shah of Persia. He was defeated in 1840 and fled to Sind. Between 1841 and 1844, he helped the British in their campaigns in Sind and Afghanistan and finally arrived in Bombay in 1845 where he was welcomed with veneration and respect and loaded with presents.[23] At the request of the British Government, he proceeded to go to Calcutta and remained there until 1848. He then returned to Bombay and made it his chief headquarters. His presence in India, and in Bombay in particular, brought him into direct contact with the Khojas and made it necessary that his influence over them be accepted. It was inevitable, therefore, that conflict should result.

Though they had been readmitted into the caste, the Barbhai

[22]This account has been based upon the evidence of Habib Ibrahim and Mahomed Ibrahim Mucha in *KC*, *T & C*, 24 June 1847; *BT*, 21 July 1851; Anstey's summary of the bill placed before the Supreme Court in 1829 in *AKC*, *TI*, 23 April 1886 and Judge Arnould's Judgement in *AKC*, 12 *BHC* 352, 363-363a.

[23]*T & C*, 21 July 1847.

remained opposed to the Aga Khan and to his claims. In part, this was a response to his financial demands and, in part, a reaction to the patently Shia image which he projected. The Barbhai were amongst the wealthiest Khojas in Bombay and they were also the most progressive and modern in outlook. For instance, they wanted to bring Western style education to the Khojas and to raise them from their generally illiterate status. In the mid-1840s, one of them, Cassumbhoy Nathubhoy, in fact started and financed a school next door to the *jamaat-khana*. Not only did the school impart religious instruction (apparently along Sunni lines) but also elementary Western learning.[24] These same men also began moving closer to Sunni forms of religion and attempting to associate themselves with the orthodox (and majority) section of the city's Muslims. Some of them made big donations to the Sunni mosque in the burial grounds and performed the greater part of their worship there.[25] Given this tendency, it was inevitable that they should oppose the Aga Khan for religious as well as for financial reasons. He was, after all, a Persian Shia, and the tenor of his activities in Bombay seemed increasingly to be to interfere with accepted Khoja customs and to orient them towards what might, for want of a better term, be called 'orthodox' Shiaism.

It was not long before the Khojas of Bombay became divided into two distinct camps: the followers of the Aga and his opponents. Equally, it was not long before differences came to a head. The occasion was provided by a dispute over a large estate worth over three lakhs of rupees left by two brothers, Sajun and Hajee Meer Ally. Habib Ibrahim and his party maintained that the usual Khoja custom must be followed and that females, and daughters in particular, should not inherit the property. On the other hand, the party of the Aga Khan, led during his absence in Calcutta by his brother, Bawkar Khan, contended that property distribution must follow Muslim law as embodied in the Koran. Thus, daughters should share equally in any division of property. The issue became a *cause celebre* and eventually reached the Supreme Court where it was placed

[24]Cf. evidence of Rahimbhoy Hemjah in *AKC*, 25 April 1866.
[25]Cf., *inter alia*, Arnould's judgement, 12 *BHC* 363a.

before Sir Erskine Perry in June 1847.[26]

Perry's judgement was important.[27] It was to remain in force and to influence succeeding judicial pronouncements regarding the property of Khojas for over half a century. Perry maintained that where customs conflicted with the express text of the Koran or with Muslim law, they could nevertheless be valid amongst Muslim sects. A reasonable custom had been proved to exist amongst the Khojas and one that was not in conflict with English Statute Law. Since its usage was well established amongst the Khojas, the Courts ought therefore to enforce it. In subsequent cases spread out over the remainder of the century, the principle was expanded: the Khojas were held to be governed by Hindu Law unless the contrary was proved. Thus, judicially, a distinction was made between the secular and temporal ethos of the Khojas, and past custom rather than religious dictate was given sanction by the Courts.[28] In the process, customs became stereotyped and were denied any natural evolution to meet the changing requirements of the caste as its character altered with growing urban prosperity.

Whatever the judicial merits of Perry's decision, it did nothing to solve the conflict amongst the Khojas. In fact, its aftermath was marked by an intensification of hostilities. The Reform Party opposed the Mukhi and Kamaria in power, held a sparsely attended meeting of their own and elected new office-bearers while the Aga Khan group continued to recognize those already in office. In April 1848, the Aga Khan ordered from Calcutta the excommunication of Habib Ibrahim and Nanjee Mahomed. In November, an action of trespass against the Aga Khan and his followers for refusing them admission to caste areas was brought for arbitration before a solicitor who proved unable to settle the issue. Meanwhile, the Aga Khan had returned to Bombay and had taken up residence in the *jamaatkhana* which hence came under his control. By this

[26]Cf. proceedings of the case in *T & C* 24 June 1847.

[27]It is reprinted in full in Perry (1853: 110 *et seq*)

[28]See, *inter alia*, judgements of Judge Scott in Mahomed Sidick *v.* Haji Ahmed, etc., in *The Indian Law Reports, Bombay Series* Vol. X—1886 (Madras, reprint, 1916) [hereafter 10 *Bom* 11] and of Judge Beaman in Jan Mahomed *v.* Datu Jaffer in 38 *Bom* 462-466.

stage he had the support of the majority of Bombay's Khojas. Concurrently, the Barbhai, now slightly different in composition from the original twelve, seceded from the *jamaat* and established a *jamaatkhana* of their own. There followed a series of broils: members of the Barbhai groups assaulted *jamaat* members and even attempted, in one notorious conspiracy case, to have them indicted for the theft of some clothing. On the other side, four members of the secessionist *jamaat* were murdered in 1850 by followers of the Aga Khan. Although the murderers were subsequently sentenced and hanged, their bodies were treated with undue honour and reverence with the connivance, if not the direction, of the Aga Khan.[29]

The dispute again reached the Supreme Court and was once again heard by Erskine Perry. The issue was over the control of caste property. On the one hand, the relators maintained that the Aga Khan had taken over all caste buildings and property and was illegally preventing them from access to it. In particular, families with vaults in the burial ground for which they had paid were denied access to them and prohibited from entering their dead in them. In addition, they maintained that the Aga Khan was not a Khoja, that he considered Khoja practices heretical, that he was not in any way connected with, or descended from, the founder, Pir Sadruddin, and that he and his ancestors had taken undue advantage of the extreme ignorance of the Khojas. On the other hand, the defendants maintained that the Aga Khan was supported by a majority of the Khojas in Bombay Town and Island, that he was their *pir* and spiritual guide and hence had an inalienable right to control their affairs and, moreover, that all *jamaat* property really belonged to him.[30]

Faced with a mass of evidence in what became known as The Great Khoja Case, Perry in one sense side-stepped the issue by refusing to define what a Khoja was. He did, however, come down squarely on the side of the opponents of the Aga Khan. In what was later sometimes referred to as the Khoja

[29] *BT*, 21 July 1851; evidence of Allarukia Soomar in *AKC*, *TI*, 14 June 1866; newspaper clipping, n.d., *c.* August 1862 in *SRO*, *JD*, 1862, Vol. 24, p. 425; *TI*, 24 April, 1866.

[30] *BT*, 21 July 1851.

Bill of Rights, he maintained that the Court had jurisdiction over the matter since it involved not merely religion but also valuable property. The property had come from voluntary contributions made by Khojas over the years, its levy had not been compulsory and no one possessed the right to make it so. The property belonged exclusively to the *jamaat* and the right to use it, to use utensils for caste dinners and to use the burial ground, was common to all Khojas. The Aga Khan had not established any right to the ownership of caste property. Also, he had no established right to interfere in caste matters like excommunication and the election of office-bearers.[31]

The party of the Aga Khan, though in a majority, thus found itself defeated. Shortly afterwards, they were forced to readmit the rival group back into the caste and the secessionist *jamaat* was abandoned. There was peace for a time until the issue flared up again early in the sixties. The offensive was first taken by the Barbhai, representing somewhat different individuals since time and other changes had taken their toll, although it continued to represent much the same kind of interests. The leaders were now Ahmedbhoy Hubibhoy (the son of Habib Ibrahim), Cassumbhoy Nathubhoy and Dhurrumsey Poonjabhoy, particularly wealthy Shetias. They and their supporters were known as the Reform Party or Dhurrumsey Poonjabhoy's Party. Early in 1861, they established a newspaper, the *Khojah Dost*, which sought to bring about reform amongst the Khojas. As the instrument of the Dhurrumsey Poonjabhoy Party, it followed their thinking, urged the reform of religious and other ceremonials and the establishment of schools for the education of the caste's children. It represented a minority and was opposed by the majority of the Khojas led by the Aga Khan. Antagonism came to a head when the *Khojah Dost* maintained that the Khojas were Sunnis and not Shias and attacked the control of the Aga Khan over caste matters. It was not long before the Aga joined the battle. In October 1861, he published a paper in which he called upon all Khojas to abandon the veil of secrecy under which they had hitherto acted and to declare themselves openly

[31]Sir E. Perry's judgement on the Great Khoja Case in *BG*, 10 October 1851 bound in *SRO, JD*, Vol. 24, 1862, p. 423.

as Shias of the Imami Ismaili faith. In future they should perform their funeral and marriage ceremonies according to Shia, not Sunni, forms and should accept the Aga's leadership as the unrevealed Imam. All Khojas who felt this way should sign a statement to this effect in a book that would be kept in the house of one of the Aga Khan's sons in Bhendy Bazar. In the end the book was signed by 1308 Khoja families in Bombay and by virtually all Khojas outside the city except for those at Mowa near Bhavnagar who felt that their trading interests would be affected if they opposed Bombay's Sunni Khojas. Although some of the Bombay signatories were boys of ten or twelve, the book nevertheless clearly showed that the majority of the Khojas accepted the Aga as well as his view of their beliefs.[32]

The caste had clearly divided into two sections, the one Sunni and the other Shia. As in the past, the battle again moved into the arena of the *jamaat* and the control of *jamaat* property. At the end of 1861, the Sunni group tried to prevent their rivals from entering the *jamaatkhana*. Order was temporarily restored by C. Forjett, Deputy Commissioner of Police, and at the request of both parties a police guard was stationed semi-permanently, to ensure the peaceful access of both groups to the *jamaatkhana*. At this stage, each side was still prepared to accept the Bill of Rights laid down by Sir Erskine Perry in 1851. The following year, during Ramadan, there was a further attempt by this Shia group to prevent the entry of the Sunnis into the *jamaatkhana* and Forjett had again to intervene.

In August 1862 matters came to a head. The Aga Khan's Party took legal advice and, as a result, decided to ignore Perry's ruling of 1851. They convened a meeting of the *jamaat* at which they decided to serve their opponents with notices calling on them to consent to the rules and regulations of the *jamaat*, to abide by all future rules and pay all contributions due by them and demanded of them in the future. (The

[32]Cf. *Bombay Telegraph and Courier*, 7 May 1861; C. Forjett, Deputy Commissioner of Police, to Acting Sec. to Govt of Bombay, *JD*, No. 728, 10 October 1862 in *SRO*, *JD*, Vol. 24, 1862, p. 397; Arnould's judgement, 12 *BHC* 354-355; evidence of Allarukia Soomar in *AKC*, *TI*, 14 June 1866.

Reform Party had immediately after the split ceased their contributions). The Reform Party of course could not accept these demands. It was formally excommunicated and denied access to caste properties. In October, the death of one of their members made them attempt a forcible entry into the *jamaat-khana* in order to complete the funeral ceremonies but they were again barred. The following month, one of Ahmedbhoy Hubibhoy's brothers died and this time, through the intervention of the police, they were permitted to enter and complete their funeral ceremonies. The tension remained; in 1864, the Sunni *mulla* was turned out of the masjid in the burial grounds and all ceremonies, whether for marriages or deaths, were thereafter conducted along Shia lines by the Aga Khan Party. Meanwhile, the Sunni group had established their own masjid and *jamaat-khana* and elected new office-bearers.[33] The state of a barely suppressed civil war continued.

The issue eventually reached the High Court in 1866 and was finally settled by Judge Arnould. By this stage, the position of each side in what became known as the Aga Khan Case had become patently clear. The Reform Party, no longer that of Dhurrumsey Poonjabhoy who, perhaps through financial pressures, now sided with his former opponents, argued that the Khojas were undisputedly Sunnis, that the Aga Khan had no sway over them and that the caste properties were rightfully theirs. The only Khojas entitled to use it were Sunnis. On the other hand, the Aga Khan Party maintained the converse: the Khojas were rightfully Shias, and such Sunni customs as they had practised had been performed as part of a policy of *taqiyya* or concealment in order to avoid persecution in a hostile and antagonistic environment. Now that the British Government promised freedom of religion, the Khojas could once again assume their rightful religious practices. Furthermore, all contributions to the *jamaat* were made for, and on behalf of, the Aga Khan. All caste property was rightfully his

[33]Cf. letter of C. Forjett to Acting Sec. to Govt., cited above, pp. 395-409; C. Forjett to Acting Sec. to Govt., *JD*, 2 December 1862 and enclosures in *SRO*, *JD*, Vol. 24, 1862, pp. 459-67; (Shia *Jamaat*) Notice to Khoja, Hasun Pooja, 23 August 1862 in ibid., p. 427; Arnould's judgement, 12 *BHC* 355-356.

and he alone could determine who might use it. They contended that he was their Imam, the lineal descendant of Ali, and had absolute power over the temporal and spiritual affairs of his followers.[34]

The hearings were protracted and complex. Finally Arnould delivered a decision that totally supported the claims of the Aga Khan and denied those of his opponents. He considered that the Aga Khan was

> the hereditary chief and unrevealed Imam of the Ismailis—the present or living holder of the Masnud of the Imamate—claiming descent in direct line from Ali, the Vicar of God, through the seventh (according to the Ismaili creed), the last of the revealed Imams.[35]

Arnould also defined the Khojas as

> a sect of people whose ancestors were Hindus in origin, which was converted to and has throughout abided in the faith of the Shia Imami Ismailis, and which has always been and still is bound by ties of spiritual allegiance to the hereditary Imami of the Ismailis.[36]

and he added that 'in order to enjoy the full privileges of membership in the Khoja community, all the terms of the above description must be complied with'.[37]

Thus Arnould totally reversed Perry's earlier decisions and gave to the Khojas a formal and precise definition of their identity. Henceforth they were not merely a closed social group whose limits were determined by birth and maintained by taboos on intermarriage and other practices through the operation of a virtually autonomous *jamaat*, but their limits were further circumscribed by the need to accept a specific creed. It was now not enough to be born into the caste,

[34]For the proceedings of *AKC*, see *TI* and *BG* for April and June 1866.

[35]12 *BHC* 343.

[36]12 *BHC* 363c.

[37]12 *BHC* 363d.

a particular dogma had to be observed also. In practical terms, this meant accepting the control of the Aga Khan, or that of his descendants. In him was vested the power of excommunication which was to be implemented at his direction by the *jamaat*; in him lay the power to appoint office-bearers to be elected by the *jamaat* while by him lay the ownership of all caste properties and not the body corporate. He was also given the right to levy contributions at will from his followers.

The movement towards a rigorous definition of what constituted a Khoja had been promoted by a number of factors. There was, first, the emergence of a reforming group. In part it was interested in promoting Western learning and, to some extent, in modernizing its brethren. At the same time, it was interested in maintaining the distinctive social identity of the caste that had evolved over the years as an amalgam of Muslim and Hindu customs. In this battle, it was successful in matters like succession and inheritance.[38] Simultaneously, its movement towards modernization also paradoxically involved a movement towards orthodox Sunni Islam as its members became increasingly self-conscious. During the nineteenth century, those who led the movement were wealthy men, traders and merchants. They were, in part at least, spurred into activity by the pecuniary demands made of them as the Aga became interested in Bombay's Khojas and in part by a determination to retain access to *jamaat* properties. The movement for reform, then, was a complex one, not easily typecast, while its expression served to crystallize groupings and attitudes and to further the debate on what precisely did constitute a Khoja.

On the other hand, the major factor in this crystallization was the arrival in Bombay of the Aga Khan and his attempt to establish his unchallenged authority over his putative followers. The issue of finance was important to him particularly in the early years of his stay when the possibility of a return to Persia as the head of a conquering army must still have been in his mind. But his view of Islam was also important. In his own way a reformer, he was determined to bring the Khojas

[38]Cf. the detailed discussions of the Khoja Law Commission of 1879 and 1880 contained in *SRO, JD*, vol. 36, 1878; vol. 35, 1879; vol. 31, 1880; vol. 31, 1881; vol. 34, 1882; vol. 27, 1884 and vol 25, 1885.

back into the path of orthodox Shiaism of the sort which he knew in Persia. Yet the direction of his efforts was contrary to that of the reformers. His efforts were ultimately to be triumphant while theirs were not, although in matters of social practices, in inheritance in particular, the courts of law continued to maintain the distinctive social customs of the Khojas, and thus to distinguish between the secular and the temporal.

Finally, it was possible to achieve a definition of the Khoja identity only in the circumstances of British India. It was the courts of law that determined the precise position of the Aga Khan and eventually gave him unchallengeable authority amongst the Khojas. It was not until India became independent and the Bombay Government passed its Prevention of Excommunication Act in 1949, that he was deprived of his power of excommunication (Hidayatullah, 1968:25).

Nevertheless, the forces that had led to the coalescing of the Reform Party were not set at rest by Arnould's judgement. Opposition continued, but thereafter the issue was a sectarian one. The Reform Party set thmeselves up with their Sunni *jamaat* and attempted, largely unsuccessfully, during the seventies to extend their influence. The Aga Khan group in the meantime attempted to attract their former opponents back into the fold. Control of the burial ground, denial of caste intercourse and financial advantage were all most potent factors for inducing a return.[39] In at least one instance, stronger methods were used: the harassment of one Sunni Khoja in 1878 proved so strong that he was driven to murder the Shia Mukhi.[40]

By the end of the seventies, there were some 300-400 Sunni Khoja families in Bombay and about a thousand Shia families.[41] Not all of the latter were as ardent as they might have been in

[39]Cf., e.g., evidence of Jairaz Peerbhoy, Goolam Hoosain Heerjee, Mahomed Dhurrumsey, Kulpan Ruttonsey in *H. vs. G.*, pp. 73, 78, 128, 129.

[40]Cf. petition from Khoja Khatao Najuani, n.d., and letter of H.F Souter, Commissioner of Police, to Sec. to Govt. of Bombay, *JD*, No. 2112, 22 July 1878, in *SRO*, *JD*, vol. 45, 1878, n.p.

[41]M. Melvill, President, Khoja Law Commission, to Sec. to Govt. of Bombay, *JD*, 23 December 1879, and M.B. Westropp to Sir R. Temple, Governor of Bombay, 31 October 1878, in *SRO*, *JD*, vol. 31, 1880, p. 7 and n.p.

accepting the spiritual supremacy and temporal sway of the Aga Khan. There were at least fifty families who differed little from other Shias though they remained within the fold. These included some of the leading Khojas, men like the first Khoja solicitor, R.M. Sayani. There were also waverers between the two groups who, through fear of oppression, maintained their peace.[42]

From such silent opponents new opposition developed. Over 1876-77, several persons were excommunicated from the Khoja Shia *jamaat* for following Atna Ashari doctrines, for believing, in other words, in the Twelve Revealed Imams rather than the Seven accepted by the Imami Ismailis. Over 1879-80, there were two further excommunications and, by 1884, the number of this new sect had grown to some twenty-five families. The major secession occurred at the turn of the century perhaps, as one learned judge considered, more for 'temporal than spiritual or religious feelings, viz., an increasing disinclination to pay the various sums which are due to the Aga Khan as Hazar Imam for the time being'.[43] Opposition which, before 1866, would have been contained within the general Khoja body now, as a result of that judgement, sought expression outside, in another Khoja sect.

Thus, during the nineteenth century, the Khojas of Bombay had changed their character. What had been a somewhat amorphous caste had had its limits redefined and narrowed along essentially new, sectarian lines. In the process, the caste lost its encompassing character and became divided. What precisely was the nature of these new groups as they developed during the new century is a matter for a further and different kind of investigation.

[42]Cf. letter of M.R. Westropp to Sir R. Temple cited in preceding footnote.

[43]Judgement of Judge Russel, September 1908 in *The Bombay Law Reporter*, Vol. XI, 1909, (*11 Bom. L.R. 424*); see also petition of Atna Ashari Shia Khoja Inhabitants of Bombay to Viceroy, 21 August 1884 and R.M. Sayani to Under Sec. to Govt., *JD*, 2 September 1884, in *SRO*, *JD*, vol. 27, 1884, n.p.

Bibliography

Bombay Government (1899), *Gazetteer of the Bombay Presidency, Vol. IX, Part II. Gujarat Population: Musalmans and Parsees,* Bombay, Government Press.

Dumasia, N. (1939), *The Aga Khan and His Ancestors: A Biographical and Historical Sketch*, Bombay, Times of India Press.

Enthoven, R.F. (1975), *Tribes and Castes of Bombay*. vol. 2., Delhi, Cosmo.

Hidayatullah, M. (1968), *Principles of Mahomedan Law*, 16th ed., Bombay, N.M. Tripathi.

Hollister, J.N. (1953), *The Shias of India*, London, Luzac and Co.

Lokhandwalla, S.T. (1967), 'Islamic Law and Ismaili Communities (Khojas and Bohras)', *Indian Social and Economic History Review*, 4, pp. 162-166.

Perry, E. (1853), *Cases Illustrative of Oriental Life and the Application of English Law to India, Decided in H.M. Supreme Court at Bombay*, London.

Picklay, A.S. (1940), *History of the Ismailies*, Bombay.

Explanation of Law Report Citations

Citations of the judgements of courts and law cases have been provided in footnotes and are consequently not included in the Bibliography. These are given in standard legal form. Thus citations include volume number, reference to the Report Series in abbreviated form after the first full citation, page or pages, and, finally, the date of publication.

5
Muslim Caste in an Industrial Township of Maharashtra

A.R. Momin

Bhiwandi is a flourishing industrial township in Thana district, situated at a distance of 30 miles from Bombay. It came into limelight during the outbreak of communal riots in May 1970 and the subsequent appointment of the Justice D.P. Madon inquiry Commission which recently submitted its voluminous report to the Government of Maharashtra.

Bhiwandi is considered to be one of the highly developed centres of the small-scale powerloom industry in Maharashtra. The cotton and silk fabrics manufactured in Bhiwandi are exported to a number of countries including the Soviet Union, Japan, United States, Germany and Bangladesh. Bhiwandi was noted as a commercial centre from ancient times, even as far back as the twelfth century (Mohiuddin, 1969:39).

The population of Bhiwandi, according to the 1971 Census, is 79,576 which excludes a large chunk of people residing in the areas which lie beyond the jurisdiction of the local municipality but which form an integral part of the township. According to a rough estimate, the total number of powerloom workers and the allied labour force in Bhiwandi is in the neighbourhood of 1,00,000.

The two major religious communities inhabiting Bhiwandi are Hindus and Muslims who constitute, respectively, 40 and 60 per cent of the total population. The powerloom industry, which is the backbone of commercial life, is predominantly in the hands of the Muslims. However, the commercial structure rests, to a significant extent, on the financial investment and entrepreneurship of Gujaratis, Marwadis and Sindhis most of whom act as financiers to the low and middle-range powerloom owners. Lately, the Hindus have also taken to the powerloom industry but their interest and involvement in the industry is not as widespread as that of the Muslims. Most of them are engaged in the services, small trade, shopkeeping and farming.

The Muslims of Bhiwandi are divided into two main ethnic groups—Kokni and Momin. The Kokni Muslims claim to be descendants of early Arab migrants whereas the Momins are descendants of a weaving caste of U.P. and Bihar which migrated to various places in the aftermath of the revolt of 1857. Besides these two, there are several other groups such as the Deccanies from Deccan, the Memons, Khojas and Bohras who came to the township in the wake of industrial expansion. Their number, however, is relatively small. Our study shall be confined to the Kokni and Momin groups who have resided in Bhiwandi for a fairly long time and are characterized by distinctive cultural features and characteristics. Our focus will be on the impact of industrialization on the caste structure of these groups as well as on inter-ethnic interaction which, we presume, underwent a significant transformation in the process.

The Kokni Muslims

History tells us that the first caravan of Arab migrants came to India in 699 A.D. In 714 a large group of Iraqi Muslims, who were persecuted by Hajjaj bin Yusuf, came to Kokan. The acculturative process gradually led to interaction and intermarriage between them and the local Hindu population, mainly the fisher-folk of Kokan. This ethnic cross-breeding produced a progeny which came to be known as Nawait. The Nawaits are the ancestors of the Kokni Muslims. The Kokni Muslims are quite proud of their supposedly Arab descent and on that count distinguish themselves from the other Muslims. On account of their foreign ancestry, the Kokni Muslims may be placed in the Ashraf category.

The Kokni Muslims are generally fairish in complexion, slender and of medium height. Their womenfolk are fair and rather palish, slender and fairly tall. They observe a strict purdah system. The Kokni Muslims, by and large, speak a dialect called Kokni which is structurally akin to Marathi but contains a sizeable stock of Arabic and Persian words.

Hierarchy

Bhiwandi has two distinct concentrations of Kokni Muslim population: Bhiwandi proper (which is commonly known as Saudagar Mohalla), and Nizampur. These two concentrations exhibit certain occupational, cultural and attitudinal characteristics. Generally, the Kokni Muslims of Bhiwandi are engaged in rice cultivation, dairy farming, forestry and, lately, the powerloom industry. There are differences between the Kokni Muslims of Saudagar Mohalla and those of Nizampur. The former have traditionally been more prosperous as most of them were engaged in the forest business and rice cultivation. The latter are mainly engaged in keeping buffaloes and selling milk. Their occupation has earned them a deprecatory label from the Koknis of Saudagar Mohalla: *bhains ke* (people of the buffaloes). The Koknis of Saudagar Mohalla, on account of having a prospering business, are more westernized in their style of living.

The Kokni Muslims of Bhiwandi possess the salient features of an ethnic group. Ethnically, they are distinct from the other Muslims—they share a number of cultural features and characteristics; they speak the same dialect; they marry only among themselves. Yet, the Kokni Muslim community has a well-defined system of ranking and stratification. This system of ranking is reflected not only in the rules of marriage and commensality but also in the burial of the dead. There are separate and demarcated areas in the Kokni Muslims' graveyards which are reserved for those families which are supposedly high in the hierarchy. Topmost in the Kokni Muslim hierarchy are those who distinguish themselves from the rest on account of purity of descent and ancestral nobility. Families with surnames like Faqih, Khatib, Patel, Bubere,

Narvil, Hani, Qazi, Tase and Muallin belong to this category. Next come people with surnames like Chivne, Bolinjkar, Bhoje and Jairumi. They are considered to be lower down in the hierarchy on account of differences in occupation and family background. Some of them are believed to have married or kept Hindu women in the nearby villages and so their families carry a stigma.

Lower than these two are the Wazahs (or Wajas as they are locally known). The Wazahs were traditionally a weaving sub-caste. Some of them formerly used to sell dry fish which is considered to be a lowly occupation in the Kokni Muslim sub-culture. Until quite recently, the Wazahs were supposed to be the lowest in the hierarchy, almost to the extent of being outside the group. They used to live in separate localities, locally known as Mohallahs. Until a few years ago, there used to be no intermarriage between the Wazahs and other Kokni Muslims. They were considered not only backward but also foolish. Till very recently, the Wazahs did not observe purdah which the Kokni Muslims of Bhiwandi consider to be a mark of backwardness.

Of late the Kokni Muslims have started giving their girls in marriage to the Wazahs as a consequence of the impact of industrialization, Islamization and the spread of modern education. However, this privilege is restricted to those Wazah boys who have acquired wealth and education and have thereby raised their status in the social hierarchy.

At the lowest rung of the Kokni Muslim hierarchy are the Telis. The Telis are oil-pressers by occupation. They came to Bhiwandi from the neighbouring villages. Though they settled among the Kokni Muslims, they were barely considered a part of the group. Their dialect, rituals and customs are the same as those of the Koknis, but there is no intermarriage between them and the latter.

Ashrafization

Among the lower groups in the Kokni Muslim hierarchy there is clearly evidenced a process which is aptly described by Vreede-de-Steurs (1969:5-6) as Ashrafization. Ashrafization is a process of social mobility whereby those whose status is low in the hierarchy try to imitate the higher groups in their style of living, customs, manners and the like so that they may be ranked with the latter. Ghaus Ansari (1960:36-62) has called them pseudo-Ashrafs.

The process of Ashrafization is clearly seen in the behaviour of the Wazahs of Bhiwandi who imitated the higher groups in matters of living, dressing and manners. Their womenfolk took to purdah. Some of them managed to accumulate wealth and thereby succeeded in entering into marital alliances with the Kokni Muslims. So, hypergamy became an important source of status mobility for the Wazahs. The process was also reflected in the attempt of the Telis to give up many of their former cultural practices and rituals which they had adopted from their Hindu neighbours.

Marriage and Endogamy

Ten to fifteen years ago, endogamy was the rule among the four sub-groups of Kokni Muslims. With the advent of industrialization, the spread of modern education and Islamization, the restrictions have been considerably relaxed. Now the higher groups have begun giving their girls in marriage to the lower groups like the Wazahs. However, the relaxation is based on considerations like wealth, standard of living, education, social status and the like. There are, however, no intermarriages between the higher Kokni groups and the Telis. Similarly, there are no marital alliances between the Kokni Muslims and the Momins.

Generally speaking, arranged marriages are still the rule among the Kokni Muslims. Occasionally there are love marriages with the consent and approval of the parents. The spread of modern education has raised the age of marriage in the case of girls. In marital alliances, traditional considerations like character and family background are being replaced by those of economic and social status. Divorce and remarriage are relatively rare among the Kokni Muslims.

The Momins

The Momins of Bhiwandi are the descendants of a weaver

caste of U.P. which migrated to places like Bombay, Bhiwandi, Melegaon and Dhulia in the aftermath of the revolt of 1857 when their traditional occupation—the handloom industry—was destroyed by the British. Prior to their migration the Momins were part of the Muslim social hierarchy of U.P. and were placed in the Ajlaf category. It is likely that the notion and practice of caste among U.P. Muslims emerged in the course of their interaction with the surrounding Hindu population. The Momins who migrated to Bhiwandi brought with them their caste structure as well.

Hierarchy

The Momins of Bhiwandi share a number of cultural characteristics. They speak a dialect locally known as Poorbi or Hindustani. They are quite conscious of belonging to a larger group called the Momin Beradari (the fraternity of Momins). Yet, they have various group affiliations. On the whole, there are two broad divisions in the Momin community: the Chaorasi *jamaat* which is an amalgam of a number of subdivisions or *jamaats*; and Phulpuri *jamaat* which consists of people whose forefathers migrated from Phulpur village in Allahabad district. Initially, the Phulpuri *jamaat* were numerically strong and economically dominant. They were also concentrated in certain Mohallas and, about twenty-five years ago, used to have a caste council. The caste council enforced well-defined caste rules and rituals on occasions like weddings and in the settlement of disputes.

The Chaorasi *jamaat* was a kind of all-caste association, with the exception of the Phulpuri *jamaat*. It included the following ten subdivisions or *jamaats*: Azamgadhi, Bhadoin, Lucknowi, Banarasi, Jahanaganji, Mahoodabadi, Khairabadi, Sagdimaharaj Ganji, Validpur Bhirai and Mubarakpuri. The names of these *jamaats* are derived from the respective villages in U.P. from where these groups migrated. Most of these subdivisions used to have their own caste councils and caste heads locally known as Sardar. Caste heads were elected on considerations like candour, honesty and impartiality. But later the position of the caste head became hereditary. Till fifteen to twenty years ago the caste councils and caste heads served as important and effective agents of control and regulation. Now, due to a variety of factors, most of the caste councils have become defunct.

Other Groups

There are a few other groups among the Muslims of Bhiwandi who resemble the Momins in matters of dialect, style of living, customs and rituals to some extent but who are not considered part of the Momin Beradari. The Dherphurre or Murgiwale are supposed to be dealers in poultry which is considered to be low down in the hierarchy of Muslim professions. The Quraishis or the butcher caste are mostly from Bareilly, Budaun, and Rampur districts of U.P. They have their own caste council and their own Sardar or caste head. The Hajjam or barbers have held on to their traditional occupation. Their womenfolk bathe the brides and wash utensils on weddings. The Bhishti or water-carriers have also retained their traditional occupation with some exceptions. They have a caste council and a caste head who is known as Chaudhari.

There are about thirty-eight households of the Shia sect. Most of them belong to the weaver caste of U.P. Their dialect is the same as that of the Momins. Most of them are engaged in the powerloom business. Formerly, there used to be intermarriages between the Shias and the Momins who belong to the Sunni sect. Now the practice is no longer prevalent and the Shias mostly marry among themselves. The Shias have separate mosques and graveyards. They have a caste council which is mainly of a religious nature. The Shias are also divided into two endogamous subdivisions: Banarasi and Azamgadhi.

There is another category of Muslims who are locally known as Mulki or Bhaiya and are new migrants from U.P. They are considered lowly and uncouth by both the Koknis and Momins. The Mulkis provide the labour force for the powerloom industry.

The Deccanies are migrants from the Deccan. They are also divided into three subdivisions: Quraishi, Sheikh and

Sayyad. Whereas the Sheikhs and Sayyads intermarry, there are no intermarriages between these two and the Quraishis. The Quraishis have a caste council and a caste head who is known as Patel.

Besides these groups, there are some Memon, Khoja and Bohra families but they are few in number. They exist as endogamous groups.

Marriage and Endogamy

The Momin Beradari consists of the Chaorasi *jamaat*, which consists of about 10 subcastes, and the Phulpuri *jamaat*. The Phulpuri *jamaat* is considered to be the highest in the hierarchy.

TABLE 1
Muslim Castes in Bhiwandi

Kokni Muslims		*Momin*		*Others*
1. Faqih		1. Phulpuri	(highest in rank)	Dherphurre
Khalib				Quraishi
Bubere				Hajjam
Patel		2. Azamgadhi		Deccanies
Narvil	of equal rank	Bhadoin		Shia
Qazi		Banarasi		Mulki
Tase		Lucknowi		Memon
Muallim		Jahanaganj		Khoja
Sayyad		Mahmoodabad	Chaorasi *jamaat*	Bohra
Agha		Khairabad		
Farid		Sagdimaharaj Ganj		
Hani, etc.		Validpur Bhira		
		Mubarakpur		
2. Chivne	of equal rank			
Quraishi				
Bolinjkar,				
etc.				
3. Muqri	Wazah			
Gorekhar				
Bobde				
4. Agaskar	Teli			
Sheikh				

Formerly, it used to be an exclusive endogamous unit. Now there are frequent marriages between the Phulpuri *jamaat* and the other subcastes. However, the Lucknowi subcaste does not get girls in marriage from the other subcastes. Similarly, there are no marriages between the Momin Beradari on the one hand and Dherphurre, Quraishi, Hajjam or Mulki on the other. There are, however, occasional exceptions.

Till recently, marriage proposals as a matter of convention used to go from the boy's side to the girl's; a proposal from the girl's side was considered ungraceful. Now the girl's parents also send the proposal to the boy's parents. Earlier, the girl's parents used to make a lot of inquiries about the boy's character, family background, etc. Considerations of wealth and poverty were not taken into account generally. Now, under the impact of industrialization and the coming of affluence, one of the major considerations in most marital alliances has become economic and social status. Traditionally, marriages were arranged by the parents. Now there are frequent cases of love marriage with the approval of the parents. The boy's say in arranging his own marriage has assumed considerable significance during the last fifteen or twenty years under the impact of industrialization and the spread of modern education. There is also a considerable increase in the age of marriage in the case of girls.

Industrialization

The Momins, when they came to Bhiwandi, brought with them their traditional skill and craftsmanship. But they had to start life from scratch. The Momins were received by the Kokni Muslims with mixed feelings. There were some who gave them shelter and moral support, others could not hide their resentment and contempt for the newcomers. Initially, a few enterprising Momins set up handlooms. Gradually, the handloom industry of Bhiwandi became quite famous for its craftsmanship. The year 1928 was a historic year for Bhiwandi when an enterprising Momin, Haji Abdus Samad, introduced powerlooms. However, it did not evoke a favourable reaction in the community. In fact, people expressed their resentment in a variety of ways. A meeting of the Chaorasi *jamaat* was convened to protest against the installation of powerlooms which, it was feared, would lead to the ruin of the handloom industry which was the major source of livelihood for the Momin community. At the meeting it was decided to take a procession to the then Collector of Thana district and to present to him a memorandum on behalf of the community expressing its strong feelings of protest. A march consisting of 1000 to 2000 people was taken out but it was of no avail as the Collector felt that he had no right to interfere in any individual's business affairs.

The powerloom industry, due largely to the foresight and initiative of Haji Abdus Samad, soon began to spread and expand. Haji Abdus Samad was a man of vision and determined action and he enjoyed tremendous power and prestige not only in the Momin community but also in the civic affairs of the town.

Industrialization and the growth of the powerloom industry in Bhiwandi received a major fillip during the Second World War. The heralding of independence in 1947 added considerable momentum to the process of industrialization. In the meantime, Bhiwandi was exposed to the urban environment of Bombay through trade and commerce. This exposure had a significant impact on Bhiwandi in terms of Westernization about which we shall have more to say in the later sections of this paper.

During the last twenty-five years, the process of industrialization has had a profound and far-reaching impact on the behaviour, attitudes, customs and institutions of the people of Bhiwandi.

The most remarkable change brought about by industrialization was on occupational mobility among the Kokni Muslims. A quarter of a century ago, the powerloom industry was supposed to be the exclusive occupation of the Momins. Since the early Momin settlers were by and large looked down upon by the Kokni Muslims, their traditional occupation—weaving—was also considered lowly and treated with scorn and ridicule. The Momins were referred to as Julaha or Hindustani with pejorative overtones. In the reaction of the Kokni Muslims towards the Momins there lurked elements of a feudal outlook.

Till then the major occupations of the Kokni Muslims used to be rice cultivation, dairy farming, and forestry which were quite paying.

It is interesting to note that the first Kokni Muslim who took to the powerloom industry, Haji Mian Patel, was scoffed at and labelled a Julaha by his people. The Momins, who had the professional and technical skill as well as the determination to establish themselves in a not too favourable social environment, steadily developed and expanded the powerloom industry. The last decade has witnessed the emergence of the powerloom industry as the dominant occupation in Bhiwandi. It brought unprecedented prosperity to the Momin community, surpassing that of the Kokni Muslims.

Thus, during the last two decades, the Momins have emerged as a 'dominant caste', to employ a suggestive phrase coined by M.N. Srinivas (1959). They enjoyed numerical strength, economic dominance as well as political power. The Kokni Muslims were struck by the rapidly growing prosperity and affluence of the Momins and this led to a change in their attitude towards the industry. Coupled with this came another stroke of bad luck. The amendment of the Bombay Tenancy and Agricultural Lands Act of 1956, giving the tiller the right of ownership of the land, deprived the Kokni Muslims of a number of privileges relating to rice cultivation which was one of their major sources of income. Then came legislation concerning the allotment of forests to cooperative societies and not to individuals as was the practice earlier. These measures severely hit the economic position of the Kokni Muslims and they were left with no alternative but to take to the powerloom industry.

Thus, the sheer pressure of circumstances induced the Kokni Muslims to take to the powerloom industry. This occupational mobility among the high caste groups in Indian Muslims society is one of the most striking developments of recent times. This phenomenon sowewhat parallels what Majumdar (1958:336-39) has described as the process of de-Sanskritization in Hindu society. As Majumdar has rightly stressed, the concept of de-Sanskritization is far more significant in understanding the dynamics of change in modern Indian society than that of Sanskritization as developed by Srinivas. A similar process in Muslim social structure, de-Ashrafization as we shall call it, indicates a tendency among the high caste groups to adopt the customs, features and rituals of the supposedly low castes which have become economically dominant. Change of occupation and willingness to establish marital alliances with the lower castes, as well as changes in the norms of commensality are some of the most important features of the de-Sanskritization process. Thus, the dominant caste becomes the source of de-Ashrafization for the high castes in Muslim society.

Another significant impact of rapid industrialization relates to the demographic composition of the local population. Industrialization and its promise of better prospects attracted thousands of people from the rural areas of U.P., Bihar, Andhra Pradesh as well as parts of Maharashtra. About 80 per cent of the labour force in Bhiwandi has come from these areas. This heavy influx of labour has given rise to a number of problems relating to accommodation, sanitation, industrial relations and the like.

Rapid industrialization has also influenced the relations between the workers and the owners. Prior to the expansion of the industry, the relations between the employer and the employee used to be quite cordial and even familial. Industrialization has given a new turn to industrial relations. The distinctions between the employer and the employee have become sharper. Occasionally there are frictions and tensions in industrial relations, sometimes of a grave nature (Momin, 1974). Not only that, the class structure of the township, which used to be quite nebulous and diffused, has undergone a change. Distinctions of rich and poor have become more pronounced and accentuated.

Above all, industrialization has given rise to a commercial cultural environment based on the ethos of commercial success, affluence, and careerism. Economic position and wealth have become the primary sources of power and prestige. There has emerged a new class of *nouveaux riche* whose sole obsession is the unscrupulous and reckless accumulation of wealth and its vain display. The new commercial culture is steadily corroding the foundations of the traditional culture which valued family background, character and deference based on personal virtues.

This commercial culture has also influenced the norms underlying marital alliances, living standards, attitudes and tastes, and even patterns of friendship. In brief, commercialism and commercial success is the leitmotif of the new industrial culture.

Education

A number of significant changes in the caste structure of Bhiwandi Muslims are linked with the spread of modern education. The history of the introduction of Western education among Bhiwandi Muslims dates from 1928 when Maulana Shaukat Ali, who was a prominent leader of the Khilafat Movement, inaugurated a school known as the Anglo-Urdu High School. This school had Urdu and English as media of instruction. A girls' section was opened in the school in 1943.

Initially, the Kokni Muslims, who were relatively better off and Westernized, took to modern education with much more interest than the Momins, most of whom were illiterate and heavily preoccupied with earning a livelihood. Gradually, as the powerloom industry expanded and the Momins attained a measure of economic security, they began sending their children to the school. However, the traditional stigma of illiteracy still hovers over the Momins. In spite of prosperity, education is not taken very seriously by the community. After the primary school level, a number of boys drop out to engage in the powerloom industry or allied occupations. The labour force consists of a floating population. People keep going to their native places for festive occasions and during spells of slackness. The education of their children inevitably suffers in the process.

It is instructive to compare the number of Muslim children attending high school with that of Hindu children. Though the Hindus comprise only 40 per cent of the total population of Bhiwandi, they have almost double the number of high schools as compared to the Muslims. The number of Hindu children attending high school is also about double the number of Muslim children doing so. In the Bhiwandi College of Arts, Science and Commerce, which is affiliated to the University of Bombay, Muslim students comprise only 30 per cent of the student population. This difference is also evident in the academic performance of Hindu and Muslim students.

The Kokni Muslims, who comprise only one-fourth of the total Muslim population in Bhiwandi, were sensitized to Western education much earlier than the Momins. The Kokni Muslims also took the initiative in sending their children to English medium schools in Thana in the 1960s. Soon thereafter the Momins also followed suit. But since education in a convent school is a relatively more expensive affair, only the well-to-do Kokni and Momin families could afford it. In course of time the number of children going to convent schools in Thana and Bhiwandi steadily rose, thanks to the coming of prosperity. Sending one's children to English-medium schools became a status symbol in the commercial culture of Bhiwandi.

The spread of Western education has had some significant consequences for the Muslims of Bhiwandi. As we shall see in detail in the concluding section of our paper, the Koknis and Momins, for a long time, and to some extent even now, have existed as culturally isolated groups. The opening of a high school where Kokni and Momin children could meet and learn together made the initial dent on this isolationism. The sharing of education in a common setting opened the possibility of exchanges and communication between the two. The old stereotypes and prejudices, nurtured during the socialization process, could now be subjected, to some extent at least, to empirical and observational test. Social psychologists have suggested that prolonged contact and exposure to one another in a common setting could be a powerful factor in changing the attitudes and stereotypes of people to an appreciable extent (Krech *et. al.*, 1962:253-62). What we are trying to say is that education extended the possible range of interaction and communication between the two ethnic groups. This possibility and its realization was extended further by the opening of a college in Bhiwandi.

A significant impact of education is reflected in the attitude of Muslim men, particularly the Momins, towards the education of girls. Traditionally, it was believed that girls should not be educated beyond a certain minimum. The primary emphasis in the socialization of girls was on learning cooking, household skills and the like. The opening of a girls' section in what later came to be known as Rais High School enlarged the possibility of girls' education up to matriculation. Industrialization and the coming of prosperity also made it possible to meet the educational expenses. The example of the Kokni Muslims, who served as a reference group for the Momins, also induced the latter to send their daughters to high school and then to college.

Another factor which added to the significance of education was its potential linkage with marital prospects. The boys began to expect and demand that their prospective wives should be educated, at least up to matriculation. Education gradually became a status symbol in the commercial culture of Bhiwandi. The linkage of girls' education with their marital prospects indirectly raised the age of marriage.

The influence of western education is also reflected in the sphere of relations between the sexes. The opening of a college has led to a greater possibility of exchange and communication between Muslim boys and girls. Education has also brought about a measure of liberalization in the attitude to, and practice of, purdah, especially among the Kokni girls who are supposed to be strict about its observance. College education has been a significant factor of change in this connection.

Another probable impact of education has been the Muslim boys' and girls' attitude towards arranged and love marriages. There have been one or two cases of love marriage among the local college students which indicates that a certain change in the attitude towards marriage is well under way among the Muslim youth. Another significant factor in this connection is the exposure to the mass media, especially the cinema, as well as contact with the liberal and Westernized environment of Bombay which is one of the most attractive centres of recreation and enjoyment for the youth of Bhiwandi.

Westernization

The process of Westernization among the Muslims of Bhiwandi first began among the Kokni Muslims. Westernization came to them through their involvement in the forest business. Contact with forest officers, who used to be Englishmen in the pre-independence days, led to an imitation of their customs, manners and habits. Initially, this was confined to the rich and the well-to-do; gradually it spread to other sections of the Kokni Muslim population who looked up to the former.

Here the case of a Kokni Muslim, Aba Divkar of Padga, a village situated about ten miles from Bhiwandi, is particularly instructive. Son of a rich landlord, Aba Divkar was admitted to an English medium school in Dehra Dun in the 1930s at the suggestion of an English forest officer. After completing his education, Aba Divkar took to English manners and dress, so much so that he was popularly referred to as Englishman. He became a member of the C.C.I. and was made honorary magistrate. He used to enjoy the company of English officers who came for hunting. Aba Divkar became a reference model for thousands of Kokni Muslims in the surrounding villages as well as in Bhiwandi. Initially, contact with the English officers was heavily concentrated in the neighbouring villages of Padga, Wada and Manor. The Kokni Muslims of these villages were looked upon as reference models by the Kokni Muslims of Bhiwandi.

Through this exposure to English manners and customs, the Kokni Muslims, initially the elite, took to wearing the English-style coat and jacket. The English custom of eating at a table was also copied by the Kokni Muslims as was the use of chairs and modern crockery. Another source of Westernization was exposure to the city of Bombay which dates back to the early 1930s.

Westernization among the Momins came initially through the Kokni Muslims and later through Western education, modern mass media and contact with the urban environment of Bombay. Under the impact of Westernization some of the traditional social features and customs are gradually being eliminated. The attitude towards the seclusion of women (purdah) is no longer very rigid and parents have become more liberal and tolerant in this respect. In this connection, the Kokni Muslims serve as a reference group for the Momins. The impact of Westernization among the Momins is evidenced in their changing style of living and in the manner in which they arrange marriages.

Westernization has carried within its matrix a slow but steady process of secularization. Apparently, secularization has affected some of the surface cultural features and practices.

Thus, a change has taken place in the sort of names chosen for children. Whereas the earlier tendency was oriented towards religious and mystic traditions, now the stress is on names which sound aesthetically pleasing. This has led to a shortening of first names. Thus, where the traditional pattern for boys would have encouraged names like Burhanuddin, Mohammad Hussain, Abdul Latif, Shamsuzzaman and Ashfaq Ahmad, the new secular pattern has induced names like Farid, Javed, Basit and Naeem. For girls the old pattern prescribed names like Mehrunnisa, Khadija, Kulsum and Zalekha, whereas the modern names are Sahira, Shabana, Leena, Almas and Saba. Changes in the naming pattern first began among the Kokni Muslims and the Momins followed suit.

The process could also be observed in the naming pattern of shops, restaurants and factories. The secularization process has also influenced marriage rituals and ceremonies. Certain rituals and customs which had religious connotations are gradually being replaced by secular and functional features. Thus, the practice of *milad* at the wedding ceremony and the custom of taking out the wedding procession (*barat*) are gradually, though not altogether, disappearing. So is the institution of *jamaat* or calling people for a formal gathering for the announcement of the wedding. The suit has replaced the traditional *sherwani*; chairs have replaced the traditional mats (*tats*) during the reception and the wedding feast; in place of the traditional *sherbat*, ice cream and cold beverages are served. In the case of girls, the *sari* is replacing the traditional *salwar-kurta*; cosmetics are increasingly in vogue.

Islamization

We refer to Islamization as that process in Indian Muslim society whereby Muslims tend to shed their supposedly un-Islamic beliefs, customs and rituals (Mandelbaum, 1970:557-59; Singh, 1974:73-80).

Among the Muslims of Bhiwandi, the beginnings of the Islamization process can be traced back to the impact of the Khilafat Movement in the 1920s. A number of influential Kokni Muslims like Mohammad Husain Madoo came under the spell of the Movement. The influential papers of those days, like *al-Hilal* and *al-Balagh*, were read with interest and excitement among the educated Kokni Muslims. The literature which was brought out in the wake of the Khilafat Movement aroused the religious consciousness of the Kokni Muslims. This, among other factors, led to a gradual shedding of many un-Islamic customs and practices relating to marriage.

The new consciousness generated by the Khilafat Movement also created a trend among the Kokni Muslims towards universalism in the context of Indian Muslim society as a whole. There arose a sense of solidarity with the totality of Indian Muslims (Millat-e-Islamiyah). Since Urdu had become a major vehicle of the new religious and political consciousness, a number of prominent Kokni Muslims who were influenced by the Khilafat Movement decided to give up their traditional dialect, Kokni, in favour of Urdu. The adoption of Urdu gradually became widespread and the present younger generation of Kokni Muslims is not very familiar with the traditional dialect.

Another significant consequence of the Islamization process, which is also linked up with industrialization and the spread of modern education, was the change in the attitude of the high caste groups among the Kokni Muslims with regard to giving their girls in marriage to the supposedly low caste groups. Thus, some people began giving their daughters in marriage to the Wazahs.

Another notable source of the Islamization process was the Tabligh movement which gained momentum during 1968-69. Initially the movement was patronized by the rich sections of the Momin community; it gradually spread to other sections of the people. On the whole, the Muslims of Bhiwandi, who broadly owe allegiance to the Sunni sect of Islam, are divided into two subsects: the Wahabis who are puritanical and fundamentalist in their approach; and the Sunnis who have syncretic inclinations in religious affairs. These divisions also influence political events in the town. The voting behaviour of the Muslims, for example, is considerably influenced by religious and denominational considerations.

Inter-Ethnic Interaction

As we have noted earlier, the Koknis and Momins have, for a fairly long time, lived together in Bhiwandi as culturally isolated groups, without much awareness of one another's distinctive life-styles, customs and rituals. The beginnings of this unhappy state of affairs can be traced back to the arrival of Momin migrants in Bhiwandi. The reception which they received at the hands of the Kokni Muslims was a mixed and ambivalent one. Some of them had sympathy for the poor migrants and were generous enough to lend them a helping hand; others made fun of their backwardness, ignorance and simplicity. By and large, the reception was not a happy and encouraging one. There were heated exchanges and occasional fights between the two groups.

The Kokni Muslims as a group have a strong feeling of community solidarity, of in-group identification. The Kokni dialect has an adage to the effect, 'carry our folk forward'. The Kokni Muslims are also characterized by a heightened awareness of status and rank. By and large, they are a culturally homogeneous group. This cultural homogeneity was preserved, among other things, by their concentration in certain localities (Mohallas).

This cultural homogeneity, reinforced by ecological segregation, strong in-group feeling as well as the cultural differences between the Kokni Muslims and the Momins, created an atmosphere of disaffection and mistrust between the two ethnic groups. This has given rise to certain stereotypes and false images which are based on distorted information and fanciful thinking. The Kokni Muslims, having long engaged in business, acquired worldly wisdom and shrewdness. This shrewdness is passed on to the younger generation in the early stages of socialization. The Koknis consider the Momins as simpletons whereas the latter regard the Koknis as selfish and cunning. The old stereotypes and prejudices still persist in the old and the younger generations, though not with the same intensity. There have been marked changes in recent years in the attitude of the Kokni Muslims towards the Momins regarding their alleged simplicity and innocence. This change is linked up with the rise of the Momins in the business sphere.

Industrialization and the spread of education have brought about a greater interaction and communication between the two groups. When the Kokni Muslims took to the powerloom industry they sought the advice and help of their Momin friends. And the Momins were gracious enough to extend a helping hand. This cooperation and interaction had some significant consequences for the relations between the two groups.

Industrialization has also made a dent in the segregation and concentration of the Kokni Muslims. There has been a good deal of inter-penetration and the old isolationism is steadily crumbling, creating more chances for intermixing and interaction.

Yet, in spite of the growing mutual awareness and increasing communication, there are no instances of intermarriage between the Kokni Muslims and Momins. Surprisingly, a number of Kokni Muslims have given their daughters in marriage to non-Kokni boys outside Bhiwandi. With the advances made by the Momins in the economic and educational fields, some Kokni Muslims are prepared to give their daughters in marriage to Momin boys. Here a peculiar situation has arisen. The Momins feel that even if they accept the Kokni Muslim girls, the latter will not accept their girls. They feel that the only consideration encouraging the Kokni Muslims to establish marital relations with them is the Momin's prosperity and economic dominance.

Conclusion

It is one of the saddest features of Islamic history that one of the basic tenets of Islam relating to the equality and brotherhood of mankind was relegated to the background by its followers. The Prophet vehemently condemned all hereditary and ancestral privileges which divide mankind; yet, once Islam spread to various parts of the world, it soon developed elements of hierarchy and stratification.

The emergence of stratification among the Arabs has a revealing historical background. As the noted Arab historian Ibn Khaldun has observed, the Arabs of the pre-Islamic era were overly conscious of their ancestral status and privileges. The predominant motif of pre-Islamic solidarity was ethnocentrism or *asabiyyah*, as Ibn Khaldun has termed it. This deep-seated sentiment of group-centredness was the basis of their notion of superiority and inferiority.

The Islamic message of egalitarianism struck at the roots of this ethnocentrism which was based on notions of ancestral purity. However, it could not be totally obliterated from Arab consciousness. Soon after the passing away of Muhammad, this deeply-entrenched sentiment reasserted itself and found expression in the emergence of groups claiming superior status on the basis of heredity and descent.

Another factor in the demise of the Islamic principle of egalitarianism relates to the conversion of millions of people in the early centuries of Islam. As Manazir Ahsan Gilani (1960:37) has noted, large sections of people embraced the new faith bringing with them their traditional beliefs and practices. In the course of time, such beliefs and practices, which were deeply rooted in notions of superiority and inferiority, re-emerged and contributed to the creation of stratified social systems throughout the Muslim world.

Contact with non-Arab groups like the Iranians and the Spaniards, who had a well-defined system of hierarchy, also influenced the emergence of stratification among the Muslims. Moreover, wherever Islam later spread, the new converts retained many of the cultural features of their old faith, as was the case in Indonesia (van Nieuwenhuijze, 1974) and India (A. Ahmad, 1962).

Indian Muslim society has been conditioned to a very large extent by historical and socio-cultural forces operating in the Indian environment. There has been a prolonged interaction between the Islamic Great tradition and the Great and Little Indian traditions. This interaction has given rise to what I have termed (Momin, 1975) the Indo-Islamic Little Tradition.[1] The daily life and behaviour of Indian Muslims is governed more by this Indo-Islamic Little Tradition than by the Islamic Great Tradition.

In large measure this is due to the fact that an overwhelming

[1]Yogendra Singh (1974: 66-80) speaks of the Great and Little traditions of Islam. The Little Tradition of Islam *per se*, independent of its regional variant, does not exist.

majority of Indian Muslims are descendants of early converts from Hinduism and most of them have retained many cultural features of their earlier faith. The Indian caste system, whose pervasiveness does not leave any aspect of Indian life unaffected, has also influenced the ethnic and religious minorities of the country like the Muslims, Christians and Parsis. A number of scholars have noted the existence of a caste-like stratification system among the Indian Muslims (Hutton, 1946; Bose, 1951; Srinivas, 1968; Dumont, 1970; I. Ahmad, 1973; and Siddiqui, 1974).

Most of these scholars are of the view that though the social structure of Indian Muslims exhibits certain features of the Hindu caste system, like hierarchy, occupational specialization, endogamy and restrictions on commensality, Muslim caste cannot be regarded as identical with the Hindu model. Most of them stress that one of the fundamental features of the Hindu caste system on which rests the hierarchical division of society, namely doctrinal justification and sanction, is singularly absent in the Muslim caste structure. They are of the view that the existence of caste among Indian Muslims can be traced to the acculturative influence of Hinduism. Dumont (1970:257) suggests that the existence of caste among Indian Muslims is conditioned primarily by proximity to the Hindu environment which predominates both generally and regionally.

Our study of caste structure among the Muslims of Bhiwandi lends support to this view. The Kokni Muslims, soon after their migration to India in the seventh century, began interacting with the local Hindu population. Their dialect, surnames, and many of their rituals and customs, which are now gradually disappearing, indicate the influence of the Hindu environment. During the last century there existed among the Kokni Muslims of Kolaba district a group known as Chorwad Koknis. They were supposed to be the illegitimate children of well-to-do Kokni Muslims but were not considered to be Kokni Muslims. During Hindu rule they were so terrified of this stigma that they even took to wearing the sacred thread. Their womenfolk also took to Hindu dress (Mohiuddin, 1969:109).

In our study, we find that the second category in the Kokni Muslim caste hierarchy is considered lowly because their forefathers married or kept Hindu women in the neighbouring rural areas. So our conclusion regarding the existence of caste-like features among the Kokni Muslims of Bhiwandi is that it can be ascribed to the acculturative influence of the Hindu environment.

The Momins, who belong to the Ajlaf category of Indian Muslim society, are descendants of the earlier converts from Hinduism. Their forefathers retained many cultural features and elements of their earlier faith. Conversion to Islam did not totally erase caste distinctions among them. Prior to their migration to Bhiwandi, the Momins formed part of the Muslim social hierarchy of U.P. So the existence of caste among the Momins, much before their arrival in Bhiwandi, was a cultural hangover of the past. The persistence of Hindu beliefs, customs and rituals among the Momins till quite recently is indicative of the pervasive influence of Hinduism.

In our view, one of the serious limitations of studies of caste among Indian Muslims is that they ignore the dimension of change which has given rise to new patterns and configurations. Our study has been mainly concerned with the impact of socio-economic changes on the caste structure of the Muslims of Bhiwandi. Here the major source of change was the process of industrialization. During the last two decades, the process of industrialization has gradually weakened the traditional bases of hierarchical ranking, rules of endogamy, occupational structure and norms of commensality, as well as the attitudes underlying them. The decisive impact of industrialization is evidenced in occupational mobility and inter-ethnic interaction. The attitude towards caste distinctions and caste privileges has also undergone a change. Ambivalence and rationalization regarding caste distinctions, which are antithetical to the principles of Islam, have replaced the traditional attitudes of pride and justification.

Our study also suggests that the traditional Ashraf-Ajlaf dichotomization of Indian Muslim society is no longer meaningful in the context of change. What is sociologically significant and has far-reaching theoretical implications is what we have termed as de-Ashrafization. Though Ashrafization and de-Ashrafization are parallel and mutually complementary processes in Indian Muslim society, it is the latter which can serve as the main indicator of the changing vistas of Muslim caste.

Bibliography

Ahmad, Aziz (1964), *Studies in Islamic Culture in the Indian Environment*, London, Oxford University Press.

Ahmad, Imtiaz (ed.) (1973), *Caste and Social Straticfiation among the Muslims*, Delhi, Manohar Book Service.

Ansari, Ghaus (1960), *Muslim Caste in Uttar Pradesh: A Study in Culture Contact*, Lucknow, Ethnographic and Folk Culture Society.

Bose, N.K. (1951), 'Caste in India', *Man in India*', 31, pp. 107-23.

Dumont, Louis (1970), *Homo Hierarchicus: The Caste System and its Implications*, Delhi, Vikas Publishing House.

Gilani, Manazir Ahsan (1960), *The Story of Muslim Schisms* (Urdu), Delhi.

Hutton, John H. (1946), *Caste in India: Its Nature, Function and Origin*, Bombay, Oxford University Press.

Krech, D. *et. al.* (1962), *Individual in Society*, New York, McGraw Hill

Mandelbaum, D.G. (1970), *Society in India: Change and Continuity*, 2nd vol., Berkeley University of California Press.

Majumdar, D.N. (1968), *Caste and Communication in an Indian Village*, Bombay, Asia Publishing House.

Mohiuddin, M. (1969), *History of Kokan* (Urdu), Bombay.

Momin, A.R. (1974), 'Maharashtra: Tensions in an Industrial Slum', *Economic and Political Weekly*, 9, Annual Number, pp. 177-81.

———(1975), Muslim Caste: Theory and Practice (Review of Imtiaz Ahmed [ed.] *Caste and Social Stratification among the Muslims*), *Economic and Political Weekly*, 10, pp. 12-15.

Siddiqui, M.K.A. (1974), *Muslims of Calcutta: A Study in Aspects of their Social Organization*, Calcutta, Anthropological Survey of India.

Singh, Yogendra (1973), *Modernization of Indian Tradition*, Delhi, Thompson, Press.

Srinivas, M.N. (1959), 'The Dominant Caste in Rampura', *American Anthropologist*, 61, pp. 1-16.

———(1968), 'Mobility in the Caste System', in Milton Singer and B.S. Cohn (eds.) *Structure and Change in Indian Society*, Chicago, Aldine Publishing Company.

Nieuwenhuijze, C.A.O. von (1974), *Indonesia in the Legacy of Islam*, London, Oxford University Press.

Vreede-de-Steurs, Cora (1969), *Parda: A Study of North Indian Muslim Women*, New York, Humanities Press.

6

Caste Hierarchy in a Meo Village of Rajasthan

Partap C. Aggarwal

Muslims deny the existence of caste or caste-like divisions in their society. They point in support of this denial to verse 13 of Sura 49 of the Koran which reads:

> O Mankind, We have created you male and female, and appointed you races and tribes, that you may know one another. Surely the noblest among you in the sight of God is the most god fearing of you. God is All-knowing, All-aware (Arberry, 1955:232).

Scholars seem to agree that in this injunction piety has been elevated above heredity as a criterion for the determination of a person's status in society. There are a number of other exhortations in the Koran which also emphasize the brotherhood of the Muslims. Therefore, it is quite clear that Islam upholds the egalitarian principle and instructs the Believers that in evaluating an individual they should not accord much importance to such factors as race, nationality, or ancestry. What matters is the degree to which a Muslim practises the teachings of the Koran. The Prophet Muhammad also repeatedly reminded his followers that they should not idolize him. He emphasized that just because he was chosen by God to convey His message to mankind, this did not alter the fact that he and his descendants were ordinary human beings.

While there can be little doubt that the Koran recommends the egalitarian principle, actual practice among Muslim communities in different parts of the world falls short of the Koranic ideal. Particularly in India and Pakistan the Muslim society is clearly stratified. First, there is a line which divides the Ashraf from the Ajlaf: the former are high and the latter low. The Ashraf are further divided into four ranked subgroups: Sayyad, Sheikh, Mughal and Pathan. Some would regard Muslim Rajputs as a fifth subgroup of the Ashraf. The Ajlaf are similarly sub-divided into a much larger number of groups. All these groups, the Ashraf and the Ajlaf, are endogamous. Furthermore, they are hierarchically arranged in relation to one another, the Sayyads occupying the highest and the Sweepers the lowest position.

Muslims insist that the subgroups of the type mentioned above are not castes. After all, they maintain, all Muslims pray together on Fridays and on other special occasions regardless of their social group. They also point out that Muslims do not object to eating and drinking together whenever an occasion arises. All this is no doubt true. The Ashraf and the Ajlaf do pray together, except perhaps some very low Ajlaf who may be excluded. And it is quite true that commensality among the Muslims of various groups is common, although many Ashrafs may in practice avoid sharing food with the low ranking Ajlafs. But congregational prayers, commensality, and scriptural prescriptions do not help us adequately to answer the question whether a caste system prevails among Muslims. This is largely a matter of definition and one can answer the question in the affirmative or negative depending on what one means by caste.

For purposes of this discussion, we shall define caste as a ranked social division in which membership is determined by birth. This definition is both simple and useful for a comparative analysis of this institution in various societies. Using this definition, I propose in this essay to discuss the caste hierarchy in a Meo village called Chavandi Kalan in Rajasthan State. The Meos are a Muslim caste who occupy a rank in relation to other Muslim and Hindu castes and this is recognized by the

Meos themselves as well as by all the others. Since hierarchy is regarded as one of the salient features of a caste society, we hope a discussion of caste ranking of the village will show how far relations among the different social groups in the village are characterized by caste considerations or are being influenced by an ideology of caste.

The Village

Chavandi Kalan is located in the Alwar district of Rajasthan State near the Rajasthan-Haryana border. Prior to independence, Alwar was a princely State under the rule of the Rajputs, but the State has now been integrated and forms a separate district. Chavandi Kalan is situated in the Tijara tehsil of the district, and Tijara village, which is the headquarters of both the tehsil and the Panchayat Samiti,[1] is about twelve kilometres to the north-east of the village.

Chavandi Kalan is not directly linked to the outside world through communication and transport facilities, but it is well within their reach. An all-weather State highway, connecting Alwar city with Tijara, passes through Bhindosi village situated at a distance of about eight kilometres from Chavandi Kalan. Chavandi Kalan is connected to this metalled road through a country road which is unsuitable for motor transport. The nearest railway station for the village is Khairthal, which is about twenty-eight kilometres east of the village. One must, therefore, go from Chavandi Kalan either to Bhindosi or Tijara and catch the bus to Alwar, or travel to Khairthal and take a train from there for the onward journey. The soil of the area is sandy and the most popular means of transportation in the area is naturally the camel. Bullock-carts are also used, but the sand is loose in the summers and the carts tend to get stuck. Generally speaking, the people of Chavandi Kalan prefer to walk up to Bhindosi or Tijara and take a bus from there for their onward journey. Most of the travelling is done between villages and

[1]Panchayat Samiti refers to the institution of local government organized at the tehsil level throughout the State under the Rajasthan Panchayat Act, 1953.

people either walk or ride camels.

Chavandi Kalan is an old village settlement. According to one of the oldest inhabitants of the village, it was founded by a Khanzada about five hundred years ago. The Khanzada settled down with a Bania companion who is said to be the ancestor of the present Bania families of the village. It is believed that through the centuries the number of families increased to five hundred. This figure is probably an exaggeration, but it is quite certain that the population of the village was much larger before 1947 than it is today.

The village had a population of 640 people in 1964, and it was divided into sixteen castes. The sixteen castes represented in the village included the Meos, four non-Meo Muslim castes, ten Hindu castes, and a caste of the Sikhs. The Meos are the most numerous caste, and the Khatris the least numerous. Except for the Sikhs, two Daḳot families and the Khatris, who settled in the village after partition, all the other castes are old residents of the village. The distribution of the population of Chavandi Kalan by caste, sex and number of households is shown in Table 1.

In Chavandi Kalan one of the first things the villagers want to know about a person is his or her *jat* or *jati*, best translated into English as caste. When referring to familiar persons as well as casual acquaintances, both their name and caste are mentioned. For example, one hears about Khemu Chamar, Sumer Meo, Gulzari Brahmin, or Behru Bania, and not just Khemu, Sumer, Gulzari or Behru. Also, in describing a social gathering, the villager normally clarifies its caste composition; for instance, a *barat* (marriage party) of the Chamars, or a fair with *saton jat* (literally, all seven castes) participating in it.

The reason for such extensive attention to caste is its important behavioural implications. Unless one knows the caste of another person one does not know how to deal with him. Conversely, upon knowing the caste of a person one gets a fair idea of how one must act. For example, if a Meo is aware that the stranger he is dealing with is a Chamar, he knows that he may not offer him any hospitality, nor treat him with deference. On the other hand, if the stranger is another Meo, he must be treated as an equal and given certain courtesies and hospitality. This does not mean that the Chamar will be totally ignored and allowed to remain hungry and exposed to the elements. In an

TABLE 1
Caste Distribution in Chavandi Kalan by Household and Sex

Caste	*Number of Households*	*Number of Members*		
		Male	*Female*	*Total*
MUSLIM				
Meo	66	198	172	370
Faqir	1	4	3	7
Lohar	1	2	2	4
Sakka	3	7	5	12
Mirasi	1	4	3	7
HINDU				
Brahmin	3	8	2	10
Khatri	1	1	0	1
Bania	4	12	13	25
Khati	1	3	2	5
Dakot	4	20	10	30
Bairagi	1	3	2	5
Jogi	1	4	1	5
Nai	2	7	2	9
Chamar	11	24	21	45
Bhangi	2	6	6	12
SIKH				
Sikh	18	48	45	93
Total	120	351	289	640

emergency, if there is no other Chamar family in the village to give shelter to the man, of course the Meo will feed the Chamar and provide him with a place to sleep. But the Meo will not allow the Chamar to sit down with him and eat from the same utensils, nor will he let the Chamar touch his water pipe. In short, interaction between castes is governed by certain rules which cannot be ignored with impunity.

Definition

A caste in Chavandi Kalan is a social group which is characterized by endogamy, hereditary membership, and a hierarchical position in relation to other castes (for detailed definitions of the caste system see Hutton, 1946; Ghurye, 1950; Srinivas, *et al.*, 1959; Beteille, 1965: 45-52; and Dumont, 1970). The sixteen castes in the village interact according to a pattern of rules and thus make up a system. It is, of course, true that castes tend to specialize in certain occupations, differ in cultural practices, and some caste groups exhibit peculiar personality traits; but these are consequences of the caste system as we have defined it, and not its characteristics. Let us therefore examine the characteristics of the caste system in Chavandi Kalan and see how the system works.

Endogamy

A major characteristic of the caste system is endogamy (see Srinivas, 1952:30; Ghurye, 1950:103; Mayer, 1960:154-56; and Dumont, 1970:108). Inter-caste marriages, with a few exceptions, are prohibited, and this rule is stringently enforced by all castes in Chavandi Kalan. Violations do occur, but in each case sanctions of varying severity are invoked, depending on factors such as degree of difference in rank between the man and the woman, social standing and the economic position of the parties involved, and also the nature of the law of the country. Details of three cases of inter-caste marriage in the village will illustrate the way endogamy operates.

The first is a Jogi-Bairagi marriage. The sister of a Jogi is married to a Bairagi in the village. Although the Jogi and Bairagi are two separate caste groups, marriages between them are approved. The two are almost equal in rank, both very low. In fact they were originally Chamars, till a person from each caste became a religious man and renounced his original caste. This is a well established means of upward mobility available to the underprivileged castes in India. Although not easy, it is recognized as legitimate. Both the Jogi and the Bairagi connote religiously inspired renunciation, and in these cases caste was the main consideration that was renounced. The two castes are, by and large, endogamous but till now inter-caste marriages have occurred.

The second case of inter-caste marriage in Chavandi Kalan is one between a Jogi man and an Ahir woman. This is considered a serious violation of the caste endogamy rule, since the rank difference between the Ahirs and the Jogis is considerable. The former are a dominant land-owning caste in parts of

Haryana, and the latter are elevated untouchables. It began as an affair of the heart in another village between a young widow and a family labourer. When the Ahirs of the village came to know about it they threatened to kill both. The couple eloped and got married in a court of law in the face of severe opposition. They were attracted to Chavandi Kalan by their Bairagi relative's assurance of help. The couple has three sons who aspire to get land from their Ahir relatives and some day be accepted in that high ranking caste. At present the family does not own any land and are treated by the villagers as other low-caste farm labourers. As far as I could observe, nobody in Chavandi Kalan was agitated about this inter-caste marriage, a major reason being that both were outsiders. The villagers did not pay much attention except for exhibiting a sense of curiosity about the unusual type of marital alliance.

A third case of an inter-caste marital alliance is between a Brahim man and a Chamar woman. Their marriage is not formally legitimized, but they live together and have children. The villagers know that they are virtually husband and wife, but there is no serious opposition. The Brahmin husband not only openly admits the fact of his relationship with the Chamar woman, but often defends his alignment with 'the rising caste' which has elected him to the Village Panchayat for two consecutive terms.

Endogamy, of course, does not rule out extra-marital sexual relations between members of different castes. It is not considered a serious offence for high caste men to have sexual relations with 'untouchable' women (see, for instance, Srinivas, 1959:10; Gough, 1955; and Beteille, 1966). In fact, the Brahmin-Chamar inter-caste marital alliance described earlier began as a clandestine sexual affair of a type that often occurs but is ignored. What is unusual is that it is no longer a secret and there is almost no opposition. But if a high caste woman has sexual relations with a low caste man, her relatives are likely to feel outraged. The violent reaction of the Ahirs to the Jogi-Ahir marriage clearly illustrates the point.

Caste endogamy is also restricted within spatial and linguistic bounds. This is well illustrated by the example of the Dakots of Chavandi Kalan. Two of the Dakot families migrated from the Punjab after 1947 and had no prior contact with the Dakots of Chavandi Kalan. Although the two groups recognize similarity of caste, they are culturally and linguistically different. Consequently, even after twenty years of residence in the same village, there is no visible move towards marriages across group lines. Thus, these two groups of Dakots constitute virtually two separate castes.

Endogamy has the effect of insulating a caste group by intensifying intra-caste interaction and restricting inter-caste contact (see Dumont, 1970:108; Beteille, 1971:531; Barth, 1969: 14). For, a good many of the social activities associated with life cycle rites, religious rituals, and recreation are performed together by caste fellows. Furthermore, since members of a caste occupy an equal social status, most meaningful friendships are formed within the caste. All this leads to cultural differences which become manifest through differences in vocabulary, ritual practices, names, and often in dress, living style, and food. In Chavandi Kalan, significant inter-caste cultural and linguistic differences are apparent.

Hereditary Membership

Closely related to endogamy is the second important characteristic of caste: hereditary membership. In accordance with this rule a child automatically becomes a member of its father's caste by virtue of the biological connection. Right to membership by birth is always honoured if the child's parents are members of a caste in good standing. Offsprings of outcastes, however, may or may not be admitted into their parent's previous caste. In fact, no other legitimate method of recruitment exists.

Marital alliance in a caste other than one's own is likely to lead to punishment for both partners rather than membership in one's spouse's caste. Adoption of a child across caste lines is uncommon, but when it occurs, the foster child retains his biological parents' caste. In Chavandi Kalan there are cases of adoption within caste, but across *gotra* lines; invariably the children retain their hereditary *gotra*. Like *gotra*, caste does not change by adoption.

Exceptions do, however, occur. It is noticeable that lower

castes, especially the 'untouchables', but also the Kamin, do often accept high caste women through marriage. In Chavandi Kalan the Jogi's Ahir wife is more or less accepted by the Jogis. When he was being harassed by the Ahirs, his relatives provided considerable support. Even the high castes make exceptions in admitting low caste wives of politically powerful individuals who can forestall sanctions by using their influence. When expedient, even large-scale inter-caste recruitment is possible. The Meos of Chavandi Kalan provide a good example of such an occurrence: for it appears that members of a variety of castes were admitted into the Meo fold after their conversion to Islam. Members of some of the existing Meo *gotras*, for instance, claim descent from various Hindu castes.

Contrary to common belief, caste membership is by no means permanent. For instance, renunciation of caste membership by individuals is not unknown in Chavandi Kalan. I met several sadhus born and known in the region passing through the village who refused to divulge to me their former caste because they felt it was irrelevant. Also, men and women are sometimes excommunicated for violating caste rules. Some outcastes are later readmitted after they have propitiated the elders, often by feasting all the caste members in the village. Others spend the rest of their lives without caste affiliation.

Hierarchy

The third, and by far the most important, characteristic of a caste system is its hierarchical arrangement (see Srinivas, 1952:25 and 1955:2-4; Mayer, 1956:3-17; Dumont, 1970:65). In other words, castes are unequal and ranked in relation to each other. In Chavandi Kalan, ranking is not done in terms of single castes, but in clusters. The sixteen castes represented in the village, regardless of religion, are divided into three ranked clusters: the Unchi Jat (high castes), the Kamin (service castes), and the Harijans (untouchables). Within each of these groups the castes are not considered equal, but their relative status positions are ambiguous, and the difference relatively inconsequential. The composition and other details of the three groups are presented in Table 2. Let us now examine each of the groups.

Unchi Jat (*high castes*): Five castes are included in this group of which the position of the Brahmins and the Banias is undisputed. The Brahmin and the Bania belong to the twice-born *varna*, occupying the first and third place respectively on a four-level scale. Furthermore, they carry on lucrative occupations of priestly work, trading and money-lending in addition to agriculture on their own land. Some of their members weild considerable political influence in the village. A Brahmin happens to be the biggest land and cattle-herd owner in the village. Consequently, he directly and indirectly provides employment to several families.

TABLE 2
Caste Hierarchy in Chavandi Kalan

Name of Caste	*Occupation and Description*	*Varna Position*
UNCHI JAT		
Brahmin	Priest and farmer	Brahmin
Meo	Muslim farmer	Kshatriya
Sikh	Sikh farmer	unclear
Bania	Trader and money-lender	Vaishya
Khatri	Punjabi trader	unclear
KAMIN		
Khatri	Carpenter	Shudra
Lohar	Muslim blacksmith	Shudra
Dakot	Brahmin beggar	Brahmin
Nai	Barber	Shudra
Bairagi	Elevated Chamar or leather worker	Shudra
Jogi	Elevated Chamar or leather worker	Shudra
Faqir	Muslim beggar	unclear
Sakka	Muslim water carrier	Shudra
Mirasi	Muslim entertainer	Shudra
HARIJAN		
Chamar	Leather worker	Low Shudra
Bhangi	Sweeper	Low Shudra

The Meos fall in this group of castes although their claim to the prestigious Kshatriya *varna* is in doubt due to their conversion to Islam. However, this doubt has not made much difference to their position, for other castes continue to treat them as high caste Kshatriyas. They retained their monopoly over landownership in the village until 1947, and remained politically dominant. In order to keep the caste system alive, the Meos made significant compromises with the ideals of their adopted religion (Islam). They observed most Hindu rituals and continued to use the services of all Hindu castes, including the Brahmins, long after embracing Islam. Since independence, the lower castes have acquired both the land and the vote, so for the Meos it seems neither necessary nor possible to keep up the ritual facade. Hence, they are replacing their Hindu rituals with equivalent Muslim ones. Yet, their place among the Unchi Jat will be assured as long as they continue to own most of the land and weild political power in the village.

The remaining two castes in this group, the Sikhs and the Khatris, have a peculiar position. Their *varna* connection is unclear and some elements of their culture resemble low caste traits. For example, it is believed that, until most Sikhs of Chavandi Kalan abandoned meat-eating and liquor drinking a few years ago, they used to eat pork which is a low-caste food. The Khatri eats meat and has habits that do not agree with high caste Hindus. Yet both the Sikhs and the Khatris are treated as high castes. All Unchi Jats sit with them on the cot, share a *chilam* (an earthen pipe for smoking tobacco), often share cooked food, and show due deference. Likewise, the Kamins and the Harijans treat the Sikhs and the Khatris as they treat other high castes. The major factor that has helped in determining the rank of both these castes is the fact that they own land. In the absence of any clear previous association with a low rank, the fact of land ownership by right tipped the balance in their favour. Interestingly enough, the Sikhs and the Khatris reacted to the situation by conforming to high-caste behaviour, adopting vegetarianism, religiousness, teetotalism, and adherence to orthodox religious beliefs and rituals.

The Kamin (*Service Castes*): Out of the nine castes in this group, three (i.e., Khati, Lohar and Nai) are clean Shudras. They practise their traditional caste occupations according to the *jajmani* (barter) arrangement. The Nai has acquired land but not enough to provide a living. The Muslim Lohar also operates according to the *jajmani* rules. Being a poor workman he has lost much of his clientele to the Khati but his caste position has remained more or less unchanged.

The Dakots of the village belong to the Brahmin *varna*, but due to their lowly occupation of beggary they are considered Kamins. Though the two refugee Dakot families own land, they have not given up their traditional occupation completely and thus their caste status has not improved. One of their striking characteristics is that, like other professional beggars, they cringe before the high castes. This has minimized their chances for upward mobility.

The Bairagis and the Jogis are elevated Chamars whose ancestors abandoned their traditional leather work in favour of religious devotion which helped remove the stigma of untouchability. Now they are classified with other Kamins. Both are upwardly mobile and are trying to acquire high caste characteristics such as land, education, and clean and lucrative occuptions.

The Faqirs, Sakkas, and Mirasis are Muslim service castes which serve the land-owning Meos according to *jajmani* rules. All three are patronized mainly by the Muslims and were attracted to Chavandi Kalan because of the presence of Meo Muslims. The Hindus do not require their services, except only rarely, and can easily do without them. Being old Muslims and serving only Meos, their *varna* association is tenuous. On the basis of their occupations and weak socio-economic status, they are grouped with the Kamins and are treated as such by the high castes.

The Harijans (*Untouchables*): There are two castes of 'untouchables' in Chavandi Kalan: the Chamars and the Bhangis. Both occupy a position at the bottom of the *varna* scale, i.e., the untouchable section of the Shudra *varna*. They constitute the most deprived section of the caste hierarchy in the village. Their occuptions require them to engage in tasks that are considered least desirable. The Chamars traditionally process animal hides and make shoes and other leather articles. The Bhangis do the scavenging: cleaning the cattlesheds of their *jajmans*, and skinning and disposing of dead animals. Members of both these castes provide extra farm hands during busy agricultural months, often at very low wages.

Because the Harijans are required to do unattractive work at relatively low wages, society apparently makes attempts to block their way out of this predicament by plying them with insults and deprivations. They are treated as untouchable, segregated in a separate hamlet, denied the basic amenities available to the rest of the village, given cast-off clothing to wear and left-over food to eat, and are made to show deference to the higher castes. All these are low status traits which, taken together, push the Harijans far below the level of the lowest Kamin caste, and widen the gulf between the Harijans and Kamins. The Harijans, being weak, bow to the inevitable and degrade themselves in the eyes of the higher castes. Naturally, of all the lines that separate the various caste groups the one separating the Harijans is the most clearly delineated and the hardest to cross.

Stability and Change

The caste system has worked smoothly in Chavandi Kalan, probably for many centuries. What has given the system its stability? An important factor seems to be cultural differentiation. Caste groups in the village possess their subcultures with variant norms and customs. This situation is brought about by endogamy and the confining of equal status interaction within the caste.

Once a caste evolves a subculture it develops its own mechanism of self-perpetuation and control of deviance. Children are socialized into the tradition and deviations from it are punished. For example, in Chavandi Kalan the Bhangis know that eating of carrion beef costs them loss of status, but they continue to eat it because: (*a*) due to their particular socialization they lack a feeling of repulsion for it; (*b*) being poor they see advantage in exploiting this source of protein; and (*c*) if a Bhangi refused to eat carrion beef he would not only be considered a snob but may even be ridiculed and punished for making others feel inferior to him.

While it is true that the mechanisms of cultural stability are quite potent, they are hardly sufficient to maintain a caste system characterized by differential rewards. Compared to other castes, the Meos in Chavandi Kalan are wealthier, politically more powerful, and enjoy higher social prestige. Knowing that the caste system favours them, they used their power to preserve it. On the other hand, the underprivileged castes, such as the Bhangis and the Chamars, know very well that they are handicapped, but they are weak in the face of the domin-ance of the Meos who control the land on which all the agricul-tural activity in the village depends. Since they see no way of improving their lot, they resign themselves to the iniquities for the economic security that the system provides to them. At least they are assured employment at a subsistence wage, and they cannot give it up in the absence of a more desirable alternative.

It is apparent that in the past the Meos used brute force to preserve the caste system. A couple of illustrations will demons-trate the manner in which they used their influence. A Meo informant told me: 'The Sakkas of our village are a crafty bunch. Their ambitions know no bounds. They are uppity. In order to acquire land they are fraternizing a Meo family. They would even allow their women to sleep with the unmarried males of this Meo family. They are doing this with a view to acquiring land. Before partition we would have beaten them up and turned them out of the village.' A second example also concerns the Sakkas. During the 1965 Panchayat elections in Chavandi Kalan a Meo and a Punjabi Hindu were competing for the post of Sarpanch (chairmanship of the Panchayat). The Meo candidate was the weaker of the two and when he did not see much hope of winning the election he tried to make an appeal to all the Muslim voters in the name of religion. A Sakka, whose sympathies lay with the Meo candidate, used to give me a great deal of information about the activities of the supporters of the Hindu candidate, hoping that I would pass the information on to the right ears. He could not talk directly to the candidate or his supporters because they did not listen to a mere Sakka who should not meddle in politics. This indi-cates how dominant the Meos were and how the lower castes were kept in their place.

In order to perpetuate the caste system the Meos made real concessions in their own behaviour. For several centuries after their conversion to Islam, the Meos continued to observe the Hindu rituals with the assistance of Hindu castes, including the Brahmins, at least partially to save the system which was so beneficial to them.

It is further apparent that the underprivileged castes understood their plight well and did not submit to it willingly. This is illustrated by the events of the post-independence period. It is quite remarkable that as soon as a real opportunity for improvement was offered to the low castes they took advantage of it with great enthusiasm.

Just before 1947, when Hindu-Muslim tensions were mounting and the Meos were still very strong in Mewat, many Hindus from Chavandi Kalan sought the safety of the neighbouring towns. The Chamars and Bhangis were the only Hindus who did not leave the village. They took the risk in the hope of acquiring land in case the Meos left for Pakistan. When the State militia entered the conflict and tried to push the Meos out of the State of Alwar, the Chamars became its allies. As soon as the Meos left, the Chamars grabbed the land. Although most of it was later returned to its Meo owners, some land belonging to Meos who migrated to Pakistan became available for redistribution. As a result, all the Chamars and the Bhangis were given land in keeping with the Government's policy of favouring the scheduled castes and tribes. The Chamars abandoned their traditional occupation of shoe-making as soon as they acquired land. They are fast abandoning their low caste characteristics and replacing them with high caste practices: vegetarianism, ritual cleanliness, religiosity, self-respect, etc. The Meos and other castes resent all this, but they can no longer forestall the improvement in the social position of the Chamars.

After independence, India adopted a democratic form of government based on the principle of universal adult suffrage. The people of Chavandi Kalan have participated in choosing representatives for the Union and State governments every five years since 1952. The underprivileged castes, such as the Chamars, particularly where they formed a sizable bloc of voters, began to realize the power potential of the ballot box. More recently, in 1961, when democratic decentralization in the form of Panchayati Raj was introduced in Rajasthan, the Chamars of Chavandi Kalan got their opportunity to gain political power. The Indian constitution provides guaranteed representation to the scheduled castes and tribes. The Chamars of Chavandi Kalan took full advantage of this provision by electing a non-Chamar from their ward, and nominating a Chamar under the guarantee provision. They voted *en bloc*, in great numbers, to exert maximum influence.

We have argued that the differential allocation of economic and political power is the key to a caste system. If this is so, one might ask why the Brahmins in Chavandi Kalan enjoyed such a high status in the absence of power? The answer is that they were supported by the dominant caste in return for their assistance in legitimizing their own position in the social system. The Brahmins knew all along that their high status was somewhat artificial and without any real benefits. For the same reason, they collaborated with the Chamars to participate in the power struggle as soon as the situation changed. Of the three Brahmin families in Chavandi Kalan, two have become land-owning farmers. One of the land-owning Brahmins has become the head of a political faction in the village and is deeply involved in village politics. He is a member of the Village Panchayat and a majority of his electorate are Chamars. He lives with a Chamar woman in the village and supports the Chamars in every possible way. The head of the third Brahmin family is a religious practitioner who has recently begun to serve the Chamars as their *purohit*.

Bibliography

Arberry, A.J. (1955), *The Koran Interpreted*, New York, Macmillan.

Barth, Fredrik (1969), 'Introduction', in Fredrik Barth (ed.), *Ethnic Groups and Boundaries: The Social Organization of Cultural Difference*, George Allen and Unwin, London.

Beteille, Andre (1965), *Caste, Class and Power: Changing Patterns of Stratification in a Tanjore Village*, Berkeley, University of California Press.

——— (1971), 'Caste, Race and Ethnic Identity', *International Social Science Journal*, 23, pp. 519-33.

Dumont, Louis (1970), *Homo Hierarchicus: The Caste System and its Implications*, Delhi, Vikas Publishing House.

Ghurye, G.S. (1950), *Caste and Class in India*, Bombay, Popular Prakashan.

Gough, E. Kathleen (1955), 'The Social Structure of a Tanjore Village', in McKim Marriott (ed.), *Village India: Studies in the Little Community*, Chicago, University of Chicago Press.

Hutton, John H. (1946), *Caste in India: Its Nature, Function and Origin*, Cambridge, Cambridge University Press.

Mayer, Adrian C. (1956), 'Some Hierarchical Aspects of Caste', *South-western Journal of Anthropology*, 12, pp. 3-17.

———(1960), *Caste and Kinship in Central India: Village and its Region*, London, Routledge and Kegan Paul.

Srinivas, M.N. (1952), *Religion and Society among the Coorgs of South India*, Oxford, Oxford University Press.

———(1955), 'The Social System of a Mysore Village', in McKim Marriott (ed.), *Village India: Studies in the Little Community*, Chicago, University of Chicago Press.

———(1959), 'The Dominant Caste in Rampura', *American Anthropologist*, 61, pp. 1-16.

Srinivas, M.N., *et. al.* (1959), 'Caste: A Trend Report and Bibliography', *Current Sociology*, 8, pp. 135-83.

7

Social Stratification among Muslim Tamils in Tamilnadu, South India[1]

Mattison Mines

There is a tendency among those who study India to speak of the Indian Muslim population as if it were a single homogeneous population. This tendency is seen both in studies with a macrocosmic orientation and in studies with a narrow scope. It is clear, however, that such a monolithic view is inaccurate. There are tremendous variations not only in the social organization of different Muslim populations in India, but also in the degree and nature of Muslim integration into the surrounding Hindu society.

In this paper I explore the nature of Muslim social stratification in the town of Pallavaram in northern Tamilnadu State, South India. My purpose is twofold. First, it is to demonstrate the social distinctiveness of this Muslim population which sets them off from the Muslims of North India, from the Moplahs and the Dakhnis of the South as well as from the Hindu Tamilians with whom they share much of their culture. Second, it is to examine the cultural and social basis of Muslim integration into

[1]This paper is based on research carried out in Tamilnadu between September 1967 and February 1969. The author wishes to express his gratitude to the Foreign Area Fellowship Programme for supporting this research. An earlier version of this paper was read at the 23rd Annual Meeting of the Association for Asian Studies, March 1969.

South Indian Hindu society and to demonstrate the ambivalent position of Muslims in urban Tamilnadu. Muslim Tamils identify with both Hindu Tamilians and the Indian Islamic religious community. Yet, because of their social uniqueness, the Muslim Tamils cannot identify fully with either.

Culturally, the Muslim Tamils consider themselves to be Tamilians. They share the Tamil language with the Hindus. Muslim intellectuals (see, for example, Raheem, n.d.) point to the contribution of Muslims to Tamil literature. Both Muslims and Hindus say that Muslim Tamils share Tamilian culture and customs with the Hindus and that even their religious practices are influenced by Hindu Tamil culture. Muslims and Hindus both emphasize that the Muslims are very much like Hindu Tamilians.

Despite such casual assessments, in Pallavaram the Muslim Tamilians and the Hindus are distinctive in their ethos and in their social structure. Muslims are egalitarian in their ethos while Hindus, in contrast, embrace an ideology of hierarchy and inequality. The Muslim ethos stresses independence and Muslims argue that the business occupation allows expression of independence. The Hindu ethos, in contrast, stresses interdependence, super-ordination and subordination. Muslim merchants point out that while Hindus can enter employment and work their way up through the bureaucratic system, a Muslim of strong character cannot because he refuses to be subordinate—the self-employed merchant is not subordinate to anyone. The Muslim has an ethic which awards high status to hard work, which stresses work as a means to success and which associates success with frugality and hard work. A man who is hard-working is a man to whom respect should be shown. The Hindu ethos associates success with leisure and low status with work. A man is shown respect not because he is hard working but because he can command others to work. Thus, the ethos of the Hindu and Muslim are distinct in several ways.

In social structural and distributional terms also the Hindus and Muslims are distinct. The Muslim social structure contrasts sharply with that of the Hindus. As we shall see, in Pallavaram the Muslim Tamils' social structure has been greatly affected by the egalitarian ideology of Islam. The Hindus' caste system, of course, is not egalitarian. With respect to residence, the Muslim Tamil is twice as likely to live in a town or city as is the Hindu. In Tamilnadu the Muslim is likely to be urban; the Hindu is likely to be a villager.

My purpose in highlighting the contrast between their respective world views and social structure is to illustrate the distinctiveness of the Muslims and Hindus in Tamilnadu. The contrast is not intended to show any casual relationship between beliefs and behaviour or between social structure and beliefs. Nevertheless, there is a striking consistency between the Hindu and Muslim social structures and ethos which reflects a core distinction between Muslim egalitarianism and Hindu inegalitarianism.

What is the nature of the Muslim Tamil subdivisions? There are four named divisions: the Rawther, Labbai, Marakayar and Kayalar. Except in the larger cities, the subdivisions appear to be distributed within territorially distinct parts of the State. Kayalars and Marakayars are found primarily along the Coromandel Coast. Most informants say that the Kayalars are a division of the Marakayars who originally come from Kayalpatnam in the extreme south. Labbais and Rawthers appear to predominate in the interior. With a few exceptions, the Rawthers live to the south and the Labbais to the north within the State.

Most informants characterize the Kayalars and Marakayars as Sunnites of the Shafi school. The fact that they are Shafiites, it is argued, corresponds with the origin of these Muslims as offsprings of Tamil women and Arab traders who, they say, were Shafiite. Rawthers and Labbais, in contrast, are Sunnites of the Hanafi school and do not claim any Arab ancestry. At least some Muslim Tamils feel that followers of these two schools should not intermarry because of slight differences in the food restrictions they observe. However, although rare, such marriages do occur in the cities.

All four of the subdivisions have various stories explaining the derivation of their name. Such stories usually indicate social origins and occupational factors. For example, the Marakayars often claim that their name comes from the fact that they came to Tamilnadu on boats and that their main occupation is that of sailor or sea merchant. 'Labbai' is often held to derive from a term of respect used for addressing the educated and refers to the Labbai's religious education. In Madurai the term is used to refer to Muslim religious practitioners. 'Rawther', many say, refers to one who rides horses and Rawthers are said to have been horse traders or cavalry men in the employ of local rulers. However, despite such origin stories, it is behaviourally difficult to distinguish the subdivisions on the basis of occupational distinctions. In Pallavaram, all groups claim that their primary occupation is that of merchant. Within this occupational category there is little differentiation with the exception of the Kayalars. The Kayalars are generally given lower status than the other subdivisions because their business speciality is considered undesirable. They are merchants dealing in raw and salted hides and in scrap.

Despite the recognition of a number of differentiating features among the Muslim subdivisions, they are not hierarchically ranked castes. All four subdivisions are of approximately equal status. Status sociograms,[2] moveable card ranking (see Marriott, 1968:138) and observations of interaction among members of different subdivisions reveal that, unlike Hindu castes, the Muslim subdivisions are not ranked.

Ranking does not occur at the level of the subdivisions as one expects with a caste system. But ranking exists on the level of the individual and is based primarily on the individual's conduct, his age, wealth, personal character and religiousness. Within Pallavaram the Muslims live intermixed and there are no restrictions on interdining. Although some occupations are considered undesirable and those that perform them are ranked low, there is no continuing stigma attached to persons who, once having performed them, have turned to different professions. There is no attributional or interactional ranking of the different subdivisions. No one in Pallavaram can rank the subdivisions attributionally, while observations of interaction also indicate equality. Members of all groups attend the same mosque, and, with the exception of the Marakayars, who are represented by only a few families, men from all the subdivisions participate in the administration of the main mosque and Islamic school. There is no recognition of untouchability

[2]The design for the sociograms used in this study was a modified version of that used by Goodenough (1965).

among the Muslim Tamils. Furthermore, interdining freely occurs at feasts with all participants sitting together, shoulder to shoulder.

In ideological terms, of course, the Muslim is highly egalitarian. The Muslim Tamils emphasize the connection between their ideology and their preference for the occupation of merchant. Business, they feel, enables a man to be his own boss—he does not have to be subordinate to anyone.

It is quite possible that the fact that the Muslim Tamils are in business in Pallavaram helps to account for the absence of interactional ranking. The business occupation enables the merchants to remain largely economically independent.[3] Merchants from all the subdivisions have approximately equal economic opportunities, each is his own boss, none of the merchants perform service functions for any of the others, and none of the subdivisions is economically subordinate to any of the others. In other words, there is no economic interdependence defining the relationship among the subdivisions. The merchant occupation, therefore, is ideally suited to an egalitarian ideology; for, as the merchants themselves stress, this occupation gives them independence and only the independent can be equal.

At first glance it appears that the egalitarian ideology does not apply in the realm of matrimony among the Muslim Tamils. Most marriages are between persons of the same subdivision, and most Muslim Tamils consider subdivision identity to be an important factor in selecting a spouse. In opting for intra-subdivision marriages the overriding concern is not, however, one of trying to maintain purity of blood, as one would expect to find associated with the system of Hindu caste ranking (see Barnett, 1970; and Dumont, 1970). The concern is for matching

[3]See, for instance, Mencher (1970:197). She has noted that an effect of increased economic opportunity in Tamilnadu has been to make it 'less and less meaningful to speak of a caste system as a rigid, hierarchical, tightly linked socio-economic system'. The Muslim Tamil merchant's situation may be comparable. The Muslims are differentiated into subdivisions, but there is no economic interdependence among the groups. Coupled with the Muslim egalitarian ideology, this fact may help to explain the absence of interactional ranking among the Muslim merchants of Pallavaram.

spouses who share the same economic backgrounds and the same cultural and, especially, religious traditions. Specific religious and social practices vary widely among the different Muslim Tamil subdivisions, and attitudes about what is orthodox and what is not vary too. Nevertheless, in the cities intermarriages do occur, although they are rare. Such marriages raise some eyebrows, because they suggest a love match rather than an arranged marriage, but these mixed couples or their children are not ostracized.

The rarity of such marriages may be in part attributed to two additional factors. First, as is customary among Tamilians generally, marriages occur frequently between relatives. This practice naturally narrows the social field from which spouses are drawn. Genealogical evidence suggests that the frequency of such marriages is higher than forty per cent among Muslim Tamils. Second, a high frequency of intra-group marriages appears to be the result of the territorial separation of the four subdivisions except in the larger cities. Intra-marriage, I would argue, should be attributed to kinship and territorial influences rather than to rules of endogamy. All Pallavaram Muslims deny that such rules exist and readily point to inter-group marriages within their own genealogies as proof that endogamy is not the rule.

As least one student (Q.H. Khan, 1910) of Muslim social stratification has argued that caste-like organization occurs among the Muslim Tamils only at the local level. As evidence for this he cites the presence of a number of Rawther and Marakayar subdivisions which, he says, are strictly endogamous. Examples of such castes are the Puliyankudiyar (men of Puliyankudi of Tinnevelly), Elaiyankudiyar (men of Elaiyankudi of former Ramnad zamindari) and the Eruthukarar (bullock-cart drivers). The identity of such groups is based on place of residence in the first two instances and on occupation in the last.

Such groups are not castes as suggested. Outside of the local area such place distinctions lose their meaning and Muslims do not use them. Similarly, occupational names depend upon actual occupation and not upon occupational heritage. Although the Kayalars are a possible exception, in Pallavaram no such occupational or place distinctions are retained as social categories and the Muslim Tamils did not recognize such names as indicative of social subdivisions. The appearance of endogamy is a result of the factors I have noted above.

Hindu caste stratification and Muslim Tamil subdivisional organization are different in two additional ways. First, the identity of Hindu castes rests on purity of blood. Members of a Hindu caste are all said to share the same blood line and hence, in this sense, are all equal. If inter-caste marriages occur, purity of blood is lost and the children of such unions are outcaste (Barnett, 1970). No such attitudes are held among the Muslim Tamils. Since purity is not a consideration, none is lost and no social ostracism occurs when inter-group marriages take place. Second, Hindu castes are ranked in terms of interaction. In Pallavaram there is no evidence that ranking based on interaction occurs among the Muslim Tamil subdivisions. As noted above, there is, however, evidence against it. It is clear, therefore, that if caste is defined in terms of occupational subdivisions, if it is defined in terms of hierarchically ranked endogamous groups which are defined in ideological or interactional terms, if it is defined in terms of purity of descent, or in terms of groups defined by explicit rules of endogamy or any combination of these criteria, then the Muslim Tamils of Pallavaram lack caste distinctions. They may have had such distinctions at one time, but there is no evidence to suggest that they still do.

Given the contrasts between Muslim Tamil and Hindu Tamil ethos and social structures, one might expect the Muslims to identify themselves less with their Hindu neighbours than with their cohorts in religion, the greater Indian Muslim population. In fact there is some evidence for this. Muslim Tamils stress the importance of the Muslim brotherhood. Also, there has been some tendency for the Muslims of northern Tamilnadu to undergo what might be called a process of 'Islamization'. Their personal names have lost their Tamil character and Arabic names have been adopted. There has been a tendency to drop the use of the subdivision names as part of personal names (e.g., Sheikh Md. Rawther). Many have urged the adoption of Urdu as the language of Muslims in India, and many Muslim Tamils in northern Tamilnadu have made the switch from Tamil as their household language to Urdu. Further, the

Tabligh[4] movement until recently has been very popular. Like Muslims elsewhere in India, the Muslims in Tamilnadu have become aware of their identity as being distinct from their Hindu neighbours. In fact, however, the Muslim Tamils are in many respects distinct from the rest of the Indian Muslim population, not only in their Tamilian heritage but also in social structural terms.

What is striking in the Indian context about the Muslim Tamils is the absence of hierarchical considerations in both their ideology and their social structure and the presence of a considerable stress on egalitarianism. While it is true that Muslims everywhere stress the Muslim brotherhood and have an ideology of egalitarianism, it is apparent that elsewhere in India the Muslim social structure involves caste hierarchies based in part on ideological considerations including those of purity of blood or descent line (Dumont, 1970:207). A number of Indian scholars have pointed out the presence of caste hierarchies among Muslims often paralleling the Hindu system (see, for instance, Guha, 1965; Fazlur Khan, 1962; and Zillur Khan, 1968). One scholar, Ghaus Ansari (1960:1-83), even suggests a common historical origin for the Hindu and Muslim caste systems of Northern India. In Southern India, D'Souza (1959:487-516) has shown the presence of a caste-like ranking among the Moplahs of Kerala.

A characteristic feature of Muslim caste hierarchies in North India and in the Deccan is the fact that the highest ranks are accorded to Muslims who claim an origin foreign to India. In the North these castes are collectively called Ashraf (honourable). Among the Ashraf those with ties closest to the Prophet rank first. The Sayyads rank before the Sheikhs, who are followed by the Mughals and Pathans (Ansari, 1960:30-31; Dumont, 1970:207-8). Many Muslims stress parallels between the Muslim and Hindu systems of caste ranking, although most agree that the absence of a consideration of ritual pollution allows for freer interaction among Muslims of different castes than among Hindus. Nevertheless, untouchability is usually

[4]Tabligh is a Muslim religious movement which urges its followers to regularize their observance of Islamic prescriptions in their daily lives.

recognized and caste endogamy is apparently observed. The Rajputs of North India offer an extreme example of such caste behaviour. Muslim Rajputs, it is said, occasionally arrange marriages with their Hindu counterparts in order to avoid marrying out of their caste. Purity of descent is, therefore, an important consideration.

In South India, among the Moplahs of the west coast, Victor D'Souza (1959) has clearly shown a similar system of Muslim caste organization. The Moplahs are divided into five ranked sections called the Thangals, Arabis, Malbaris, Pusalars and Ossans. The Thangals trace their descent from the Prophet's daughter, Fatima, and are of the highest rank. Next in rank are the Arabis, who claim descent from Arab men and local women and who have retained knowledge of their Arab lineage and have adopted matrilineal descent. The Pusalars, or new Muslims, are converts and so are of low status. The Ossans are barbers and by virtue of their lowly occupation are ranked lowest.

The social distance among these castes is very great. They practise endogamy. In interaction those of a higher caste are treated deferentially. The sections eat separately, they have separate mosques, separate religious organizations and separate burial grounds (D'Souza, 1959:504).

It is apparent that the absence of caste among the Muslims of Tamilnadu contrasts strikingly with its presence among the Muslims of North India, the Deccan and the Malabar coast. This contrast is made sharper by the stress placed on ultimate foreign origin for determining status among Muslims elsewhere in India.

The Muslim Tamils distinguish themselves from the Muslims of the Deccan and from those of North India also in their acceptance of their Tamil heritage. As such, they see themselves as an integral part of the local population and not as the descendants of a former ruling elite of foreign origin. They embrace the idea of a Muslim brotherhood, but at the same time they feel that they are true Tamilians. The Muslim Tamils further distinguish themselves from the greater Indian Muslim population by claiming to be better Muslims than the others. They feel that they observe the tenets of Islam more closely than do the others, whom they describe as being decadent.

It is apparent that while the Muslim Tamils identify closely with the Hindu Tamils, they are in fact different from that population in ethos and social structure. The Muslim Tamils of Pallavaram are aware of this difference. Because of their Islamic belief they also identify with the greater Muslim population of India. Yet this identification is by no means complete. They live in a Tamilian cultural environment and view it as their own. Furthermore, they appear to be distinct in social structure from the Muslims living elsewhere in India. One informant, a Muslim who had gone to Pakistan at the time of partition and then returned to Pallavaram disillusioned, expressed this neither-nor identification clearly. He said he went to Pakistan in order to participate in the Muslim brotherhood but returned to Tamilnadu because there was less divisiveness between Muslim Tamils and Hindu Tamils than there was among the Pakistani Muslims. The Muslim Tamils of Pallavaram are a surprisingly egalitarian population living in a hierarchically structured society. Identifying with both the Hindu Tamilian society and the greater Muslim population they are integrated members of neither.

Bibliography

Ansari, Ghaus (1960), *Muslim Caste in Uttar Pradesh: A Study in Culture Contact*, Lucknow, Ethnographic and Folk Culture Society.

Barnett, S.A. (1970), 'Approaches to Caste and Change in South India', Mimeographed.

D'Souza, Victor S. (1959), 'Social Organization and Marriage Customs of the Moplahs on the South-west Coast of India', *Anthropos*, 54, pp. 487-516.

Dumont, Louis (1970), *Homo Hierarchicus: The Caste System and its Implications*, Delhi, Vikas Publishing House.

Guha, Uma (1965), 'Caste among Rural Bengali Muslims', *Man in India*, 45, pp. 167-69.

Goodenough, Ward H. (1965), 'Rethinking "Status" and "Role": Toward a General Model of the Cultural Organization of Social Relationship', in M. Banton (ed.), *The Relevance of Models for Social Anthropology*, ASA Monograph No. 1, London, Tavistock Publications.

Khan, Fazlur R. (1962), 'The Caste System of the Village Community of Dhulundi in the District of Dacca', in John E. Owen (ed.), *Sociology in East Pakistan*, Dacca, Asiatic Society of Pakistan.

Khan, Qadir H. (1910), *South Indian Musalmans*, Madras.

Khan, Zillur (1968), 'Caste and Muslim Peasantry in India and Pakistan', *Man in India*, 47, pp. 138-48.

Mencher, Joan P. (1970), 'A Tamil Village: Changing Socio-economic Structure', in K. Ishwaran (ed.), *Change and Continuity in India's Villages*, New York, Columbia University Press.

Marriott, McKim (1968), 'Caste Ranking and Food Transactions: A Matrix Analysis', in Milton Singer and B. S. Cohn (eds.) *Structure and Change in Indian Society*, Chicago, Aldine Publishing Company.

Raheem, Abdul (n.d.), *Muslim Tamil Paravarhal*, Madras.

8

Endogamy and Status Mobility among the Siddiqui Sheikhs of Allahabad, Uttar Pradesh[1]

Imtiaz Ahmad

One of the characteristic features of the caste system has been said to be the regulation of marriage. Each caste is characterized by the obligation of endogamy to marry within the group. No doubt, there are numerous exceptions to the rule of endogamy as is clearly demonstrated by the Nambudri Brahmins and Nayar castes in Malabar, by the Kulin Brahmins in Bengal, and by the Patidar caste in Gujarat; but castes are, by and large, associated with rules which require endogamy. Wherever infringement of the rule of endogamy is allowed, as seems to

[1]This paper is largely based on personal interviews with thirty-five informants of the Sheikh Siddiqui caste. Four of them were over seventy years old, nine were between fifty-five and seventy years old, and the remaining were still in their middle age but were reputed to be keenly interested in the affairs of their caste and possessed a great deal of information about their caste history. Genealogical charts for four ascending generations were reconstructed with the help of these informants and the information supplied by them were subsequently cross-checked with others. I also gained access to an old genealogical chart maintained by one of the informants and the data reported here were also cross-checked against it. Given the somewhat limited nature of this study, the analysis presented here is largely tentative and requires to be corroborated and substantiated by more detailed and intensive fieldwork.

be the case in the instances just cited, the approved degrees of marriage outside the caste are usually hypergamous. Marriages outside the caste are allowed when such marriages involve those of girls of one caste marrying into a caste or sub caste of relatively higher status. The marriage of girls into castes inferior to their own are neither approved nor tolerated. Such marriages may take place today within the framework of the Civil Marriages Act and probably took place earlier in some areas such as the Punjab where marriages between Khatris and Aroras were common, but they were not accepted by the vast majority of the Hindus throughout the country. There are, in fact, indications that earlier it was somewhat difficult to secure the services of a Brahmin priest to perform a marriage between a boy of an inferior caste and a girl of a superior caste. It was only under Arya Samaj rites that such marriages came to be solemnized as a normal Hindu practice.

Endogamy and hypergamy within the context of the caste system serve essentially as mechanisms for the maintenance of the boundary of a caste or social group. However, they can also serve as mechanisms for social mobility for an upwardly mobile group. In this essay, I shall describe how a Muslim social group successfully used endogamy to build up its distinctive group identity as well as to transform it suitably and subsequently employed both endogamy and hypergamy to raise its social standing within the hierarchy of Muslim groups. The group is the Sheikh Siddiquis of Allahabad district. It is today divided into two 'marriage circles' one of which is strictly endogamous while the other has followed a pattern of selective hypergamy. I shall show that social mobility centering around the recognition of their status as Sheikh Siddiquis has been the primary concern of members of both these marriage circles but their approach to the problem has diverged. One group has sought to secure recognition of the claim to Sheikh Siddiqui status through a persistent and somewhat strict adherence to endogamy. On the other hand, the members of the other marriage circle[2] have tried to achieve the same goal

[2]Dumont used the word 'marriage circle' as an equivalent for the vernacular term *beradari*. I find this translation somewhat erroneous and unsatisfactory. The vernacular word *beradari* implies that the members of

through a systematic and selective use of hypergamous marriage alliances.

Endogamy among the Muslims

Even though endogamy has been frequently reported to be a characteristic of Muslim social groups, there seems to be some difference of opinion about the level at which the principle of endogamous marriage alliance operates among them. Dumont, for example, has asserted that 'among the Ashraf there is no (absolute) endogamous grouping in the sense in which we have given the term . . . , the Ashraf are contaminated by caste spirit although they have not succumbed to it' (Dumont, 1970:207). He then distinguishes the so-called Ashraf groupings from the non-Ashraf and concludes, 'These groups indeed seem to be endogamous in the Hindu sense of the term, and quite a large number of Hindu customs which they have preserved have been mentioned, some to do with marriage' (Dumont, 1970:208). A similar distinction has been made by some other authors as well (see, for instance, Ansari, 1960; Zarina Ahmad, 1962; Misra, 1964; and Vreede-de-Steurs, 1969).

Dumont's conclusion that 'among the Ashraf there is no (absolute) endogamous grouping' while the non-Ashraf groups are 'endogamous in the Hindu sense of the term' is based on three obvious misconceptions. Firstly, he assumes that the Ashraf and Ajlaf are empirically valid sociological categories and certain clear-cut features distinguish them at local levels. The Ashraf-Ajlaf dichotomy evolved out of the initial attempts of the Census Commissioners to arrange Muslim castes into a hierarchy and its use has been continued in theoretical discussions of the subject (see, for instance, Ansari, 1960; Zarina Ahmad, 1962; Misra, 1964; and Vreede-de-Steurs, 1969), but the empircial

the group share a common feeling of brotherhood and are thus united through that feeling. The Sheikh Siddiquis regard themselves as members of a single *beradari* to the extent that they can be treated as a *beradari* in the absence of that institutionalized expression of the feeling of brotherhood called panchayat. Caste brotherhood would appear to be a more appropriate translation of the word *beradari*. I use the word 'marriage circle' to denote a unit of endogamy within a caste.

relevance of these categories remains open to question. Elsewhere (Ahmad, 1966) I have questioned the utility of the Ashraf-Ajlaf dichotomy for an understanding of the system of social stratification among the Muslims. I showed that this dichotomy was comparable to the *varna* scheme among the Hindus, but its relevance for understanding the local or regional rank of castes was considerably limited. At the local level, I argued, the social groups were ranked on the basis of mutual interactions with common obligatory behaviour demanded from their members. This interactional hierarchy did not always correspond to the theoretical rank order based on the position of a caste in the Ashraf and Ajlaf categories.

The point I am trying to make can be illustrated by reference to an actual empirical situation. In Rasulpur, a village where I initially conducted an enquiry on the nature of caste stratification among the Muslims, there were altogether ten different Muslim caste groups. Two of them were groups who would generally be placed in the Ashraf category on the basis of their names and would be considered superior to all others. Yet, the terms 'Ashraf' and 'Ajlaf' did not form part of the vocabulary of the people. It was mentioned only once by a member of the Sayyad caste. Subsequent enquiries showed that the members of other castes, including the Sheikhs, were not even aware of the distinction. Moreover, the rank of each caste, with the possible exception of the Sayyads whose descent was said to raise them above all else, was based on their position within the local economic and political structure. The Sheikhs, who would rank below the Sayyads according to the logic underlying the Ashraf-Ajlaf dichotomy, occupied a position equal to the Rajput Muslims, a group whose Hindu antecedents are still widely known. Nevertheless, the position of the Sheikhs in an adjoining group of villages, collectively referred to as the Sheikhana (the circle of the Sheikhs), was vastly different from that of the Sheikhs in Rasulpur. In short, then, the dichotomy between the Ashraf and the Ajlaf is a palpably false one and it does not seem to have always had a direct referent in local social hierarchies.

Secondly, Dumont's insistence that the pattern of endogamy among the non-Ashraf Muslim groups alone compares with the pattern of endogamy among the Hindus arises from a basic inability to see the distinctions that obtain among the higher Hindu castes and the so-called Hindu occupational castes on this aspect. Dumont's point that there is a basic Hindu sense of the term endogamy would be well taken if it could be shown that the patterns of endogamy among the traditionally superior Hindu castes, often identified as *dwijas*, is similar to the pattern of endogamy among what are traditionally characterized as occupational castes and are identified either as low-level Sudras or untouchables. But this is not borne out by empirical observation. Even casual observations seem to suggest that the so-called occupational castes among Hindus are more rigidly endogamous than the superior castes. Wherever the hypergamous marriage pattern prevails, it usually involves castes of relatively superior standing. Even the cases of hypergamous castes cited by Dumont (1970:207) involve only those castes which are either well above the line of pollution or are clearly recognized as belonging to the category of *dwija* castes. For example, Dumont points out that hypergamy prevails among the Nambudri Brahmins and Nayars in Malabar, the Kulin Brahmins in Bengal and the Patidars in Gujarat. Yet, such hypergamous unions are not found among the lower castes in these regions, and they continue to remain endogamous in contradistinction to the model provided by the locally superior castes.

The persistence of a rigidly endogamous pattern among the occupational castes in an area even where the superior castes marry hypergamously is not a matter of mere coincidence. It seems to be related to the internal structure of the occupational castes, to their conditions of living and the function hypergamy is supposed to perform as a pattern for the formation of marriage alliances. For one thing, it can be seen that in the case of the occupational groups there are many external factors which enforce a somewhat more rigid pattern of endogamy. Principal among them are the specialization of occupation, the presence of caste panchayats and internal government contributing to a greater cohesion within the castes.[3] Moreover, even if theoretically

[3]The relevance of these factors would be readily obvious if one were to imagine how a potter's daughter, for example, would feel if she happened to find herself hypergamously married in the Smith, Barber, or Weaver castes. Her entire socialization would make her a stranger in those castes and create difficulties in her adjustment to their way of life. Since the entire

permitted according to orthodox Hindu customs and sanctions, hypergamy is never resorted to by a group as a matter of normal practice. Hypergamous marriages occur when a group is seeking to raise its social status and uses its hypergamous unions as a means of legitimizing its claims to superiority.[4] Given the close link between hypergamy and social mobility, one would naturally find that the tendency toward hypergamy would be stronger and more widespread among groups which are already close to the top of the hierarchy than among those who are still in the middle or too far down the hierarchy to be able to stake a sufficiently strong claim to superiority.

Lastly, Dumont's assertion that among the Ashraf there is no absolute endogamous grouping seems to be based on a confusion about what actually constitutes the real unit of endogamy. The Ashraf as a general category is composed of four major groups called the Sayyads, Sheikhs, Pathans and Mughals, and there is a widespread belief that these four groups are the Muslim prototypes of castes. Ghaus Ansari, thus, characterizes these four groups as castes and attempts to discuss their relative positions in a hierarchy. But a closer scrutiny of empirical evidence suggests that the Sayyads, Sheikhs, Pathans and Mughals are not castes at all; rather, they are categories somewhat similar to the Hindu categories like Brahmin and Kshatriya. Just as Brahmins and Kshatriyas actually represent categories rather than castes, so are the Sayyads, Sheikhs, etc., categories which include a large number of people who identify themselves as members of different groups. To take only one example, the Sheikhs are divided into a series of smaller groups which share a common name, trace their descent from a common ancestor and, while they all characterize themselves as Sheikhs, scrupulously distinguish themselves from other groups of the same order. These

range of the customs, practices, and conditions of life of these castes are conducive to endogamy, social mobility within castes characterized by strong internal caste panchayats is fostered more frequently by the adoption of external symbols of status rather than by hypergamy. The efforts towards social mobility of these castes is, for the same reason, somewhat arrested and less frequently productive of positive results.

[4]This point is repeatedly confirmed in the literature on the Hindu caste system. See, apart from Dumont (1970) who indicates this possibility at several places, Pocock (1957), Srinivas (1952) and Beteille (1965).

groups are secondary divisions while the division of the Ashraf category into Sayyads, Sheikhs, Pathans and Mughals is a primary status division.

The secondary divisions are not castes either, or at least they cannot be characterized as such. On the contrary, they are sub-categories. For instance, the Sheikhs are often divided into three or four major sub-categories. One would find that members of the same sub-category claiming the name of that sub-category may be found to live in different cultural regions or occasionally in different areas within the same cultural region. This does not, however, mean that they either interact as members of one caste-like grouping or are regarded as such. On the contrary, members of the same named sub-category are often divided further into segments on the basis of marital links and geographical identification. Firstly, the members of a particular segment are identified, or identify themselves, with a particular region. In the rural areas, this identification is expressed by naming the geographical area identified with a particular segment after the name of that segment. Thus, the set of villages which are identified with the sub-category of Kidwai Sheikhs is known as Kidwara. No doubt, Kdwai Sheikhs may also live in other regions but they are treated as members of a different group.

The second basis which separates the segments is marriage links. All the members of a segment are endogamous, showing a greater emphasis or preference for marriage within the segment. The marriage of segment members with members of other segments which may bear the same generic name, such as Sheikh Siddiqui or Ansari, are not approved. In effect, then, the segment is not merely a local unit but is also endogamous. Thus, it is the real unit of endogamy and should be considered as the Muslim equivalent of Hindu endogamous castes. Generally, however, the sub-category or the primary category (e.g., Sayyad, Mughal and Pathan) has been regarded as the real unit of endogamy. The real units can be identified only on the basis of local enquiry, and there have been few empirical studies of Muslim social groups. Small wonder, then, that it should appear that there is no endogamous grouping among the so-called Ashraf Muslims.

Once it is recognized that the real unit of endogamy is not the primary or the secondary category, but a further segment of the latter defined by marriage and geographical location, it would also become clear that the character of endogamous grouping among the Muslims is not particularly different from that which prevails among the Hindus. The Hindus are broadly divided into four *varnas*: Brahmin, Kshatriya, Vaishya, and Sudra. The Kshatriya category is again divided into two sub-categories called the Suryavanshi Kshatriyas and the Chandravanshi Kshatriyas. Each one of these sub-categories lives in several areas, but it does not mean that all the Chandravanshi and Suryavanshi Kshatriyas necessarily constitute single homogeneous castes. On the contrary, the Suryavanshi Kshatriyas living in any one particular geographical area consider themselves a separate group and confine their marriages within it. Like the segments referred to among the Sheikhs, this geographical unit would appear to be the real endogamous grouping rather than the category Kshatriya or the sub-categories Suryavanshi and Chandravanshi.

It is clear, then, that the distinction which Dumont and others draw between the Muslims belonging to the Ashraf category on the one hand and the non-Ashraf groupings on the other is not borne out by empirical evidence. On closer scrutiny, it is evident that a more meaningful distinction can be drawn between the higher Hindu castes and the so-called Ashraf Muslim groups on the one hand and the lower Hindu castes and non-Ashraf Muslim social groups on the other. While the latter are strictly and rigidly endogamous, the former are generally endogamous but do occasionally combine endogamy with hypergamy. Or, to put the matter somewhat differently, whenever hypergamous marital alliances occur either as part of a long-standing tradition of hypergamy or as a step in a group's search for a new status identity, such groups normally occupy a superior status within their community. Hypergamous marriages either do not occur at all among lower groups no matter whether they are Hindu or Muslim or, if they occur at all, they are generally stigmatized. This is not to rule out the possibility of the occurrence of hypergamous unions among the lower castes. Human nature being what it is, hypergamous marriages can, and do, occur among lower castes or between members of lower and higher castes just as hypogamous alliances can and do sometimes occur. Occasionally, a Smith may decide to elope with a Potter or Pasi woman and may subsequently take her as his wife. Or, a Rajput or Kayastha may take a Potter wife. But both these types of marriages, while they may be sanctioned by Hindu law, are stigmatized. In the first case, both the Smith and his Potter bride may be excluded from their respective castes. In the second case, the Rajput would be subjected to perpetual social stigma and disapproval. In short, the point that I am trying to make is simple: whereas hypergamous marriages are generally sanctioned, the degree and extent to which hypergamy can be practised by a group is determined by factors closely related to the objectives hypergamous marriages can serve and the ultimately favourable effects those marriages are capable of having for that group.

The Sheikh Category

Before analyzing the structure of marriage circles among the Sheikh Siddiquis and the role of hypergamy in their search for a new status identity as Sheikh Siddiquis, it would perhaps be useful to discuss briefly the Sheikh category as a whole and closely examine its internal social organization. Such a discussion will serve to isolate the social referents of the group under discussion and its general structural position within the social hierarchy of Muslim social groups. It should also serve to clarify what specific group we really have in mind when we speak of the Sheikh Siddiquis and the extent to which it can be treated as a caste grouping.

Literally, the word 'Sheikh' means chief or leader and is used in its Arabic form as an honorific title for the head of a tribe, lineage or family. However, in India the term has come to enjoy a somewhat specific meaning and connotes a status group. It is used throughout the subcontinent to refer to persons who claim to have descended either from the Arab tribe of Koraish, the tribe to which Prophet Muhammad belonged, or from one of the close associates or friends of Muhammad. In India, such persons are generally supposed to be of noble birth and, along with the Sayyads, Pathans and Mughals, are distinguished from the converts of indigenous origin. Like the Sayyads, Pathans and Mughals, the Sheikhs also occupy a fairly high social position within the idealized scheme of social hierarchy among the Muslims. Along with the Sayyads, who claim to have descended directly from the Prophet Muhammad through his daughter Fatima and Ali, and the descendants of the Afghans and Mughals, the Sheikhs are considered to constitute a category of social groups somewhat analogous to the *dwija* castes among the Hindus (Gait, 1911:342-82) and these four groups are collectively referred to as the Ashraf (Ansari, 1960:34; Zarina Ahmad, 1962; Zillur Khan, 1968:138; Dumont, 1970:208; Misra, 1964: 309).

The Sheikhs are widely dispersed throughout the whole subcontinent with a somewhat heavier concentration in the Indo-Gangetic plains. Schwartzberg (1968:208) found them predominating over the entire area 'extending southward from the Nepalese border all along the border of East Pakistan (now Bangladesh) to the Bay of Bengal' (1968:207-8). This area is, according to him,

> marked throughout by an usually high percentage of the population in but a single caste, the Sheikhs, who comprised almost the whole of the resident Muslim population. Prior to partition this group would have comprised close to 50 per cent of the total population of the area depicted, but an overflow of modest proportion to East Pakistan and an inflow of Hindus in much larger numbers have considerably reduced their relative strength. . . . Were the Sheikhs Hindu, rather than Muslim, their dominant position, regionally, would be assured, since no other group even approaches them in numerical strength. But as members of a communal minority the Sheikhs presumably find their strength vitiated, since there is always the risk that in situations of conflict the otherwise factious Hindu community would unite against them. Yet, within their own hamlets, villages or clusters thereof, where they tend to constitute a very large proportion of the total population, it is probable that they exercise authority much as they did before Indian independence. Villages or hamlets tend to be, on the whole, clearly Muslim dominated or clearly Hindu dominated, Muslim villages having far fewer castes in general than those dominated by Hindus. The non-Muslim groups who are most commonly found in large numbers in Sheikh villages

> are depressed Hindu castes or tribal or semi-tribal people, who are, for the most part, petty cultivators, fishermen, and agricultural labourers (Schwartzberg, 1968:108).

Schwartzberg refers to the Sheikh as a single caste and this tendency has been quite common in the literature on Muslim castes (see, for instance, Ansari, 1960; Zarina Ahmad, 1962; Misra, 1964; Vreede-de-Steurs, 1969; Dumont, 1970; Guha, 1965; and Khan, 1968), but this usuage is quite erroneous. The Sheikhs do not constitute a single homogeneous caste at all, but represent instead a congeries of a large number of separate subgroups each of whom shares certain characteristics of a caste. For example, the Sheikhs are divided into a number of subgroups based on descent and source of origin and their members not only identify themselves as members of separate groups but also try to preserve and highlight their separate group identity through a careful use of surnames. Ghaus Ansari (1960:38-41) has noted that the members of each separate subgroup within the general Sheikh category suffix a particular title or name, such as Qureshi, Ansari, Kidwai, Usmani, etc., which serves to indicate the source from which they trace their descent and distinguish them from members of other groups within the Sheikh category. Of course, this does not mean that these distinctions are necessarily reckoned or recognized by outsiders. Generally speaking, the members of two or more subgroups rarely live in the same locality, except in urban centres, and the distinctions are not directly relevant. Wherever members of more than one Sheikh subgroup live within the same locality, the different groups maintain their distinct identity, but outsiders see them all as a single group—that is, as Sheikhs. This is to be expected, especially since the internal divisions within any social category are likely to be irrelevant to outsiders (see Mayer, 1960:1-9).

The different Sheikh subgroups are distinguished on the basis of a number of criteria. At least four principles can be easily identified: (a) they are based on affiliation with an Arab tribe; (b) they are based on descent from a person of definite and distinctively Arab origin whose close ties with the Prophet Muhammad are known; (c) they are based on names of places in Arabia or Persia; and (d) they are based on someone who is said to have been of foreign origin and who is supposed to have come with the invading Muslim armies in the early phases of the expansion of Islam into India. The essential point about these subgroups is that they are always regarded as foreign and their members emphasize their foreign origin either by tracing their roots to one of the historic personages or tribes of early Islamic Arabia, or by identifying themselves with a place which lies in Arabia or Persia, or by claiming descent from a person who supposedly came from the heartland of Islamic civilization into India.[5]

Each of the subgroups within the Sheikh category is hierarchically arranged, ranking being based on descent and the source of derivation of the group. The criterion of ranking is the same that applies in determining the relative standing of the different categories within the Ashraf stratum. Thus, the degree of distance from the Prophet serves to define the relative standing of the subgroups. Highest in the hierarchy of Sheikh subgroups are the Qureshis who trace their descent from the tribe of Koraish to which, as indicated earlier, the Prophet Muhammad himself belonged. Next in order of precedence are the descendants of the three Caliphs, Abu Bakr Siddique, Usman and Umar.[6] There is a hierarchy, however, even within the descendants of the first three Caliphs. The highest in rank order are the descendants of the first Caliph, Abu Bakr Siddique,

[5]This tendency has often tended to create an extra-territorial orientation to the members of these groups and suggested that the loyalties of the Muslims lie outside the subcontinent. This last point is somewhat controversial and cannot be discussed here at length but it seems that there is an obvious error of interpretation of the meaning of the supposed linkage to foreign sources and its effects upon the extra-territorial orientations of the Muslims. As a matter of fact, those who consider this as evidence of an extra-territorial orientation of the community and compare it with the identity principles among the Hindus commit an obvious error in comparing a social group, the cultural heartland of whose civilization lies outside India with another whose civilizational heartland lies within the subcontinent. A more appropriate comparison would be between Muslim groups in India and Indians in East-Africa or Fiji. Evidence available so far shows that a tendency toward extra-territorial identification exists among Hindu groups removed from the heartland of Hindu civilization (see Singer, 1967:93-116).

[6]The fourth Caliph, Ali, was the son-in-law of the Prophet and his descendants are regarded as Sayyads rather than as Sheikhs.

who was also a close and trusted friend of Muhammad, followed by the descendants of the other two succeeding Caliphs. Following the descendants of the Caliphs are the descendants of close associates or friends of Muhammad, especially those who accompanied him to Medina. Lastly, below these groups are the descendants of those who are supposed to have been of Arab or Persian origin and supposedly came with the invading Muslim armies. However, the hierarchy of the subgroups of the Sheikhs is largely theoretical and idealized. It has already been indicated that the members of the different Sheikh groups do not live in the same locality. There is, consequently, no interaction among them that could serve to indicate their relative standing. Secondly, each group is largely endogamous. Under the circumstances, disagreement among the Sheikh subgroups about their relative standing is quite common, especially among groups which claim descent from persons of supposedly foreign origin who came with the invading armies.

Even the Sheikh subgroups described above are not castes, though popular usage treats them as such. Communities bearing the same sub-category name are often dispersed in several districts, but this does not mean that they are all members of the same caste. On the contrary, they distinguish themselves from one another both verbally and through endogamy. Occasionally, the distinction is also expressed by clearly marking off the villages where the members of the group sharing a notion of common group identity are living in a separate area. Thus, the area adjoining Rasulpur has a population of Siddiqui Sheikhs who are distributed in thirteen villages over a radius of approximately thirty miles. These Sheikh Siddiquis marry among themselves and consider themselves as members of the same group. Sheikh Siddiquis also live in other villages and in Rudauli town about seventeen miles away, but the Sheikh Siddiquis of the circle of fourteen villages, collectively called Sheikhana, neither recognize these other Sheikh Siddiquis as members of their caste nor inter-marry among them. Thus, from the point of view of the Sheikh Siddiquis themselves, the Sheikh Siddiquis of the area called Sheikhana and the Sheikh Siddiquis of other areas regard themselves as members of different castes.

The Sheikh category is based on ethnic differentiation and

it is assumed that the different social groups claiming Sheikh descent represent a slow and gradual emigration of persons from Arabia. But the number of Sheikhs in the country as a whole raises serious doubts about the fact that all the Sheikhs are actually of foreign origin. For instance, the total number of persons claiming that they belonged to the Sheikh caste was well over 1,300,000 in 1931 and this represented an increase of over 150 per cent over those who made this claim in 1901. If it is remembered that there were no immigrations during the period 1901-31 from Arabia, it would be obvious that this remarkable increase could not have been possible except by the slow and gradual induction of members of other castes into the Sheikh category. The available evidence seems to suggest that the Sheikh category always remained somewhat open and fluid. Mobile groups seeking a new status identity frequently used the Sheikh category as a means of raising their status. Generally speaking, the Sheikh claim was somewhat easier to sustain than a claim, let us say, to Sayyad status on account of the ease with which Sheikh status could be claimed. In staking a claim to superior status, the mobile group was expected to show genealogical links with a historic personage from Arabia. Such links could always be shown with relative ease to anyone of the immigrants rather than to the descendants of the Prophet Muhammad. Gait rightly noted that the Sheikh category is comparable to the Kshatriya category among the Hindus and groups have frequently used it to stake a claim to superior status in the social hierarchy of Muslim castes (1911:308).

The fact that the Sheikh category has always remained open and fluid has led some scholars to make a distinction between genuine Sheikhs and spurious Sheikhs (see, for instance, Misra, 1964:312). But this distinction would be highly ambiguous and arbitrary. A group would be characterized as a spurious Sheikh group only so long as its claim to Sheikh status was questioned by others. But given the fact that a group could eventually get recognition of its claim in the course of a generation or two, the distinction would be difficult to sustain. At any given time, the claim of some groups to Sheikh status would be accepted and recognized while the claims of some other groups would be questioned. Then, at a later point in time, some of the groups whose claim to Sheikh status was not recognized earlier would be accepted as genuine Sheikhs while new groups with claims to Sheikh status would have emerged. Under the circumstances, attempting to divide the Sheikhs into genuine and spurious would be a never-ending task. In fact, the Sheikh Siddiquis are themselves a case in point of the fluidity of the Sheikh claim and the ambiguity of the distinction between genuine and spurious Sheikhs.

The Sheikh Siddiquis

The Sheikh Siddiquis of Allahabad district today claim to be the descendants of Abu Bakr Siddique and this claim is recognized by others. But this recognition has come only within the last quarter of a century. In fact, the Sheikh Siddiquis are converts from the Kayastha caste from among the Hindus. Over the generations, the group has succeeded in completely obliterating its Hindu ancestry and has created a new social identity for itself as the descendants of Abu Bakr Siddique. This process has been aided by certain historical developments which came in the wake of British rule; urbanization and the gradual movement of the members of the caste from their original location in Allahabad district to urban centres in Uttar Pradesh and Pakistan; the economic and occupational differentiation within the caste; and the ability of a section of the caste to contract marriages into social groups of supposedly Sheikh status. Nevertheless, systematic and sufficiently persistent enquiries within the area of their original residence do still yield information that shows that these Sheikhs were originally Kayasthas and their Sheikh status is a matter of recent acquisition.

The Sheikh Siddiquis originally lived in the Chail tehsil of Allahabad district. It is said that they were distributed in over thirty villages at the time of their conversion to Islam and the entire area comprising those thirty villages is still collectively referred to as Kaethana, probably a corruption of the word Kayasthana, meaning the home of the Kayasthas. Legendary accounts preserved by the local Bhats and occasionally confirmed by the settlement records suggest that the Kayasthas were land record-keepers before their conversion to Islam. The precise circumstances of the conversion of the Sheikh Siddiquis to Islam are not known. It is, however, known that when they converted to Islam they were allowed to retain their traditional occupation as land record-keepers, a fact which is also attested to by the fact that the members of the caste often served as *patwaris* well after the annexation of the area by the British. Today, the occupation is no longer a monopoly of the Sheikh Siddiquis partly because it is no longer considered very attractive and partly because the educated members of the caste have moved to urban centres and taken up employment in Government offices. This movement is said to have commenced with the establishment of the provincial capital at Allahabad. It opened up new employment opportunities and the Sheikh Siddiquis cashed in upon those new opportunities because, apart from the financial advantages, they aided their search for a new status identity.

Today the Sheikh Siddiquis are not associated with any single occupation, traditional or modern. On the contrary, they are distributed among a variety of different occupations: some are still agriculturists, some are employed as lower grade civil servants in administration, some work as teachers, accountants, and salesmen, etc. It is, however, noticeable that the Sheikh Siddiquis have a definite preference for lower administrative jobs. For example, a survey of the families who could be contacted showed that 67 per cent of the Sheikh Siddiquis in the present generation on whom data were available work as clerks in government offices while the remaining are distributed in other lower jobs. Until the creation of Pakistan, the Sheikh Siddiquis did not, with a few notable exceptions, occupy senior administrative jobs. However, since the creation of Pakistan several members of the caste have migrated to that country and have succeeded in securing senior administrative positions by virtue of their educational qualifications. Such occupational mobility was made possible particularly by the dearth of educated and experienced personnel in the initial stages after the creation of Pakistan.

The conversion of the Sheikh Siddiquis to Islam was a group process. The whole of the Kayastha caste was converted rather than individuals. The conversion of the whole group made the transition from Hinduism to Islam and the accompanying positional changes somewhat easier for the caste members.

Some marginal adjustments were required, especially with the other Hindu castes with whom the Sheikh Siddiquis must have interacted closely, but these adjustments could be made without any great difficulty as the corporateness of the group remained intact. Moreover, since the area was already inhabited by certain other Muslim groups, especially those who enjoyed land grants under previous rulers, whatever the group lost by way of social intercourse among the Hindus was eventually gained among the Muslims.

Convert groups to Islam are generally characterized as New Muslims and they are looked down upon by the social groups which are known to be of foreign origin or who have succeeded in eliminating the stigma of recent conversion. This gave rise to certain differentiations in the adjustment of the Sheikh Siddiquis, after their conversion to Islam, in the different villages. In villages which were largely or predominantly Hindu, the Sheikh Siddiquis were excluded from the framework of interaction with the Hindu castes but they continued to enjoy a somewhat superior status as a Muslim group. But in villages where there were numerous other Muslim groups of superior status, the Sheikh Siddiquis were not merely excluded from the social hierarchy of Hindu castes, but were also relegated to a somewhat lower position even within the hierarchy of Muslim castes.

The conversion of the Sheikh Siddiquis from the Kayastha caste actually made relatively little obvious difference to the caste and it continued to retain its traditional customs and practices much as before. The two specific customs which were considered as betraying the Hindu origin of the caste were said to be *pankti* and *charava. Pankti* literally means a row and refers to the row in which people in the village sit down to eat at communal feasts. There were few occasions in the rural areas when members of all the castes could interdine, but whenever such occasions arose the Sheikh Siddiquis sat down to eat in a separate row. Nowadays, the Sheikh Shiddiquis do not object to sitting with other castes of relatively equal or superior status but it is said that until about seventy years ago they formed a separate row at intercaste dinners. Ceremonial community feasts often invoke sarcastic comments about the tendency of the Sheikh Siddiquis to sit separately at intercaste dinners and they are often ridiculed for their earlier snobbishness. Somewhat to the amusement of other participants, the members of other social groups comment that the Sheikh Siddiquis sat in a separate row as if the other castes were inferior to them. In any case, the implication of these comments is that the Sheikh Siddiquis were so high browed as to regard even castes superior to them as lowly and that this was a pretence.

The second custom which was said to betray the Hindu ancestry of the Sheikh Siddiquis was the custom of *charava*, especially the particular form that it assumed among them. *Charava* literally means an offering but in the context of the Kayasthas it refers to the offerings of sugar, dry fruits, and other similar items sent to a bride's house at the time of marriage. Among the Hindus of the area, the principal items of the *charava* were two: dry fruits and clothes for the bride. The dry fruits were packed in colourfully decorated earthen pitchers while the clothes were tied in a particular type of thread (*kalava*) considered auspicious. Again, turmeric paste was liberally applied to all the pitchers as it was supposed to bring good luck. On the contrary, among the Muslims the *charava* was not sent in earthen pitchers but rather in large brass trays (*tasht*) covered with embroidered scarfs. The Sheikh Siddiquis followed the Hindu custom of sending these offerings to the bride at the time of a marriage. This was considered by other castes as evidence of their neo-Muslim status.

To begin with, the Sheikh Siddiquis do seem to have accepted their status as neo-converts and the social position which went with that status. However, a change in their attitude occurred around the close of the nineteenth century. This change was precipitated by two simultaneous and somewhat closely related developments; the spread of education and the enlargement of the opportunity structure brought about by the establishment of the provincial capital at Allahabad. The Sheikh Siddiquis were land record-keepers and were consequently already heirs to a somewhat limited literary tradition. When Western education was introduced in the region, the Sheikh Siddiquis took advantage of the new education, though the members of the caste did not necessarily go in for higher education. For instance, until 1940, the caste could count only four Bachelors of Art and one Master of Art among their numbers. The majority of the members of the caste studied only up to high school or below. But education up to middle and high school was sufficient in those days to secure Government employment as clerks and the aspirations of the group were probably limited to the lower grades of the civil service at that time. It is only during the present century that the group has undergone a somewhat extended diversification of occupations, and sons and daughters of the caste have gone into senior administrative positions and the professions.

New Status Identity

The Sheikh Siddiquis who received Western education and moved into urban based occupations at the beginning of this century eventually grew dissatisfied with the stigma of Hindu ancestry that continued to be attached to their caste and their status as neo-Muslims. They wanted to shake off their Hindu ancestry and wanted to be recognized as Sheikhs. There were, however, two major difficulties in the way. Firstly, their Kayastha antecedents were quite well known in the area and many of their caste customs and practices betrayed their Hindu antecedents. Secondly, their caste was entirely endogamous and they could not cite any instances of marriage alliances with families of accepted Sheikh status, or even with those who might previously have been Hindu converts but had succeeded over the generations in establishing a Sheikh identity for themselves. In order to overcome the first difficulty, it was necessary that the caste should discard some of its more obvious Hindu customs and practices and adopt those customs which were characteristic of proper Sheikh groups. Equally, in order to support and reinforce the claim to Sheikh status, it was essential that caste members should selectively enter into marriage alliances with groups of known Sheikh origin so that it could be shown that the group was actually Sheikh and its members had formed marriage alliances with Sheikh groups whose high birth was recognized.

The first of the difficulties that the Sheikh Siddiquis faced in their search for a new status identity was comparatively easily resolved. Self-conscious members of the caste who had received Western education and had consequently succeeded in raising their economic and political status by working for the Government, started a movement for the abandonment of Hindu caste customs and practices and advocated the adoption of Islamic customs and practices associated with the Sheikh style of life. This movement was specifically directed towards giving up the twin practices of *pankti* and *charava* to which reference has been made earlier. The practice of sitting in a separate row consisting exclusively of Sheikh Siddiquis at intercaste dinners was abandoned and the members of the group began to sit with other castes of comparable social status. Since the decision to sit in a separate row had been taken by the Sheikh Siddiquis themselves and had not been imposed upon them by other castes as a status differentiating mechanism, the attempts to sit in a common row with castes of comparable status aroused some comments but no apparent opposition. Secondly, the practice of sending offerings of clothes and dry fruits to the bride's house on the occasion of marriage was also modified; instead of earthen pitchers previously used for the purpose the caste adopted the use of large brass trays as is customary among the Muslims of recognized Sheikh standing in the region and elsewhere. Simultaneously, certain other changes in dress and religious rituals were undertaken and a more rigid and orthodox observance of religious prescriptions and rituals was adopted.

In the literature on the social organization of Muslim groups in Indo-Muslim society, these changes are commonly referred to as Islamization (see, for instance, Misra, 1964:213 and Vreede-de-Steurs, 1969:5).[7] The term Islamization lacks a

[7]Cora Vreeda-de-Steurs has, however, drawn a distinction between what she calls Ashrafization and Islamization. She uses the word 'Ashrafization' to denote attempts at social climbing by groups or individuals through hypergamy and the adoption of the way of life of higher classes, and reserves the term Islamization for the process whereby groups and individuals wishing to distinguish themselves from non-Muslims rid themselves of the so-called un-Islamic customs and practices (Steurs, 1969:5-6). Islamization actually has two sides to it: one may be called its structural implications and involved attempts at social climbing by groups and individuals through the adoption of customs and practices of the upper class Muslims. This process has structural implications because it results in positional changes for the members of the mobile group. On the other

clear-cut definition though it has been used extensively while describing efforts at social mobility of Muslim social or caste groups. It is usually used to describe the tendency of a group to build up an identity as one of pure and noble Muslim descent by patterning its style of life on an Islamic model. But while the adoption of the customs and practices of the higher classes is undoubtedly a feature of Islamization it has been generally assumed that the elements which are adopted by a group as a part of that process are necessarily drawn from the Shariat. This is not always so. On the contrary, some of the elements adopted by mobile groups in the course of Islamization are not necessarily drawn from the Koran or the Hadiths, and often have no sanctions in the Shariat. They are adopted because the group thinks them to be essential to its self-definition as Muslims of high social standing. Islamization, thus, refers not merely to the adoption of social and cultural elements drawn directly from the Shariat, but rather to the process or processes of adoption and spread of those cultural or social elements which a particular Muslim group may have come to recognize as the basis of its self-definition as a Muslim group of high and noble standing in the course of its social history.

The subjective element in what constitutes Islamization for a particular group is quite important and an illustration from the Sheikh Siddiqui caste serves to highlight its significance. Prior to their Islamization, the Sheikh Siddiqui women usually wore *saris* as their normal dress. However, the *saris* were regarded by the Sheikh Siddiquis as a Hindu dress and it was gradually replaced by the tighter and more uncomfortable *churidar pyjamas*. The members of the caste thought that the *churidar pyjama* was a more typical Islamic dress suited to a caste that claimed to belong to the Sheikh status. There is nothing in the Koran which says that the *sari* constitutes any less an Islamic form of dress than the *churidar pyjama*, but the members of the caste felt that the *churidar pyjama* reinforced their image as Muslims

hand, the cultural aspect of Islamization involved the attempt of a group to distinguish itself from non-Muslim groups through gradually projecting an Islamic image. For an elaborate and detailed discussion between the structural and cultural aspects of Islamization and their implications for Islamizing groups, see my paper entitled 'Sanskritization, Islamization, and Indian Society' (Mineographed).

of high social position. It is clear, then, that the question whether a particular item adopted as part of Islamization is truly Islamic or not is decided not on the ground that it is sanctioned in the Shariat, but rather on the ground that the Islamizing group considers it as basic to its self-definition as a Muslim group of high social standing.

Side by side with the gradual Islamization of their caste customs and practices and the style of life generally, the Sheikh Siddiquis also pressed their claim to be recognized as Sheikhs. Its members, and particularly the more self-conscious ones amongst them, emphasized that they were descendants of the first Caliph, Abu Bakr Siddique, through a priest who had accompanied the Ghaznavid army and was known to have descended from the Caliph. In the course of time a suitable genealogy was fabricated which showed the Sheikh Siddiquis to be the descendants of Abu Bakr Siddique through this priest in the Ghaznavid army.

The Sheikh Siddiquis were a locally influential and well-off group and their attempts to claim Sheikh Siddiqui status do not appear to have given rise to any serious opposition from other castes. As a matter of fact, the other caste groups in the area remained indifferent to the Sheikh Siddiqui claim as it made very little difference to them what status claim the Sheikh Siddiquis preferred. Commensal relations between the Sheikh Siddiquis and other high Muslim castes of the area were reciprocal, and they were not affected by whether the Sheikh Siddiquis retained elements of their Hindu origin or discarded it. On the other hand, as far as marriages were concerned, each caste was endogamous in the area and there was no change in the pattern of marriage alliances caused by the Sheikh Siddiqui claim to the Sheikh status. Clearly, there would have been social protests if Sheikh Siddiquis had tried to break the endogamy of other castes, but this they were not in a position to do. Consequently, the Sheikh claim to be recognized as the descendants of Abu Bakr Siddique apparently aroused no serious opposition from the other high castes of the area.

Islamization certainly helped to elevate the prestige of the Sheikh Siddiquis within the hierarchy of local Muslim castes, but it failed to bring about the recognition of their status as Sheikhs. There *still* remained the fact that the Sheikh Siddiquis had not been successful in forming marriage alliances with recognizable Sheikh groups, and the other high Muslim castes of the area refused either to give their daughters or to accept girls from the Sheikh Siddiquis in marriage. Unless the Sheikh Siddiquis could demonstrate definite marriage links with groups of recognized Sheikh status either within their original area or outside, their claim to Sheikh status could be accepted tentatively but not necessarily taken as established. And this was especially so because the group was known to have descended from the Kayastha caste among the Hindus and its Hindu antecedents were a matter of common knowledge in the area.

Ideally, the Sheikh Siddiqui would have preferred to form suitable marriage alliances with groups of recognized Sheikh status and to cite that fact in support of their claim to be recognized as Sheikh Siddiquis. But this was difficult both because the Hindu ancestry of the group was commonly known in the area and because the groups of known Sheikh status were unwilling to give their daughters in marriage to, or to take girls from, the Sheikh Siddiquis. Consequently, the Sheikh Siddiquis had to try to make a virtue of the fact that they had failed to form marriage alliances with groups who were recognized to be Sheikhs. The Sheikh Siddiquis then claimed that their failure to form marital links with other groups of high status did not arise from their Kayastha ancestry and the reluctance of castes of high status to enter into marriage alliances with them. On the contrary, they asserted, this was so because they themselves refused to marry into other castes. Its members claimed that their group was characterized by a special ritual quality which was said to be inherent in the blood and bones of the caste members (*hargor*). This ritual purity of the blood and bone was supposed to be best preserved when marriages were confined within the group. Marriages with outsiders, whether hypergamous or hypogamous, were supposed to adversely affect this ritual quality of the caste. Thus, the Sheikh Siddiquis argued that their caste was endogamous not because the other high castes refused to marry with them but because they themselves did not marry into other castes as a mechanism for the preservation of their purity of the blood and bone.

The belief in the ritual purity of the blood and bone was symbolized through the caste genealogy (*shijra*). It has already been mentioned that, along with the rise of mobility aspirations, the caste members had fabricated a genealogy which traced the origin of the group to the descendants of Abu Bakr Siddique and showed that the ritual purity of the blood and bone had been preserved through a somewhat strict adherence to endogamy. The genealogy, thus, became a symbol through which the status of the caste as Sheikh Siddiquis was made public. It served as the objective evidence of the fact that the group not only possessed ritual purity but had successfully preserved that purity through carefully regulating its marriage alliances.

Endogamy and emphasis upon ritual purity of the blood and bone helped the group to project an exclusive image of itself, but the need for arranging hypergamous marriage alliances still remained quite imperative. In Indian Muslim society, such marriage alliances serve as a mechanism for the reaffirmation of the fact that a group really enjoys a high social status. The more aware members of the group continued their efforts in the direction of forming suitable hypergamous marriage alliances, and their efforts were finally rewarded a decade or so later.

At the turn of the present century, the capital of the province was shifted from Allahabad to Lucknow. Many of the Sheikh Siddiquis who had been in Government service in the secretariat had to move to the new capital at Lucknow. The spatial mobility generated by this shift produced two direct consequences for the social mobility efforts of the Sheikh Siddiquis. On the one hand, it removed them from the immediate social context and control of their kindred group and made it possible for them to follow an independent course in their search for a new status identity. On the other hand, it also removed them from the locality within which their antecedents were a matter of common knowledge and made it possible for them to claim their status as Sheikh Siddiquis with greater force. Since their kinship connexions were unknown in the new locality, they could choose not to state their old caste antecedents, and, by changing their caste name and displaying their newly acquired wealth and influence, pretend to be what they fancied and expect to get away with it.

One of the implications of both these consequences was that the members of the caste found themselves in a position to discard their previous identity as new Muslims altogether and seek validation of their new status identity through forming suitable marriage alliances into castes of accepted Sheikh status. Of course, whether or not they ultimately succeeded in forming such alliances depended upon their ability to find a suitable family willing to enter into a marriage alliance with them.

In theory no one is supposed to countenance inter-marriage with a 'stranger'. The presumption always is that such a man is of low status (Yalman, 1960:99). But by making a show of wealth and personal status one can often persuade a family of somewhat dubious social status to accept a stranger as a son-in-law. Some of the Sheikh Siddiquis thus succeeded in finding families of dubious Sheikh status willing enough to marry their daughters to them.[8] Consequently, the first set of hypergamous marriage alliances entered into by the Sheikh Siddiquis were not with members of recognized Sheikh status. On the contrary, it was with the daughters of an allegedly barber family which had gradually succeeded in building up a Sheikh identity through prosperity in trade and migration to Kanpur, an industrial urban centre. The Sheikh Siddiquis pretended that their new relatives were of the same high social standing as themselves even though they might have known that this was not so. Subsequently, however, the Sheikh Siddiquis succeeded

[8]The first set of marriages of Sheikh Siddiqui men outside the caste were second marriages and their previous spouses had belonged to the caste. Three explanations can account for this pattern. Firstly, it may be due to the fact their first marriages had been arranged while they were still rather young and had little say in the selection of their spouses, but when they married a second time they felt freer to follow their own volition in the matter of spouse selection. Secondly, it is quite possible that when they married a second time, usually after the death or divorce of their previous wives, they were living in urban centres away from their close relations and did not feel constrained by the social control of their caste. Lastly, it is quite likely that the Sheikh Siddiquis distinguish, like the Hindu caste groups, between primary and secondary marriages (for an elaboration of this distinction, see Dumont, 1970:53-54), and the less prestigious secondary marriages were allowed to be arranged outside the caste while their primary marriages had been arranged within the caste. Unfortunately, this point was not investigated and cannot be confirmed here. It should be noted, however, that Sheikh Siddiqui men succeeded in each case in marrying women who had not married previously and their marriages had the effect of splitting the caste into two separate and exclusive marriage circles.

in forming marriage alliances with members of other families, some of whom were of recognized Sheikh descent.

A distinct pattern is visible in the marriage alliances entered into by the Sheikh Siddiquis with outside castes. At first the Sheikh Siddiqui marriage alliances with outsiders involved only Siddiqui men; the daughters of the caste were married endogamously. It was only later that they started marrying their daughters to outsiders. This step was taken because of the differential significance of the marriage of boys and girls and the strategy of the group in their efforts at social mobility. Like the Hindus, Muslim social groups in India differentiate between the marriage of a daughter and a son of the caste, and the two carry different implications for the status of the group. Giving a girl in marriage is considered a sign of lower status and the group giving its girls in marriage is regarded as lower to the group which receives them. Conversely, the act of acquiring a girl in marriage tends to place the caste in a position of social superiority to the group to which the girl belongs. The decision of the Sheikh Siddiquis to take girls from outside groups, while they married their own girls endogamously, was dictated by the possible implications that marrying their girls with outsiders might have.

If the Sheikh Siddiquis married their girls into the same families from whom they acquired brides, it would have implied that they were either equal or inferior to them in social standing. And this would have hardly helped in raising their own social status or fulfilling their aspiration to be recognized as genuine Sheikhs. What would actually have helped their chances to be recognized as Sheikh Siddiquis was if they could demonstrate their superiority over the groups from whom they took girls in marriage. On the other hand, their claims to Sheikh status were likely to be strengthened if they took brides from other Sheikh groups and married their own daughters within the caste. In that case they could assert that they were a group of such high social standing and birth that, while they acquired girls from other Sheikh groups, they did not find them sufficiently high to give their daughters in marriage. One obvious implication of their refusal to marry their daughters into outside groups would have been that those outside castes would be made to appear inferior to them. Of course, once their claim to social superiority became established in this way, they could begin to marry their daughters into Sheikh groups, suggesting this time that they married their daughters only into families of undisputed and impeccable social standing.[9]

In recent years the Sheikh Siddiquis have begun to marry their daughters into outside groups. It is, however, noticeable that the daughters of the caste flow in a different direction from the one from which brides are obtained. The Sheikh Siddiquis do not marry their daughters into the same families from which they acquire their brides. On the contrary, they acquire brides for their sons from one set of families and marry their daughters into another. In this way, the caste shows its social superiority to some castes and claims social equality with others. However, in those cases where the families from whom the Sheikh Siddiquis acquire brides have succeeded in securing a girl from the families to whom they give their daughters, the Sheikh Siddiquis have been quick to point out that the latter are not necessarily superior to them. In this way they have often been able to show themselves superior even to those families from whom they accept grooms and where the presumption is that those castes are superior to them in social standing.

Since the act of giving a girl of the caste in marriage has wider implications for a group and its search for a new status identity, it also presents somewhat greater constraints and implications for the mobile group. In the normal course of events one would expect that the father of a girl would ideally prefer to marry his daughter within the caste to a man of relatively equal status and wealth so that his own social status is not impaired and his daughter can enjoy the physical comforts that she may be used to in her own home. But such a marriage is likely to

[9]This seems to be a standard strategy of mobile groups in their search for a new status identity. I found much the same pattern among the Mainpuri Chauhan Muslims, a convert Rajput caste, in Rasulpur village. The Mainpuri Chauhans have been trying to claim the status of Khanzadas. Several Chauhan boys have been married into other castes of Pathan status, but there was not a single instance of the marriage of a Chauhan girl in any of the other Pathan castes. It is only in recent years that the Mainpuri Chauhans have begun to marry their daughters into some selected Pathan families of impeccable status. The Chauhan practice of not giving their daughters in marriage to the groups from whom they take girls in marriage has the effect of placing those groups in a somewhat inferior position to them.

produce no advantages for the mobile group in its search for upward social mobility. In order to be able to use the marriage of a daughter to his advantage, the father would find it imperative to marry her to a man of impeccable status. But if such a man, especially if he is himself well off, is likely to find a girl of comparable wealth and status within the caste, or, even if he decides to marry outside, he is more likely to find a wife for himself from a family of poorer economic background but of high social standing. Consequently, a father whose own social standing is not impeccable is likely to find it difficult to arrange the marriage of his daughter to a man of equal wealth and higher social standing than himself. But if he is willing to marry his daughter to a man of high status but poor economic background he has a fair chance of success. Given the high value of social status among them, the Sheikh Siddiquis have married their daughters up the social hierarchy into castes of superior social standing after a considerable economic sacrifice on the part of the girls' parents. Invariably, they have married their daughters to boys who enjoyed high social standing but were of poorer economic background.

Each Sheikh Siddiqui family, it has been mentioned, maintains a genealogy (*shijra*) which traces the genealogy of the family and its past and present marital ties. The social and personal status of the families from which brides have been acquired and to which girls of the caste have been given in marriage are carefully recorded in the genealogy. The genealogy is used whenever marriages are arranged outside the caste. Since, until three generations ago, marriages among the Sheikh Siddiquis were arranged among known kinsmen, there was no need to maintain a genealogy as the groups' marital links were known to both families entering into a marriage alliance. But today these genealogies are frequently consulted, especially when marriages with outsiders are contemplated. As soon as the negotiations are started, the inter-marrying families exchange their respective genealogies. Occasionally, detailed investigations are initiated for the verification of the genealogy. It has been noted, however, that the Sheikh Siddiquis are somewhat wary of such investigations. They either avoid marrying into families or groups which are likely to investigate their genealogy or summarily break off negotiations whenever they learn that an investigation of their genealogy is under way. More generally, they prefer to marry into families where a pretence of investigation is made and negotiations are completed without either party trying seriously to find out the historical antecedents of the families. This naturally suggests that the Sheikh Siddiquis still feel somewhat shaky about their claim to Sheikh status and wish to avoid situations wherein their Kayastha antecedents may be discovered, thereby nullifying their past efforts towards the acquisition of a new status identity for themselves.

Marriage Circles

The first marriage alliance of the Sheikh Siddiquis outside the caste was formed three generations ago. Even though the alliance was hypergamous and was formed with the specific and explicit purpose of aiding the efforts of the caste for social mobility and for reinforcing its claim to be recognized as Sheikh Siddiquis, it nevertheless had the effect of splitting the caste into two separate marriage circles. One of them consists of the descendants of those families whose members married endogamously and continue to do so even today. For the sake of convenience, we shall refer to it as the endogamous marriage circle. The members of this marriage circle distinguish themselves from the members of the other marriage circle on the ground that the latter have married outside the caste and they do not marry with them. They believe that the ritual quality of the blood and bone is adversely affected if a member of the caste marries outside it, and they claim that the members of the other marriage circle have lost the ritual purity of the blood and bone by marrying outside the caste even if their marriage alliances were hypergamous. The endogamous marriage circle comprises the larger section of the caste and includes the majority of the caste members.

The other marriage circle is exogamous and consists of the descendants of those families which had formed the first marriage alliances outside the caste. Its members either marry endogamously amongst themselves or outside into castes of supposedly recognized Sheikh status. There have been no instances of marriages between the members of the endogamous and exogamous marriage circles since the split between them first occurred. It forms a small segment of the caste and consists mainly of the members of four lineages only. Its members also believe in the notion of the ritual purity of the blood and bone, but they argue that their ancestors had not compromized the purity of their blood by marrying outside their caste as they had married only into families of recognized Sheikh status. According to them, the ritual quality of their blood would have been compromized if they had married into castes which were of Pathan or Mughal status. Since all the marriage alliances that they formed were with families of recognized Sheikh status, the question of compromizing the ritual purity of their blood does not arise at all according to them.

A careful examination of the data on marriage for three generations since the split within the caste occurred shows some interesting differences in the marriage patterns of the two marriage circles. Even though the endogamous marriage circle has a definite tendency towards endogamy, its marriage pattern is much more diversified. For example, out of 170 marriages in three generations for which data are available, the majority were between persons who belonged to the caste but were quite unrelated to one another prior to their marriage. Moreover, wherever marriages between relatives took place, such marriages were between persons who were distantly related. There were very few cases of marriages between close kinsmen. The actual frequency of cousin marriages is particularly low and accounts for barely 14 per cent of the marriages that have taken place in the three generations since the split first occurred within the caste. The frequencies of the degree of relationship between spouses in the three generations in the endogamous marriage circle are presented in Table 1.

The situation of the exogamous marriage circle is quite different. Even though the marriage circle has been called exogamous because its members have married hypergamously outside the caste group, actually it displays a tendency towards close family endogamy and cousin marriages. Table 2 presents the frequencies of the degree of relationship between spouses in the last three generations. It will be seen from this table that the actual frequency of marriage alliances outside the marriage circle is not as high as it might appear from its name.

TABLE 1
Frequencies of Degree of Relationship Between Spouses in Three Generations in the Endogamous Marriage Circle
(Figures in Parenthesis show Percentages)

Degree of Relationship	*Present Generation*	*First Ascending Generation*	*Second Ascending Generation*	*Total*
FaBrDa	3 (5.5)	2 (3.4)	4 (7.0)	9 (5.3)
FaSiDa	1 (1.9)	3 (5.1)	1 (1.8)	5 (2.9)
MoBrDa	6 (11.2)	7 (11.9)	5 (8.7)	18 (10.6)
MoSiDa	3 (5.5)	4 (6.8)	2 (3.5)	9 (5.3)
Other Relatives	17 (31.5)	20 (33.9)	22 (38.6)	59 (34 7)
Unrelated	24 (44.4)	23 (38.9)	23 (40.4)	70 (41.2)
Total	54 (100)	59 (100)	57 (100)	170 (100)

Out of 89 marriages for which data are available, only 22.9 per cent are with outsiders. The overwhelming majority of the marriages are between persons who are related; 19 per cent are between paternal cousins, 28 per cent are between maternal cousins, and the remaining 20 per cent are between distant relatives within the marriage circle. In short, though the marriage circle is exogamous in the sense that its members do sometimes marry into other castes, the actual incidence of close cousin marriages is actually higher than in the endogamous marriage circle.

The incidence of close family endogamy and close cousin marriages, especially of the father's brother's daughter type, has usually been assumed to be associated with the desire to maintain property within the family in the face of Koranic rules of inheritance (see Granquist, 1931:78; Zarina Ahmad, 1960:48).[10] If this explanation is to be valid for the Sheikh

[10]Fredrik Barth offered an explanation of this type of preferential marriage among the Kurds in terms of lineage solidarity. He argued that a pattern of father's brother's daughter marriage solidified the minimal lineage in factional struggles and served to reinforce the political

TABLE 2
Frequencies of Degree of Relationship Between Spouses in Three Generations in the Exogamous Marriage Circle

(Figures in Parenthesis show Percentages)

Degree of Relationship	*Present Generation*	*First Ascending Generation*	*Second Ascending Generation*	*Total*
FaBrDa	2 (5.9)	4 (14.8)	4 (14.3)	10 (11.2)
FaSiDa	1 (2.9)	3 (11.1)	3 (10.7)	7 (7.8)
MoBrDa	3 (8.8)	2 (7.5)	2 (7.1)	7 (7.8)
MoSiDa	8 (23.5)	6 (22.2)	4 (14.3)	18 (20.1)
Other Relatives	7 (20.6)	6 (22.2)	5 (17.9)	18 (20.1)
Unrelated	4 (11.8)	1 (3.7)	4 (14.3)	9 (10.1)
Outside Castes	9 (26.5)	5 (18.5)	6 (21.4)	20 (22.9)
Total	34 (100)	27 (100)	28 (100)	89 (100)

Siddiquis, and possibly for other Indian Muslim groups as well, it is necessary that the Koranic rules of inheritance regarding the division of family property should be followed. But there is no evidence that the Koranic rules of inheritance have been followed among the Sheikh Siddiquis. On the contrary, the Sheikh Siddiquis follow the customary law which is quite similar to the traditional Hindu practice regarding inheritance. According to traditional and customary laws, the daughter is not eligible to a share of father's property upon the latter's death. If she is unmarried at the time of her father's death, she is entitled to receive dowry at the time of her marriage. If she is widowed or divorced and reverts back to the family, she is entitled to maintenance from her brothers. But beyond these

implications of the lineage system (Barth, 1954:171). This explanation is again unsatisfactory when applied to the Sheikh Siddiquis, because they are not organized according to the lineage principle characteristic of the Kurd tribes.

privileges, she is not entitled to any other share in her father's property. It is obvious, then, that the high incidence of close family endogamy and cousin marriage among the Sheikh Siddiquis, and possibly other Muslim groups as well, requires a separate explanation.

The explanation would seem to lie partly in the demographic consequences of the division of the caste into two mutually exclusive marriage circles. When the entire Sheikh Siddiqui caste constituted a single unit of endogamy, the demographic situation allowed the dispersal of marital links throughout the caste. Firstly, on account of the large size of the group, the number of marriageable boys and girls available at any time from within the caste tended to be fairly high, and there was consequently no compulsion to confine marriages to close kins. Secondly, since the caste possessed a certain degree of corporateness, the status of each family within the caste was supposed to be equal and marriages with persons not previously related did not carry any serious implication for a family in terms of the ritual purity of blood and bone. The fragmentation of the caste altered this situation. The endogamous marriage circle, which comprised the larger segment of the caste and continued to possess a corporate character much as before, allowed the dispersal of marriages characteristic of the caste before the split. But the exogamous marriage circle was greatly circumscribed and its members could not follow a pattern of dispersed marriages. Though they could marry into other castes, such marriages were subject to the limitation that they had to be arranged with families or groups of supposedly established Sheikh status and these could not be contracted on any large scale. Consequently, compelled by their failure to find enough families or groups willing enough to give their daughters or accept Sheikh Siddiqui girls, the members of the exogamous marriage circle were forced to follow a pattern of close family endogamy whenever they could not succeed in arranging marriages outside the circle.[11]

[11]Observations in a predominantly Muslim village of Bara Banki district of Uttar Pradesh confirm the significance of demographic factors in the incidence of close family endogamy. It was found there that close family endogamy prevailed only among the castes which were limited in size and whose members were confined to a few villages. It was parti-

The tendency towards close family endogamy in the exogamous marriage circle would seem to arise partly from the search of its members for a Sheikh status identity and their desire to raise their social status through intermarriage with families of established Sheikh descent. Since the inception of mobility aspirations amongst them, the members of the circle had tried to arrange marriages with Sheikhs of impeccable descent, or at least supposedly established Sheikh descent, and to cite that fact in support of their claim to be Sheikhs. Such marriages were contracted wherever possible. Given the difficulty of being able to contract such marriages with outsiders always, the pattern of close family endogamy was used to further buttress their claim of ritual purity of blood and bone and to enhance their chances of contracting marriages into families of Sheikh descent. They were able to assert, somewhat more forcefully than would have been possible otherwise, that they were of such pure descent that they confined their marriages to a close family circle as a rule and married with outsiders only when they were sure of the latter's genealogical antecedents. Such assertions naturally carried greater conviction as their genealogy showed a definite pattern towards close family endogamy.

Conclusion

This paper has been concerned with a discussion of the Sheikh Siddiquis of Allahabad district in eastern Uttar Pradesh. The Sheikh Siddiquis were originally Kayasthas and were converted to Islam *en masse.* Within the span of this century, the Sheikh Siddiquis have succeeded in building up a new status identity for themselves as descendants of the first Caliph, Abu Bakr Siddique, and their Hindu antecedents, though a matter of common knowledge at one time, have been gradually obliterated over the years.

cularly found to prevail among the Mainpuri Chauhans, a caste of Rajput converts. The Chauhans are restricted to a single village. Castes characterized by the presence of a caste panchayat covering a number of villages in the region did not practise close family endogamy. Such endogamy was, in fact, taboo among some of the artisan and menial castes such as weavers, oil-pressers and barbers.

This social transformation was made possible by two closely related social processes: abandonment of traditional customs and rituals which betrayed their Hindu ancestry, and establishment of marital links with families of supposedly recognized Sheikh origin and descent. The first set of marital links with outsiders of assumed Sheikh origin were established three generations ago and had the effect of splitting the caste into two mutually exclusive marriage circles distinguished by the attitudes of their members to marriage outside the caste. One of them is called the endogamous marriage circle. Its members confined marriages within the circle and looked down upon marriages outside the caste as they assumed that such marriages were likely to impair the ritual purity of the blood and bone of the caste. The other is called the exogamous marriage circle. Its members followed a pattern of close family endogamy, but married outside into families of impeccable descent wherever such marriages were possible. There was no intermarriage between the members of the two marriage circles.

Recently, the attitudes of the Sheikh Siddiquis belonging to both the marriage circles have been undergoing a change. They allege that there is a great dearth of eligible Muslim boys nowadays as Muslim youngmen frequently migrate to Pakistan in search of employment and the few Muslim boys who prefer to stay on in India are easily 'roped in' by families of better economic and social status. Consequently, they no longer place much emphasis upon ritual purity of blood and bone or on descent and are willing to marry their daughters to eligible boys of comparable rank. For the same reason, however, the marriages of eligible Sheikh Siddiqui boys can now be arranged into families of recognized Sheikh descent and are often used to raise their social standing and to reinforce their claim to Sheikh status.

Bibliography

Ahmad, Imtiaz (1966), 'The Ashraf-Ajlaf Dichotomy in Muslim Social Structure in India', *Indian Economic and Social History Review*, 3, pp. 268-78.

Ahmad, Zarina (1960), *Muslim Caste in Uttar Pradesh*, Unpublished M.A. Dissertation, University of London.

———(1962), 'Muslim Caste in Uttar Pradesh', *Economic Weekly*, 14, pp. 325-36.

Ansari, Ghaus (1960), *Muslim Caste in Uttar Pradesh: A Study in Culture Contact*, Lucknow, Ethnographic and Folk Culture Society.

Barth, Fredrik (1954), 'Father's Brother's Daughter Marriage in Kurdistan', *Southwestern Journal of Anthropology*, 10, pp. 164-71.

Beteille, Andre (1965), *Caste, Class and Power: Changing Patterns of Social Stratification in a Tanjore Village*, Berkeley and Los Angeles, University of California Press.

Dumont, Louis (1970), *Homo Hierarchicus: The Caste System and its Implications*, Delhi, Vikas Publishing House.

Gait, E.A. (1911), *Report of the Census of India*, 1911, Delhi, Superintendent, Government Printing.

Granquist, H. (1931), *Marriage Condition in a Palestinian Village*, Helsinki, Societas Scientiarum Fennica, Commentationes Humanarum Litterarum III. 8.

Guha, Uma (1965), 'Caste among Rural Bengali Muslims,' *Man in India*, 45, pp. 167-69.

Khan, Zillur (1968), 'Caste and Muslim Peasantries of India and Pakistan' *Man in India*, 47, pp. 138-48.

Mayer, Adrian C. (1960), *Caste and Kinship in Central India: A Village and its Region*, London, Routledge and Kegan Paul.

Misra, S.C. (1964), *Muslim Communities in Gujarat*, Bombay, Asia Publishing House.

Pocock, D.F. (1957), 'Inclusion and Exclusion: A Process in the Caste System of Gujarat', *Southwestern Journal of Anthropology*, 13, pp 19-31.

Schwartzberg, Joseph E. (1968), 'Caste Regions of the North Indian Plains', in Milton Singer and B.S. Cohn (eds.), *Structure and Change in Indian Society*, Chicago, Aldine Publishing Company.

Singer, Philip (1967), 'Caste and Identity in Guyana', in Barton M. Schwartz (ed.), *Caste in Indian Overseas Communities*, San Francisco, Chandler Publishing Company.

Srinivas, M.N. (1952), *Religion and Society among the Coorgs of South India*, Oxford, Oxford University Press.

Vreede-de-Steurs, Cora (1969), *Parda: A Study of North Indian Muslim Women*, New York, Humanities Press.

Yalman, Nur (1960), 'The Flexibility of Caste Principles in a Kandyan Community', in E.R. Leach (ed.), *Aspects of Caste in South India, Ceylon and North-West Pakistan*, Cambridge, Cambridge University Press.

9

Status and Power in a Muslim Dominated Village of Uttar Pradesh

Zarina Bhatty

The concept of dominant caste has been quite familiar to students of Indian sociology for well over a decade. Since Professor Srinivas' first exposition of it (see Srinivas, 1959), the concept has been used extensively in the study of the relationship between secular power and ritual rank (see, for instance, Bailey, 1957; Mayer, 1958; and Beteille, 1965), the structure of authority at the village level, and Sanskritization (see Srinivas, 1966; Dube, 1968; and Beals, 1960). However, a great deal of the discussion on the concept has been based on the study of predominantly or exclusively Hindu villages. There has been no study of the role and significance of the dominant caste in pre-dominantly Muslim villages. This essay deals with the dominant caste in a Muslim dominated village, focussing upon the link between status and power in a changing socio-economic framework characterized by the abolition of zamindari and the introduction of changes which followed in its wake.

Kasauli,[1] the locale of our study, is a village in an old

[1]Kasauli is a pseudonym. Fieldwork was carried out in Kasauli during 1962 and 1964. It was financed by a Junior Research Fellowship of the University Grants Commission. Grateful thanks are due to the Commission for the Fellowship which made this study possible. I am also grateful to the people of Kasauli for their hospitality during my stay in the field and for answering my queries.

zamindari settlement in the erstwhile Oudh region of Uttar Pradesh. It lies 25 miles east of Lucknow and 8 miles from the town of Bara Banki. The population of Kasauli is split between Muslims and Hindus, with the former having a slight majority (51 per cent). Political and economic power rests almost entirely in the hands of the Muslims for historical reasons rather than as a consequence of the slender majority of Muslims in the population. For this reason I justify myself in calling Kasauli a Muslim village.

Kasauli represents a typical example of the persistence of the traditional caste system despite the numerous quantitative and qualitative changes through which the village has been passing, specially since 1947. I shall argue in these pages that the caste structure of the village rests squarely on its power structure and that structural changes in the traditional caste system can be expected only if the traditional power structure is effectively challenged. I shall further argue that the power structure derives its potency mainly from the economic viability and superiority of the dominant group. I shall demonstrate my arguments through the story of Kasauli where a Muslim lineage of Kidwais constitutes the dominant group.

Before 1950

As the relative distribution of land ownership between different caste groups has played a principal formative role in the power structure of Kasauli, it would be useful to briefly outline the historical background of the region.

Muslims came to this region, formerly known as Oudh, mainly through conquest. Subsequently, they added to their numbers by converting Hindus to Islam. It appears from what little historical evidence is available that the Muslim conquest of Bara Banki was effected earlier and perhaps more thoroughly than other parts of Oudh. As far back as 1030 A.D., a General named Syed Mahmood of Ghazna established his headquarters in a village called Satrikh in Bara Banki district. Later, in 1191, another General, under orders from Mohammed Ghori, thə then ruler of Delhi, conquered the last Hindu kingdom of Kanauj. From then on, through seven centuries, numerous shifts and changes occurred which are of no consequence to us here. In 1720, Emperor Mohammad Shah awarded the Governorship of Oudh to a nobleman called Muhammad Amin. Later, interpreting correctly the signs of decay in the Delhi Empire, he became independent of the Crown and established his own dynasty in Oudh. His dynasty ruled through ten successive rulers or Nawabs, who progressively fell prey to the same forces of decay which were undermining the seat of power at Delhi. Wajid Ali Shah, the last of the Nawabs, was a very incompetent libertine and under his misrule the State of Oudh deteriorated to such an extent that the British, now the dominant power in India, decided to annex it with the North Eastern Province of Agra and named the region as the United Provinces of Agra and Oudh. Subsequently, the province was simply known as United Provinces and the name of Oudh was dropped for all practical purposes. After independence, the abbreviated title of the province, U.P., was retained but it now stood for Uttar Pradesh.

At the time of their annexation of Oudh the British Government in India made revenue settlements with the existing landowners, a large number of whom were Muslims. Except for some tentative moves towards change, the British finally opted for a policy of *status quo* for reasons of expenditure rather than progress. This meant retention of the land ownership structure and acceptance of the landed gentry as the dominant economic group. Administratively, the settlement was a simple one. It called upon the landowner or zamindar to pay a fixed amount, incorporated in the settlement, as revenue to the government. In lieu of this, he acquired the right to deal with his tenants in whatever manner he pleased. By this uncomplicated arrangement, power was effectively transferred to the zamindar so far as the rural countryside was concerned. This power was variously exercised by the zamindars but always to their advantage with less or more oppression. The Government's authority in the villages was only marginal, if at all.

Most zamindars did not cultivate their lands directly and many of them became what came to be called absentee landlords. They let their lands to tenants either on rent or on an agreed basis of sharing the crop. The zamindar could evict the tenant at will and increase the rent as and when it pleased him.

The economic and political power of the zamindar was thus firmly established in the village. As the economic and political power structure had evolved from within the caste structure of a Hindu society, the Muslim zamindars also assumed ritual supremacy, claiming higher caste status than their tenants. Muslim tenants as well as other occupational groups were mostly converts from Hinduism and had retained their caste status in the village hierarchy which conformed to the Hindu caste society. Although contrary to Muslim ideals of social equality, a society of rigid social stratification akin to the Hindu caste system functioned effectively wherever relations between various groups were well-defined and regulated on the basis of occupations, the nature of occupations determining to a large extent the hierarchical position of each caste with the dominant caste at the apex of the whole structure.

In fact, the structure of Muslim society in India did not at any time exhibit the Islamic ideal of social equality. An elaborate system of social stratification had been in practice from the very beginning of Muslim rule in India. Greater honour and respect was paid to the foreign ruling classes than to those of Indian extraction. People invented foreign ancestry for themselves in order to improve their social status (see Ashraf, 1959; Nizami, 1961; and Yasin, 1958) Historians confirm the importance of foreign ancestry during the period of Mughal rule. It provided the basis for greater honour and respect and the highest claim to social status (Yasin, 1958).

The sense of superiority derived from foreign ancestry is an important criterion of social stratification among Muslims in India (see Ansari, 1960; Dumont, 1970). The entire Muslim society is divided into two major sections, the Ashrafs and the non-Ashrafs. The Ashraf castes are: the Sayyads, the Sheikhs, the Mughals and the Pathans. All four castes claim higher status than non-Ashraf castes by virtue of their foreign descent. The non-Ashraf castes are all alleged to be converts from Hinduism. Among the Ashraf castes too there is a division for the purposes of marriage alliance. The first two, that is, the Sayyads and the Sheikhs, intermarry and the Mughals and Pathans also intermarry, but marriages between Sayyads or Sheikhs and Pathans or Mughals are not accepted socially. However, there is commensality between all four Ashraf castes. There is no commensality between any of the four Ashraf castes and the non-Ashraf castes, while among the non-Ashraf castes rules of commensality and marriage are governed by norms of the cleanliness or uncleanliness of different occupations.

In Kasauli there is one lineage of Sayyads, but the Sheikhs, through the subcaste of Kidwais, dominate numerically. There are no Mughals and Pathans. There are eighteen non-Ashraf castes excluding the Sipahi caste which is placed on the lower fringe of the Ashraf and the upper fringe of the non-Ashraf castes. The Sipahis claim to have been soldiers in the Muslim armies, and do not have any specified occupation. Some of them cultivate land but resent being called cultivators, others serve the dominant caste as domestic servants.

The eighteen non-Ashraf castes follow specific occupations and relate to each other in an hierarchical pattern. This, in order of precedence, is as follows: Julahas (weavers), Mirasis (singers), Darzis (tailors), Halwais (sweetmeat makers), Manihars (bangle sellers), Nais (barbers), Bakar Kasabs (butchers dealing in mutton only), Kasabs (butchers dealing in mutton and beef, and also in hides and skins), Behnas (cotton carders), Behen-Kasabs (a mixed caste, with butchers and cotton carders), Telis (oil pressers), Kabariyas (vegetable sellers), Gujars (dairymen), Kasgars (potters), Dhobis (washermen), Faqirs (landless labourers who also watch graveyards and beg for food), Nats (acrobats) and Banjaras (gypsies).

At the top of the hierarchy is the dominant caste. It has a unilinear relationship with all the castes in the village in the sense that it enjoys a uniformly superior status in relation to all other castes. The non-Ashraf castes are both superior to some and inferior to others, thus incorporating a duality in their hierarchical status. Each non-Ashraf caste being bound to an occupation, its status is largely determined by the nature of its occupation. At a broad level, two criteria seem to apply in grading the nature of the occupation. First, and perhaps more important, is a certain socially accepted notion of purity or impurity, cleanliness or uncleanliness, in terms of which the contents of an occupation, including materials handled, can be measured. Second is the proximity, in a physical sense, of the occupation to the Ashraf castes. Nats, who skin dead animals and make drums, find a place close to the bottom of the scale while

Julahas and Darzis are at the top. Dhobis, who must wash soiled clothes, are closer to the Nats than to the Julahas. Mirasis, on the other hand, have a rank next only to the Julahas mainly because of their proximity to the Ashrafs. They are singers and their women dance to provide entertainment. This precise function is also performed by the Nats, and their women also dance to entertain, but while the Mirasis sing and dance only for the Ashrafs, the Nats do it for the public at large. The distinction makes the Nats cheap and the Mirasis exclusive. Thus the Mirasis speak Urdu instead of the local dialect, and often literate, can say their prayers, and their women wear *ghararas* (long, flared skirts) as the Ashraf women do. Any broad treatment of the subject of caste hierarchy, however, leaves much unsaid. It is not the purpose here to examine the caste structure exhaustively, but merely to outline it and to stress that except at such a broad level any uniformity in the criteria for caste gradation for Indian Muslims, or even for Muslims in a region, is not easily discernible.

The dominant lineage of Kidwais claim Sayyad ancestry but are known in the region to be Sheikhs. They explain that, because the title of Sayyad was the highest, it was often assumed by non-Sayyads trying to upgrade their caste status, and since it had become difficult to distinguish the spurious from the genuine, they had decided not to call themselves Sayyads and let it be known that they were Sheikhs. The Kidwais claim to have descended from Kazi Kidwa, a son of the Sultan of Rum (Turkey). Kazi Kidwa, after falling out with his brother, migrated to India with his wife and son. He became a disciple of Khwaja Moinuddin Chishti of Ajmer, a renowned saint of the time. Within a short time he gained the Saint's favour and was given the title of Saint-brother. Khwaja Chishti sent him to Ayodhya to spread Islam, where he is alleged to have won over fifty villages to Islam. These fifty villages were later awarded to him and became known as Kidwara. Kasauli is one of these fifty villages.

In Kasauli, there is a tomb in which, it is said, Kazi Kidwa's grandson was laid to rest. It is further said that this grandson had achieved great spiritual eminence and for that reason an *urs* (a commemorative fair for a holy man) is held every year at the site of the tomb. The *urs* acts as a constant reminder of the high and pure ancestry of the Kidwais and every year reaffirms the superiority of their caste. Besides the dominant lineage of Kidwais there are four other lineages of Kidwais in the village, but they are not the descendants of the grandson of Kazi Kidwa whose tomb is located in Kasauli. This provides the basis for the dominant lineage to claim superiority over the other Kidwai lineages.

Prior to the Zamindari Abolition Bill, the Kidwais let out their land to both Hindus and Muslims in the village. The Hindu tenants were principally cultivators while the Muslim tenants used their small plots to supplement their income which was mainly derived from their specialized occupations. The occupational castes—Mirasis, Dhobis, Nais, Manihars, etc.—served all Kidwai lineages, but in particular the dominant lineage. The relationship between the occupational castes and the Kidwais was based on the *jajmani* system[2] and the dominant lineage of Kidwais was referred to as *sarkar*, which literally means government. In reality, too, the only effective government in the village was provided by the dominant lineage. In this single appellate *sarkar* one thus finds the confluence and the consolidation of economic power and political authority in the dominant lineage.

Not only in Kasauli but elsewhere too the dominant zamindar was the *sarkar*. His right to the ownership of land, virtual or real, was accepted both by the Government and the people and provided the foundation of his economic supremacy. The unwillingness or inability of the Government to extend its rule effectively into the village willy-nilly invested the zamindar's economic dominance with political power. While for the Government the zamindar was the only political link with the people, the bureaucracy was either held at bay as a matter of policy or, being manned mainly from the class of zamindars (the Indian complement), was unwilling to undermine the authority and power of the zamindar class.

The mechanics of exercising political power rested in the

[2]An essentially feudal system in which the lower castes rendered certain customary services to the zamindars and received certain customary benefits from them. To the rendering of caste services a ritualized expression is given at the time of ceremonial occasions in the zamindar's household.

system of settling disputes within the village community. In Kasauli every non-Ashraf caste had a panchayat of its own. Minor disputes among the members of the caste were settled by ti. Major disputes and those disputes over which the caste panchayat had failed to reach accord were referred to the *sarkar* for their decision. The nature of disputes which were thus treated varied over a wide range—from disputes over property to matters relating to divorce, personal quarrels or family vendettas. The effective sanction against non-compliance with the *sarkar's* decision was suspension of the *jajmani* rights,[3] eviction from tenancy and, in the last resort, expulsion from the village through forcible seizure of the house site.

Three sources of the political power enjoyed by the dominant lineage in Kasauli can now be identified: (i) Their vastly greater command over economic resources reinforced by an institutional framework in which the superiority of their bargaining power tended to be absolute; the latter for two reasons: (a) the endemic weakness of the poorer classes in a subsistence and stagnant economy and (b) the absence of any counter-vailing endogenous (of the nature of a trade union) or exogenous force (such as the Government) to offset the inherent advantage of the dominant lineage, (ii) The operation of the *jajmani* system which imposed on the lower castes the rendering of services to the dominant lineage obligatory. The rewards for these services, being customary, were delinked from the market and the gains from the transaction were overwhelmingly in favour of the *sarkar*. This derived from the fact that the utility of the customary benefits accruing to a member of the lower caste was very high since he lived at the subsistence level whereas the total utility sacrificed (in payments of benefits to the lower castes) by the *sarkar* was comparatively low. Thus, the lower castes were willing, individually and collectively (as an arithmetic sum and not by a joint decision), to make considerably greater sacrifices of utility (in terms of labour) to retain the benefits from the *sarkar* than the utility sacrificed by the *sarkar*. As the sacrifice of utility customarily made by the members of the lower castes individually was generally less than what he would be willing to

[3]Just as the zamindar had the right to expect customary services from the lower castes the latter had the right to certain benefits.

make, the *sarkar* enjoyed a surplus which was directly converted into power and authority over the lower castes. (iii) The system of settling disputes through the caste panchayats with the final judicial powers resting absolutely in the *sarkar* subjugated the lower castes to the will of the *sarkar*. While the elevation of the *sarkar* to this status was socially prescribed, it was in fact a natural concomitant of their economic power. This is clearly evident from the nature of sanctions against non-compliance with the decision of the *sarkar* in a dispute referred to them.

Two facts stand out clearly: (i) the sources of power were interlinked and their impact was cumulative; (ii) the base of the power structure rested on the vastly superior command of the *sarkar* over economic resources in the context of a subsistence economy on the one hand, and a policy of minimum intervention by the Government on the other.

After 1950

In 1950, the U.P. Land Reforms and Zamindari Abolition Bill came into effect. It was a good piece of legislation which aimed at drastically overhauling the landownership and tenancy system of the State. It was inspired by the notion that land should belong to the tiller and that the institution of absentee landlordism should be abolished. It is not necessary here to go into the various provisions of this Bill in detail. Broadly, it prescribed a ceiling to the ownership of agricultural land based on a somewhat rough notion of what a farmer could cultivate himself. Every landowner was to engage in cultivation himself but could let out some portions of his land to tenants. However, the tenant was protected and if he were to cultivate the same plot of land for more than two years he could claim the ownership of the plot and could have it by making payments according to a prescribed formula. The landowners could also acquire permanent and heritable rights over land, known as *bhumidari* rights, by paying prescribed amounts to the government.

The provisions of the Bill were severe but unfortunately they had become comman knowledge before the Bill came into force. Consequently, anticipating the Bill, the dominant Kidwai lineage in Kasauli was able to retain (as many others did) a substantial area of land under their control by a series of manipulations. The land was distributed within the joint family and each owner was shown as a cultivator. In practice, they continued to let out land on an arrangement which described the tenant as a hired servant. The latter accepted the arrangement on account of his inherent economic weakness and his inability or unwillingness to take advantage of the law. If a tenant was expected to cause difficulties, he was not allowed to cultivate the same plot for more than two years. This led to a well managed reshuffling of tenants every two years. Simultaneously, the dominant lineage began to cultivate relatively large farms directly with the help of hired labour drawn from among the landless labourers.

The minor Kidwai lineages were not equally fortunate. Lacking power, their manoeuvrability was limited and consequently they lost a good part of their land to the tenants who acquired legal rights over the land they were cultivating. Also, lacking the means they were not able to buy *bhumidari* rights. The economic condition of these lineages has therefore deteriorated.

The demand for the services of some of the occupational castes has declined even in respect of the dominant lineage of Kidwais. Over the past twenty years or so, the younger members of this lineage have gone for higher education and sought employment in the cities. The services that they might have required had they stayed in the village are not required except on occasions when they come to the village on vacation or to be present at a ceremonial occasion. The opportunities for making a living in their specialized occupations having dwindled (more for some and less for others), these non-Ashraf castes are turning to cultivation and seeking land from the dominant lineage for cultivation. In these circumstances, the Kidwais have appeared to them as friends in need and, therefore, worthy of even greater allegiance[4] than was traditionally given to them within the framework of the *jajmani*

[4]A distinction is made here between dependence and allegiance. The former is the result of economic and political realities; the latter is induced historically through accepted social values, attitudes and modes of behaviour. While the two are mutually inter-related from the point of view of the dependent group or class, they represent the negative and positive aspects of their relationship with the dominant class.

system. The Kidwais, on their part, have found the shift in circumstances entirely to their advantage as they are in need of tenants whose allegiance can be relied upon. Thus, though the services of the occupational castes are less needed, their dependence on the dominant lineage through their additional role as tenants has increased, strengthening the *jajmani* system instead of weakening it as one might have expected.

The question that one might legitimately ask at this stage is: why have the occupational castes not opted to move away from the dominance of the *sarkar*? Part of the answer is apparent from what has been said earlier, viz., that within the village alternative opportunities for earning a livelihood in occupations outside the ambit of the control of the *sarkar* were practically negligible. The other part lies in the unwillingness of the occupational castes to move out of the village in search of opportunities for work or their inability to find such work when sought. My enquiry suggests that they were hampered more by their unwillingness to move out than by their knowledge of lack of opportunities elsewhere or their experience of failure in finding opportunities farther afield. I explain their unwillingness to move on the ground that the village economic and political structure has not been disturbed to any appreciable extent, so that the traditional sense of security in one's own village has not been shaken. The common aspiration is to make good in the village itself. This aspiration has been encouraged by the willingness of the *sarkar* to let out land to occupational castes in addition to continuing the use of their specialized and occupational skills to the extent possible. In thus continuing to project their protective role, the *sarkar* have effectively inhibited mobility.

In fact, opportunities for work have grown in Kasauli in other ways also. The village was electrified as far back as 1957. It was already served by canal irrigation and now has tubewells as well. In the past twenty years, significant changes in the cropping pattern of the village have occurred. Essentially, the shift in crop preference has moved towards two cash crops: poppy seeds from which opium is extracted and sugarcane—both high value crops. In the kharif season paddy has replaced a good deal of millets. Very few of the pulses and oilseeds grown earlier are grown now. Along with a change in cropping pattern there has been a marked increase in crop intensity. The productivity of the land has consequently improved markedly and with it the incomes of farmers as well as agricultural labourers have increased, though not evenly between small and big farmers or between farmers and agricultural labourers. Higher incomes have induced greater demand for consumption goods which in turn have generated employment and incomes in other occupations. Two flour mills have been set up, one by a Bania and the other by a member of one of the minor lineages of Kidwais. A power-loom has also been established by the U.P. Kargha Cooperative Union. These industries have provided employment as well as some diversity to the village economic structure.

Kasauli, three miles from the nearest railway station, is now well connected by road. The principal goods that move out by road from Kasauli are poppy seeds, sugarcane and foodgrains. Sugarcane goes to the sugar mill situated 10 miles away. The establishment of the sugar mill and the construction of the road leading to it have clearly been responsible for the adoption of sugarcane as one of the principal crops grown in Kasauli. Other infra-structural developments have been a primary school with a *pukka* building, a hospital with beds for in-patients and facilities for minor operations, a post office and a grain storage in the office building of the Regional Cane Co-operative Union.

Expansion of trade has led to an increase in the number of shops as well as in the quantity and variety of goods handled by each shop. Trades, such as, the butcher's (Kasai), tailor's (Darzi), dairyman's (Gujar) and vegetable vendor's (Kabariya), have found sustenance from the growing purchasing power in the village. The market place, though modest in size, is today well lit by electric lights and presents a lively scene in the evenings with people moving about and shops doing good business.

For all this development, it is commonly believed in the village, the dominant lineage of Kidwais is responsible. This belief is well founded in good part. The dominant lineage of the Kidwais has led the way in adopting the new agricultural technology and has actively participated in propagating it amongst the other farmers. Mr. N., the elder member of the dominant lineage, is the Chairman of the District Cooperative

Bank and is known to help the residents of his village to obtain credit. He is also the General Secretary of the U.P. Sugarcane Association and was instrumental in having the sugarmill located within a short distance from the village and connecting the two with a metalled road. This sugar mill has been a boon to the village. It is said that he is also responsible for having the offices of the U.P. Sugarcane Association located in the village. This has not only added to the prestige of Mr. N. in the village but has made the village prominent in the sugarcane business. Mr. N.'s son who looks after the family farm is also a building contractor and has constructed several Community Development projects in Kasauli and other villages in the region. Many ignorant village folk give him the credit for these projects. Mr. N.'s elder brother was a member of the U.P. Legislative Assembly since its inception until the last election. One of his nieces is a member of the U.P. Legislative Council and is an aspirant for a seat in the Parliament.

Quite clearly, the dominant lineage of Kidwais from Kasauli lost no time in moving with the times. With independence in 1947, it was clear that the new Government intended to bring about radical changes in the village economic structure aimed at drastically curtailing the economic control and power of the zamindar. It was evident that these changes would greatly attenuate the economic dominance of the Kidwais, and their status as the principal political link with the Government would totally disappear and be replaced by new direct links with the Government and its agencies. In fact, it was quite on the cards that shorn of a good part of their economic resources by an act of the Government they would stand out as some sort of culprits on whom the wrath of the Government had fallen. The Kidwais, by design or accident, took effective steps to protect themselves in both respects. Anticipating the provisions of the Land Reforms and Zamindari Abolition Bill, they managed to retain a good part of the land in their possession thus avoiding any serious erosion of their command over economic resources. Simultaneously, they aligned themselves with the dominant political party and, using earlier and new associations, secured a nomination for a State Assembly seat. It was easy for them to win an election from the home constituency given their inherited prestige and prominence. Positions were then secured in organizations, such as, the Cooperative Bank and the U.P. Sugarcane Association, which were directly relevant to the economic life of the region. Thus, the link shattered by the abolition of zamindari was reforged and the political prestige and power of the dominant lineage of Kidwais successfully retained.

Having protected themselves, the dominant lineage wisely nurtured its power. It actively participated in bringing greater prosperity to the village. It effectively provided the needed political link with the Government from which the village benefited. Where previously the Government's arm never directly reached the village, today, through its efforts to develop and to regulate, it directly intrudes in the life of the village in many ways. The entry of the dominant lineage into active politics and into positions of consequence has greatly smoothed the new relationship between the people of Kasauli and the Government.

None of this, I wish to emphasize, would have been possible had the dominant lineage fallen a victim to the Land Reforms and Zamindari Abolition Bill as their minor lineages did. Shorn of their economic strength they would have lost their dominant position in the village power structure and without these assets would have hardly succeeded in injecting themselves successfully in State politics. The Bill, therefore, failed to disrupt them and, being led competently and intelligently, they learnt to create the conditions for their survival and progress in the new environment. The Kidwais today are as powerful in Kasauli, if not more than they ever were before the enactment of the Bill.

Let us now refer back to the nature of economic interdependence between the *sarkar* and the occupational castes. We had drawn attention to its two principal features, viz., (a) the *quid pro quo* of services rendered and payments or rewards made contained in the *jajmani* system was outside the ambit of the market; and (b) the transaction was heavily loaded in favour of the *sarkar* on account of the very wide gap in the income and wealth levels of the two parties and the subsistence and stagnant economy of the occupational castes. It was from the second feature that the *sarkar* derived their power. The question that we might ask now is: In what way were these features altered as a result of the changes we have described? Feature (a) went through a subtle transformation. The importance of services rendered to the *sarkar* reduced as the need for them declined, but simultaneously other developments engineered by the enterprise of the *sarkar* protected the incomes of the occupational castes. The demand for the goods or services of a number of the occupational castes rose as a result of an increase in the aggregate purchasing power of the village as a whole and as avenues for supplementing service incomes by cultivation and wage employment (particularly in the sugar industry) were created. As the emergence of the new opportunities were attributed directly or indirectly to the *sarkar*, their relationship of interdependence was not affected; in fact, it was strengthened.

However, the market had now intruded into economic transactions entered into by the occupational castes. While previously, goods supplied by them were against customary payments which were often related to the income (crop size, as payments were made in kind) of the buyer and not precisely to the quantity of goods supplied, now practically all goods are sold at a price (money or barter), except to the dominant lineage on ceremonial occasions when some customary recompense is made for them. Castes providing services, such as, laundry (Dhobi) or hairdressing (Nai), are, nevertheless, still transacting business in a good part on customary payments. The principal change here has been that, while before Dhobis or barbers did not compete with each other as each was allowed a certain number of families, now they are competing with each other. Another manifestation of the intrusion of the market is the decline of certain occupations, principally, pottery (Kumhar) and oil crushing (Teli). In some cases the market has brought in competition from the products of superior technology which have both quality and/or price advantage. This is true of the barber's occupation as well with the advent of the safety razor and the emergence of haircutting saloons.

As regards feature (b), the gap between the income and wealth levels of the *sarkar* and the occupational castes has, if anything, widened. But the occupational castes are tending to emerge out of the subsistence type of economy. The earlier state of stagnation has been given a shake or two. Development and growth is occurring in many ways and, though some people are still at the subsistence level, others have moved up. But the horizon of opportunities is still viewed by most as confined to the village. The incentives to move out have been weak or, rather, the sense of security in the village structure has been for the present strengthened by the new developments and has effectively countered the incentives to move out. Some enterprising people who have moved out of the village economy represent exceptions.

Thus, the *sarkar* has retained its economic power and control as well as its political dominance. Its relationship of interdependence with the occupational castes has continued unimpaired. The ritual aspect of services rendered to the *sarkar* in the *jajmani* system continues unaltered. The role of the *sarkar* in settling disputes not sorted out in caste panchayats is still played as before.[5] Among the occupational castes, however, there is some evidence of new stresses and strains on account of individuals having improved their lot either by leaving the village or by exploiting opportunities within the village. The case of a young man from the Mirasi (singer) caste illustrates the situation very aptly. This Mirasi had migrated out of the village and made good in occupations other than that of his caste. He had moved up in his status and position in the caste structure outside the village. When the time for his marriage came, his family arranged for a girl from among the Mirasis in Kasauli. To this girl the young man was engaged on the condition that, as his fiancee, she should cease pursuing the traditional occupation of the caste, viz., singing and dancing. This condition was agreed upon as there was already a trend to withdraw from the profession and not to perform for all and sundry. But before the wedding could take place, a ceremonial occasion arose in the family of the dominant lineage at which the Mirasis were called upon to sing and dance according to custom. The parents of the girl, and presumably the girl herself, chose to perform at this occasion

[5]A Gram Panchayat does exist in Kasauli with one of the Kidwais from the dominant lineage as its Sarpanch. However, it had a record of rarely meeting at the time of my enquiry and not a single dispute was taken to the Gram Panchayat. The role of the Gram Panchayat was being performed by the dominant lineage.

for the *sarkar* even though it clearly meant breaking the girl's engagement. Take another instance. The womenfolk of the Manihars (bangle seller) used to sell bangles by going to the houses of all castes, including non-Ashraf, but now with their income levels having risen these women do not go to any house except the houses of the dominant lineage, and even there they are liable to come veiled (wearing a *burka*).

Thus, while the vertical dimension of the caste structure (relationship between the occupational caste and the *sarkar*) has remained intact, some chinks have appeared in its horizontal dimension (relationships between the various occupational castes). There are, however, two elements in the economic changes that have occurred over the past two decades which might be the thin edge of the wedge in the vertical dimension of the caste structure. One of them is the progressively increasing intrusion of the market in the relationship of interdependence between the occupational castes and the *sarkar*, and the other is the emergence of a wider range of opportunities for the occupational castes accompanied by a rise in their income-consumption level and the prospects for further improvement.

But important though these changes are, by themselves they may not make a significant impact. They provide, as it were, one blade of the scissors. The other blade could take one of two forms: either the dominant lineage breaks up by a split from within or another competitive economic power (including the Government in any of its manifestations) enters the scene from outside.[6] In other words, the monopoly of economic power enjoyed by the dominant lineage is replaced by competition among those who have control over the means of livelihood of the occupational castes. Alternatively, the monopolistic power of the dominant lineage is confronted by a monopolistic power from the occupational castes, which amounts to the adoption of a collective approach by the occupational castes, similar in nature to a trade union. Of these possibilities, the former is more probable.

[6]The object of the Land Reforms and Zamindari Abolition Bill was precisely this, but it obviously failed to achieve it.

Bibliography

Ansari, Ghaus (1960), *Muslim Caste in Uttar Pradesh: A Study in Culture Contact*, Lucknow, Ethnographic and Folk Culture Society.

Ashraf, K.M. (1959), *Life and Conditions of the People of Hindustan*, Delhi, Jeevan Prakashan.

Bailey, F.G. (1957), *Caste and the Economic Frontier: A Village in Highland Orissa*, Manchester, University of Manchester Press.

Beals, Alan R. (1960), 'Leadership in a Mysore Village', in Richard Parke and Irene Tinker (eds), *Leadership and Political Institutions in India*, Bombay, Asia Publishing House.

Beteille, Andre (1965), *Caste, Class and Power: Changing Patterns of Social Stratification in a Tanjore Village*, Berkeley and Los Angeles, University of California Press.

Dube, S.C. (1968), 'Caste Dominance and Factionalism', *Contributions to Indian Sociology*, New Series, 2, pp. 51-81.

Dumont, Louis (1970), *Homo Hierarchicus: The Caste System and its Implications*, Delhi, Vikas Publishing House.

Mayer, Adrian C. (1958), 'The Dominant Caste in a Region of Central India', *Southwestern Journal of Anthropology*, 14, pp. 407-27.

Nizami, K.A. (1961) *Some Aspects of Religion and Politics in India during the Thirteenth Century*, Aligarh, Department of History, Aligarh Muslim University.

Srinivas, M.N. (1959), 'The Dominant Caste in Rampura', *American Anthropologist*, 61, pp. 1-16.

——(1966), *Social Change in Modern India*, Berkley and Los Angles, University of California Press.

Yasin, M. (1958), *A Social History of Islamic India*, Lucknow, Upper India Publishing House.

10

Caste Stratification among Muslims in a Township in Western Uttar Pradesh[1]

S.P. Jain

An interesting conclusion which one can draw from available studies on caste is that most scholars have confined themselves to a study of the caste system among the Hindus. Very little attention has been paid by sociologists and social anthropologists to the form and pattern of caste-like groups among other religious minorities of the country, in particular the Muslims who occupy an important place in the Indian social structure. Although the Muslims form the second largest religious group and have a special place in the Indian social structure due to historical and political reasons (Dumont, 1970), whatever has been published so far with respect to the organization of caste among the Muslims is, by and large, fragmentary and does not expose the inherent characteristics of their social structure.

The objective of the present paper is to highlight the salient features of the stratification pattern among the Muslims of north India in terms of the caste system. In doing so, an attempt will

[1]The data used in the present enquiry are drawn from the research material collected by the author in a North Indian town for his Ph.D. thesis (Jain, 1967). He wishes to thank Professor V. S. D'Souza for his guidance and supervision.

be made to examine the extent to which caste status is related to some of the main elements of social structure in a given community. The data forming the basis of the present paper have been derived from a study of a middle-sized town community of North India (see Jain, 1975). Although the sample of this study consisted of both Hindu and Muslim respondents, only the Muslim population (155) from the sample has been taken into account for the purpose of the present paper.

Kabirnagar

The community under study (which we shall hereafter refer to by a pseudonym—Kabirnagar) is a middle-sized town in the State of Uttar Pradesh in India. It is situated in the northwest corner of the Rohilkhand division of the State. According to the *District Census Handbook* (India, 1962), the physical area of the town is 195 acres. Since the occupational pattern of the population did not fulfil the urban conditions, it had been declassified in the category of village, though its population was 18,133. As can be observed from Table 1, the population of the community has been rising since 1921. Prior to this, the population had, in fact, gone down by 195 persons during the earlier two decades, namely, 1901 to 1921. However, the population of the town gradually increased from 9,434 in 1921 to 18,133 in 1961.

TABLE 1
Population of Kabirnagar (1911-1961)

Years	*Population*	*Variation*
1901	10,062	--
1911	9,829	— 223
1921	9,434	— 395
1931	11,130	+1696
1941	11,799	+ 669
1951	15,132	+3333
1961	18,133	+3035

Source: India (1962).

Kabirnagar can easily be considered a community representing the social structure of Western Uttar Pradesh. Its population is broadly divided into two religious groups, namely, Hindus (approximately 38 per cent) and Muslims (approximately 62 per cent). Each of the two religious groups is sub-divided into several castes as follows:

I. *Hindu Castes*: 1. Acharaj, 2. Bagwan, 3. Barhai, 4. Brahmin, 5. Chamar, 6. Dhangar, 7. Jain, 8. Jotshi, 9. Kumhar, 10. Mali, 11. Rastogi, 12. Sunar, 13. Tyagi.

II. *Muslim Castes*: 1. Ansari, 2. Barhai, 3. Chaudhry, 4. Darzi, 5. Dhuna, 6. Ghosi, 7. Halwai, 8. Kalal, 9. Kasai, 10. Kazi, 11. Khatik, 12. Luhar, 13. Mahgir, 14. Nai, 15. Sheikh, 16. Sayyad, 17. Teli.

Although the community in question has developed from a big village settlement, it still retains many rural characteristics and thus displays an inter-mixture of rural-urban features. On the one hand, one sees unplanned buildings, streets so narrow as to hardly allow a cart to pass through, and drains coming out directly on the streets. On the other hand, one comes across big school buildings, shopping centres and industrial establishments on its fringe. Mud settlements may also be seen existing side by side with cement dwellings of uneven size. Besides, a large number of temples and mosques are also to be found. All these physical features of the town provide it with the typical character of a rural-urban milieu.

The members of the two religious groups mostly live in separate residential areas. Similarly the people belonging to different castes within each religious group also, to a great extent, exhibit residential segregation. This is most conspicuous from the fact that a number of residential areas are known by the name of the particular caste which predominates in that particular residential locality.

The residential areas of the community are marked not only by residential segregation based on religious differentiation of the population, but also by the size of the houses and the quality of the material from which they are constructed. The houses in the residential areas of higher caste people, whether Hindus or Muslims, are larger in size and built of good material whereas the areas inhabited by poor people present a reverse picture. Thus, the residential pattern of the community depicts the difference in the socio-economic life of the two religious groups.

Of the people who are gainfully employed in Kabirnagar, as many as 24.8 per cent are engaged in cultivation. The next single largest number is of those engaged in manufacturing (11.2 per cent) followed by those engaged in trade and commerce (9.2 per cent). Of course, the percentage of those who are working in different types of unspecified jobs is also quite high, namely, 24.3. But as the nature of their jobs is not known, they cannot be treated as a single occupational group. As may be seen from Table 2, the people in the rest of the occupational categories are found in varying numbers, ranging from 6.3 per cent in mining, quarrying, etc., to 2.2 per cent in transport, storages, etc. Evidently, the occupational structure of Kabirnagar is rural-based.

TABLE 2
Occupational Pattern of Kabirnagar

Occupational Category	*Number*	*Percentage*
1. Cultivators	1,265	24.8
2. Agricultural Labourers	218	4.3
3. Mining, Quarrying, etc.	342	6.3
4. Household Industry	685	13.5
5. Manufacturing	571	11.2
6. Construction	192	3.8
7. Trade and Commerce	466	9.2
8. Transport, Storage, etc.	111	2.2
9. Other Services	1,239	24.3
Total	5,089	100.0

Caste Ranking Methodology

Although the concept of caste status has long been in currency, the use of caste ranking as a measure of caste status is just beginning. There are very few studies which have taken this aspect directly into account. Particular mention may be made of Marriott (1959 and 1960) and Mahar (1959). According to Marriott, the interaction among the various castes should be the main criterion for caste ranking whereby 'castes are ranked according to the structure of interaction among them'. On the other hand, Pauline Mahar attempted to extract a scale of inter-caste pollution. The technique required to rank the various castes is, however, different; here the caste rank is measured by a technique in which the caste members themselves, or a set of judges selected randomly, are asked to rate the various castes according to their prestige and then arrange them into convenient categories of prestige.[2]

Keeping in view the assumption that a community characterized by caste stratification tends to be divided into a number of groups arranged in a status hierarchy, caste status was directly measured by asking the members of the community to grade the various castes according to their prestige. It was assumed that the degree of caste stratification would depend upon the degree of unanimity among the respondents in their grading. Accordingly, 36 Hindus and Muslim respondents (male adults) were randomly selected as a 'panel of judges'. They were asked to grade the 17 Muslim castes residing in Kabirnagar in order of prestige ranking. The respondents were supplied 17 cards, each one bearing the name of one caste but placed in alphabetical order. Each respondent was expected to rearrange the cards of the different castes on the basis of his own judgement of the prestige status of each caste. The rank orders so given to the different castes by a particular respondent were entered on a separate sheet for further tabulation. Having elicited the judgement of a respondent and having entered it on a separate sheet, the cards were rearranged in alphabetical order and supplied to another respondent. This process continued till we obtained the judgement of our panel of respondents.

From the ranks assigned to the different caste groups by the respondents the median judgements and the differences between the first and the third quartiles were derived. The median judgements helped us in assigning relative positions to the various castes in a descending order. The frequency distribution giving the number of respondents ranking the castes as first, second, etc., was also obtained. The statistical parameter, the most appropriate measure to explain the distribution, is the median.

[2]The validity of this technique has been demonstrated in the well known studies of Kaufman (1944) and D'Souza (1959). In this study, eighteen people of both sexes, belonging to eleven different castes, were asked to answer thirteen questions about each of the other twenty-one castes in the town.

This bifurcates the total population on the rank axis. Similarly, the third quartile breaks it at a point up to which 75 per cent of the total population is distributed. The differences between the first and the third quartile are, therefore, used in ascertaining the degree of consensus among the respondents in assigning a particular rank to a given caste. The variations in the median judgements are also expected to show the degree of agreement among the respondents with regard to the prestige positions of different castes in a hierarchical order. It should, nevertheless, be mentioned here that the positions of the different castes so arrived cannot be treated as a strict boundary line between any two castes. What actually can be derived by such an analysis is the degree of agreement among the respondents with regard to the position of a particular caste. Thus, the variations in the median score are indicative only of their positions relative to one another.

Caste Ranking

The data with regard to the different castes of Muslims are presented in Table 3. It shows that the median of the judgements of the Muslim respondents for the 17 castes gradually varies from 1.40 to 16.22 and that of the Hindu respondents from 0.91 to 16.33. The gradual variations in descending order clearly indicate that people have assigned different positions relative to one another to different caste groups. This is true for respondents of both the religious groups. Broadly, it shows that there is no unanimity among the respondents with regard to the position of each caste. This is evident from the fact that the maximum quartile difference in the case of Muslim respondents is 6.50 (Ansari and Dhuna) followed by Teli (4.66) and Khatik and Kalal (4.50 each). On the other hand, the maximum quartile difference in case of Hindu respondents is 8.33 (Ansari and Halwai). Then come Dhuna (6.0), Khatik (5.50), Darzi (4.65), Teli (4.50) and Kalal (3.71) in that order. The minimum quartile difference is 1.33 (Kasai).

If all the respondents were to grade each caste in a random fashion, the quartile difference would have been as high as 7.5. On the other hand, in case of complete unanimity in ranking

TABLE 3

Median Judgements given to Muslim Castes by Muslim and Hindu Respondents

By Muslim Respondents				By Hindu Respondents			
Muslim Castes	*Rank Order*	*Median Judgement*	*Quartile Difference*	*Muslim Castes*	*Rank Order*	*Median Judgement*	*Quartile Difference*
Sheikh	1	1.40	1.83	Chaudhry	1	0.91	1.41
Chaudhry	2	1.80	1.75	Sayyad	2	1.50	2.66
Sayyad	3	2.00	1.57	Sheikh	3	1.90	0.98
Ansari	4	4.50	6.50	Kazi	4	4.66	1.95
Kazi	5	5.00	3.30	Ghosi	5	5.80	2.25
Ghosi	6	6.00	1.60	Ansari	6	6.00	8.33
Halwai	7	7.00	3.67	Halwai	7	6.00	8.33
Barhai	8	7.33	2.50	Barhai	8	8.33	2.00
Darzi	9	9.50	4.00	Darzi	9	9.00	4.65
Luhar	10	10.00	3.50	Luhar	10	9.62	1.40
Dhuna	11	11.00	6.50	Dhuna	11	11.00	6.00
Khatik	12	11.50	4.50	Nai	12	11.60	3.00
Nai	13	12.00	3.25	Teli	13	11.66	4.40
Teli	14	12.50	4.66	Khatik	14	12.00	5.50
Kalal	15	12.75	4.50	Kalal	15	14.00	3.71
Mahgir	16	14.66	2.50	Mahgir	16	15.00	3.29
Kasai	17	16.22	1.33	Kasai	17	16.33	0.66
Average quartile difference 3.37				Average quartile difference 3.24			

positions, the quartile difference would have been 0.5. There are certain castes about whose positions there is some degree of unanimity among the respondents. For example, the minimum quartile difference for Sayyad and Ghosi is 1.57 and 1.60 respectively as judged by Muslim respondents as against 0.66 (Kasai) and 0.98 (Sheikh) respectively as judged by Hindu respondents.

Thus there is some disagreement among the respondents of the two religious groups with regard to the social positions given to Muslim caste groups. For instance, Sheikh was placed in the top position by Muslim respondents whereas Hindu respondents ranked Chaudhry on this position. Similarly, a significant difference is observed in the positions assigned to Sayyad, Ansari, Ghosi, and Kasai by respondents from both the religious groups. More specifically, the Muslim respondents have placed Chaudhry, Sayyad, Sheikh, Kazi, Ghosi, and Ansari on the 1st, 2nd, 3rd, 4th, 5th and 6th ranks respectively. Agreement with regard to the positions of several castes is, however, found from 7th rank (Halwai) up to the 11th (Luhar). Some disagreement regarding the positions of Nai, Teli, and Khatik is also evident. The Muslim respondents have assigned these castes 13th and 14th and 12th ranks while Hindu respondents have placed them on 12th, 13th and 14th ranks respectively. Kalal, Mahgir, and Kasai have been given the lowest positions by all respondents. How the respondents of the two religious communities have graded the different castes is more evident from Figure 1. It clearly shows the difference between the ranking of the two sets of respondents.

On the basis of the analysis of data it can be said that the different Muslim groups do enjoy different degrees of prestige relative to one another and they form a hierarchy in the social structure of Kabirnagar (Jain, 1971). Further, the Muslims possess a comparable, if not an identical, 'caste' system. However, as may be seen from Figure 1, unanimity among the Hindu and Muslim respondents with regard to the rank of castes was limited only to certain castes.

Do the positions accorded to the different castes by the respondents compare with the traditional hierarchy of the castes? A broad comparison of the particulars with respect to the traditional caste hierarchy among Muslims, as reported

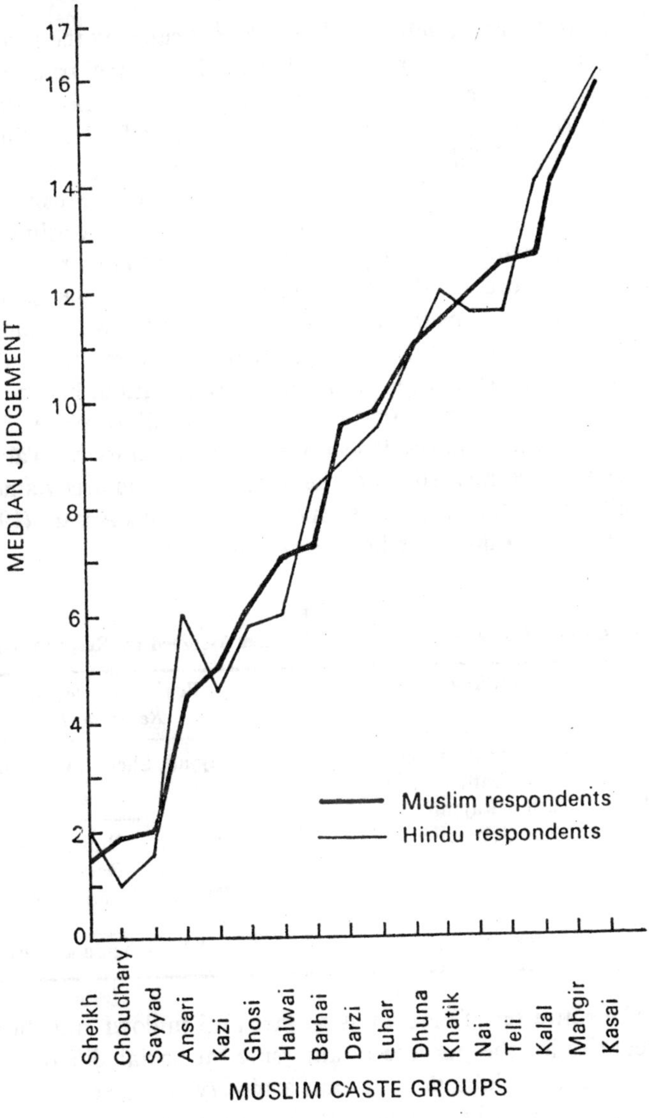

Figure 1
Muslim Caste Ranking in Kabirnagar by Muslims and Hindus

by Ghaus Ansari (1960), and the ranks indicated by the respondents, show a high degree of similarity. Since the traditional caste structure was based on ethnic and other considerations, minor modifications have had to be made in a few cases in the arrangement of different castes to facilitate comparison. We accorded greater weightage to the judgements of the Muslim respondents as it was felt that the opinions of the Muslim respondents would be more dependable and closer to the traditional ideal than those of the Hindu respondents. For the sake of comparison, we thus placed Kalal, Mahgir and Kasai among the unclean castes. While doing so, personal judgement, based on our observations gained during field investigation, had to be used. We had observed that most of the Muslims place these three castes on the lowest ladder of the status hierarchy. Table 4 presents a comparison of the traditional hierarchy among Muslims in Uttar Pradesh as reported by Ghaus Ansari (1960) and the caste ranking indicated by our data.

TABLE 4

Traditional Caste Status and the Position Assigned by Respondents

Hierarchy	*Traditional Status*	*Ranks Assigned by Respondents*
I	*Ashraf*: Sayyad, Sheikh, Mughal, Pathan	Sayyad, Sheikh, Chaudhary, Kazi
II	Muslim Rajputs	—— —— ——
III	Clean Occupational Castes	Ansari, Ghosi, Halwai, Barhai, Darzi, Luhar, Dhuna, Khatik, Nai and Teli
IV	Unclean Castes	Kalal, Mahgir and Kasai

The entire set of castes was further broken down into broad categories for the purpose of analysing the social differentials. This was, no doubt, done in an arbitrary manner and there was no alternative which could have provided a suitable framework for delineating a meaningful categorization of the caste hierarchy. However, in order to eliminate personal bias as far as possible, the different castes were placed in a particular category by taking into consideration the differences between median judgements and also the numerical strength of a particular caste in our sample. Thus, all the seventeen castes were compressed into four broad categories, namely, the upper, the upper-middle, the lower-middle, and the lower.

The results of the exercise are presented in Table 5. It shows that, out of the total sample of 155 respondents, the maximum (47 per cent) belong to the upper group followed by the lower group (22 per cent); the number of respondents who belonged to the upper-middle and lower-middle groups was 20 per cent and 11 per cent respectively.

TABLE 5

Muslim Caste Stratification in Kabirnagar

Caste	*Caste*	*Sample (per cent)*
Upper	Chaudhry, Sayyad, Sheikh	47.00
Upper-Middle	Ansari, Kazi, Ghosi, Halwai	20.00
Lower-Middle	Barhai, Darzi, Luhar, Dhuna	11.00
Lower	Khatik, Nai, Teli, Kalal, Mahgir, Kasai	22.00
Total	17	100.00 (155)

Caste and Social Differentiation

Is the caste stratification of the Muslims of Kabirnagar reflected in terms of social differentiation? In order to study this phenomenon we shall examine some of the key elements of social structure in relation to caste hierarchy in the following pages. The elements selected are occupation, education and leadership.

Caste and Occupation

Some sociologists have found an intimate relationship between the hierarchy of caste and a man's occupation. It has been concluded that members of higher castes are generally distributed in occupations of higher prestige while the lower castes are concentrated in occupations which are considered lower in prestige. How far this is true with respect to the members of different Muslim castes may be seen from a comparison of caste status and occupation set out in Table 6.

It is evident from Table 6 that those following the occupation of skilled manual workers are in a majority in the upper-middle and lower-middle groups, namely, 51.6 and 58.8 per cent respectively. In the lower castes also the percentage of such persons is fairly high (49.0). The occupational pattern of the upper caste people is, however, different. There are 47.3 per cent agriculturists followed by 25.7 per cent unskilled manual workers among them. It could thus be stated that the occupational pattern of the different groups is characterized by the fact that the lower-middle and upper-middle caste respondents are mainly engaged in skilled occupations, though the lower caste people also have the same base. Further, nearly one-fourth of the upper and lower caste respondents are skilled manual workers. The occupational base of the upper and upper-middle castes is essentially agriculture.[3]

Caste and Education

Several studies have again revealed an intimate relationship between caste hierarchy and education. It has been found that the people belonging to the higher caste categories provide more education to their children than the people belonging to the lower ones. For instance, Desai (1953) reports that educational attainments are intimately related to the hierarchy of caste. The higher the caste of the individual, the higher would be his educational attainment. But most of the studies on the relationship between caste and education have been concerned with Hindus and as such their conclusions may or may not be true for Muslim castes. In such a situation, one would assume that caste and education among Muslims are by and large related in a similar fashion as among the Hindu castes.

Table 7 presents the caste rank and educational standing of the Muslim respondents in Kabirnagar. It would be observed from the data presented that an overwhelming majority of the

[3]In this study we have used the occupational classification prepared by Sovani (1959) in a slightly modified way.

TABLE 6

Distribution of Muslim Castes by Occupational Categories

Caste	*Unskilled Manual Workers*	*Skilled Manual Workers*	*Lower Professions*	*Small Business*	*Highly Skilled Manual Workers*	*Clerks and Shop Assistants*	*Intermediate Professions*	*Medium Business*	*Agriculturists*	*Others*	*Total*
Upper	25.7	5.4	2.7	6.7	2.7	2.7	2.7	—	47.3	4.0	100 (74)
Upper-Middle	6.5	51.6	9.7	3 2	—	—	—	9.7	19.4	—	100 (31)
Lower-Middle	—	58.8	—	17.6	23.5	—	—	—	—	—	100 (17)
Lower	27.0	49.0	3.0	12.0	—	—	—	—	3.0	6.0	100 (33)

TABLE 7
Educational Attainments among Muslim Castes

Status	*Illiterate*	*Primary*	*Middle*	*High School and above*	*Total (N=155)*
Upper	76.0	9.0	8.0	7.0	100 (74)
Upper-Middle	87.0	10.0	3.0	—	100 (31)
Lower-Middle	88.0	6.0	—	6.0	100 (17)
Lower	100.0	—	—	—	100 (33)

respondents in each caste category were illiterate. The rate of illiteracy is to the extent of 76 per cent among the upper, 87 per cent among the upper-middle, 88 per cent among the lower-middle and 100 per cent among the lower groups. But one conspicuous fact that stands out is that the rate of illiteracy increases as we proceed from upper to the lower caste categories, though the actual difference is not much. Coming to the level of education, it is observed that the people of higher castes have attained more education than the lower castes. The only exception found is with respect to the lower-middle castes, where 6 per cent of the respondents belong to the educational category of high school and above.

Having analyzed the pattern of educational attainment among the four caste categories, let us now see if the same trend is continued with respect to the educational aspirations of the people. This is necessary because the actual level of education attained by the members of a particular group may not necessarily mirror its values. It is possible that some people, though they belong to a lower caste, may like to give their children a better education than they had themselves, but are unable to do so for economic reasons. In order to verify how far this is true we present the pattern of educational aspirations among the different castes in Table 8.

It is evident from Table 8 that, on the whole, the educational aspirations of the respondents for their children are very low. There does not appear to be a sharp relationship, as the following description would reveal, between the position of a caste in the hierarchy and the educational aspiration of its members. As many as 47.3 and 17.5 per cent respondents from the upper and 32.3 per cent and 6.5 per cent from the upper-middle castes aspire for secondary and college education for their children. The respondents of the lower-middle and lower castes also aspire for almost exactly the same educational levels for their offsprings as those above them on the social scale. However, what is surprising is that a fairly large percentage of the respondents belonging to the upper and upper-middle castes aspire to give their children only primary education. It is noticeable that as many as 17.6 per cent of the respondents from the lower-middle castes aspire to give their children technical education. On the whole, the respondents of this caste-group aspire for higher educational levels in fairly large numbers as compared to the other castes.

TABLE 8
Educational Aspirations of the Muslim Castes

Caste	*Primary*	*Secondary*	*College*	*Professional*	*Technical*	*Uncertain*	*Total (N=155)*
Upper	18.9	47.3	17.5	8.1	4.1	4.1	100 (74)
Upper-Middle	38.6	32.3	6.5	12.9	—	9.7	100 (31)
Lower-Middle	5.9	29.4	23.6	5.9	17.6	17.6	100 (17)
Lower	33.3	36.4	18.0	—	—	12.3	100 (33)

On the whole a majority of the respondents aspire for secondary education. Next to this are the people who aspire for primary and college education. Interestingly, more respondents from the lower castes were uncertain about the education of their children than those of the upper castes.

Caste and Leadership

Leadership forms an important element of a community's social structure. Studies on the subject have conclusively shown that the status of a caste plays an important role in the leadership pattern and decision-making process in a given community.

Table 9 presents the data with respect to the caste background of Muslim political leaders in Kabirnagar which allows us to see how far caste and leadership status are inter-related among them.

TABLE 9
Muslim Political Leaders by Caste Rank

Code No. of Leader	*Caste of the Leader*	*Caste Status*
5	Chaudhry	Upper
40	Sheikh	Upper
2	Sheikh	Upper
39	Chaudhry	Upper
3	Sheikh	Upper
8	Sayyad	Upper
9	Sayyad	Upper
12	Sayyad	Upper
18	Sayyad	Upper
7	Kazi	Upper-middle
10	Sayyad	Upper
11	Sayyad	Upper
34	Ansari	Upper-middle
38	Sayyad	Upper
1	Sheikh	Upper
4	Chaudhry	Upper
6	Chaudhry	Upper
35	Ansari	Upper-middle
37	Sayyad	Upper
48	Sayyad	Upper
55	Chaudhry	Upper

The table clearly shows the overwhelming preponderance of upper caste Muslims in the political leadership of the community. Out of a total of 21 Muslim political leaders in Kabirnagar, the majority is from the upper Muslim castes, namely, Chaudhry, Sayyad and Sheikh. This would seem to confirm the finding that leadership positions are monopolized by upper caste categories and lower castes enjoy little, if any, control over leadership and decision-making. This is true even of a township like Kabirnagar which reflects an admixture of both rural and urban characteristics.

A similar trend is observed with respect to Muslim social leaders. Table 10 shows that all but one of these leaders were from the upper castes, namely, Chaudhry, Sayyad and Sheikh.

Thus, we can conclude easily that leadership among the

TABLE 10
Muslim Social Leaders by Caste Hierarchy

Code No. of Leader	*Caste*	*Caste Status*
4	Chaudhry	Upper
18	Sayyad	Upper
2	Sheikh	Upper
7	Kazi	Upper-middle
9	Sayyad	Upper
40	Sheikh	Upper
5	Chaudhry	Upper
1	Sheikh	Upper
35	Ansari	Upper-middle
3	Sheikh	Upper
37	Sayyad	Upper
38	Sayyad	Upper

Muslims of Kabirnagar is confined mainly to those belonging to the high castes. There are very few cases where a leader belongs to the upper-middle caste category and none belong to the lower-middle and lower caste categories. However, it should be noted that our data cannot show conclusively that there do not exit any leaders among the lower-middle or lower caste Muslims of Kabirnagar. Since this study was confined to the leadership available in the town as a whole, only those leaders who were on the top in the total community could find place in our analysis. It is quite possible that there may be leaders even among the lower caste Muslims but that their roles are confined to their own caste circles. Even if we accept this, the fact cannot be ignored that the factor of 'status' among the Muslims of Kabirnagar is as potent as anywhere else.

Conclusion

Our study of caste structure among the Muslims of Kabirnagar has brought to the fore the following conclusions: that (i) there does exist a pattern of caste hierarchy among the Muslims of Kabirnagar; (ii) people do recognize this pattern of stratification; and (iii) caste stratification directly influences access of persons to particular occupations, education and leadership positions.

Since the foregoing analysis is based on data collected in a middle-sized community of western Uttar Pradesh, the conclusions cannot be generalized in view of the cultural diversities obtaining in different parts of the country. In this sense, the pattern of stratification as revealed here may not be all that applicable to other parts of the country.

Bibliography

Ansari, Ghaus (1960), *Muslim Caste in Uttar Pradesh: A Study in Culture Contact*, Lucknow, Ethnographic and Folk Culture Society.

Deasi, I.P. (1953), *High School Students in Poona*, Poona, Deccan College Post-Graduate and Research Institute.

D' Souza, Victor S. (1959), 'Social Grading of Occupations in India', *Sociological Review*, 10, pp. 145-59.

Dumont, Louis (1970), *Homo Hierarchicus: The Caste System and Its Implications*, Delhi, Vikas Publishing House.

India, Government of (1962), *Census of India, 1961: Uttar Pradesh*, District Census Handbook, Delhi, Manager of Publications.

Jain, S P. (1967), *Social Structure of a Hindu-Muslim Community in Uttar Pradesh*, Unpublished Ph.D. Thesis, Panjab University, Chandigarh.

———(1971), 'Religion and Caste Ranking in a North Indian Community', *Sociological Bulletin*, 20, pp. 134-44.

———(1975), *Social Structure of Hindu-Muslim Community*, Delhi, National Publishing House.

Kaufman, H. (1944), *Prestige Class in a New York Rural Community*, Memior No. 260, Ithaca, Cornell University Agricultural Experiment Station.

Mahar, Pauline M. (1959), 'A Multiple Scaling Technique for Caste Ranking', *Man in India*, 39, pp. 127-47

Marriott, McKim (1959), 'Interactional and Attributional Theories of Caste Ranking', *Man in India*, 39, pp. 92-107

———(1960), *Caste Ranking and Community Structure in Five Regions of India and Pakistan*, Deccan College Monograph Series No. 23, Poona, Deccan College Post-Graduate and Research Institute.

Sovani, N.V., *et al.* (1959), *Poona: A Resurvey*, Poona, Gokhale Institute of Economics and Politics.

11
Caste among the Muslims of Calcutta

M.K.A. Siddiqui

The concept of caste is basically opposed to Islamic ideology. Caste implies 'a hierarchy of endogamous groups organized in a characteristic division of labour' (Sinha, 1967:94), while Islam stands for the perfect equality of all individuals and groups in the social and religious spheres.

Early Islam brought about radical changes in the society under its influence and put its egalitarian principles into practice so that the traditional foundations of Arab hierarchy, as shown by Ibn-e-Khaldun, the philosopher-historian of the fourteenth century, were completely shaken (Grunebaum, 1961: 199). Birth as a basis of superiority or inferiority was deemed absolutely irrelevant and piety alone came to be regarded as a criterion of individual distinction (Koran, S.XLIX 13-15:1407). Koranic injunctions rendered immaterial the distinctions of colour, race and region.

But with the passage of time and as Islam spread to distant lands, some sort of stratification re-appeared in Muslim society, though it took various shapes and forms according to the nature of the adjustments which Islam made on coming into contact with regional traditions and other civilizations, as also to the nature of its historical development. For example, veneration of the Prophet led to the development of a new criterion of nobility based on kinship with him. Such categorizations as

'Arab' and 'Ajam', 'Sarih' and 'Mawali' also led to conflicts which have sometimes resulted in the victory of the underprivileged, as for example the Mawalis in Iran who secured an equal status with the Arabs for themselves. This trend towards stratification was strengthened by the introduction of the practice of limiting marriage relationships within a specified range of kins known as *kufv*.

In India, a land of an elaborately stratified society, very few sociological studies of the Muslims, who constitute a considerable part of the population, have been made. However, right from the middle of the nineteenth century a number of glossaries of castes and tribes belonging to various regions of India—such as those by Elliot (1869), Ibbetson (1920), Risley (1891), Crooke (1906), Nesfield (1885), Thurston (1909), Iyer (1909), Rose (1911) and Russell and Lal (1916)—have suggested the existence of a number of Muslim groups of various backgrounds which are almost analogous to *jatis*. A number of social scientists, like Max Weber (1947), Hutton (1946), N.K. Bose (1958) and M.N. Srinivas (1964), have also, through their various writings, suggested the existence of some caste attributes in Muslim society in India. In recent times Ghaus Ansari (1956 and 1960), Z. Ahmad (1962), Raghuraj Gupta (1956) and a few others have attempted either synchronic or diachronic studies of the Muslims of Uttar Pradesh and reported the presence of caste or caste-like features in their society. A few more recent studies of the rural areas of West Bengal and of Southern Bihar by Bhattacharya (Chapter 12) and Ali (Chapter 1) respectively do not rule out the existence of certain features of the caste system among the Muslims in those areas.

In a study based on both the Eastern and Western wings of Pakistan, Zillur Khan contended that the stratification of Muslim society in India and Pakistan was based on gradations inherent in the historical development of Islamic society and that it would have existed even without the influence of the social environment (Khan, 1968:133). The development of caste among the Muslims, on more or less similar lines as caste among the Hindus, is seen by Khan not as a result of acculturation as of the fact that Hindu and Muslim peasants remained isolated in worlds of their own until India won independence from British rule. This contention, however, does not bear scrutiny in the light of social history. Nevertheless, Khan neither denies the egalitarian principle of early Islam nor does he disprove the existence of a rigid stratification in Muslim society on the Indian subcontinent.

The present study is an attempt to analyze what Muslim society is like in a cosmopolitan situation with reference to the dominant milieu or the 'situational model', i.e., the system of caste. A city is usually considered a melting pot of castes and ethnic boundaries. This should be true to a greater extent with regard to a cosmopolitan city like Calcutta. Also, Islam is seen as essentially an urban religion, unfolding itself in an urban milieu (Grunebaum, 1961:173). If the characteristics of rigid stratification based on birth are not of fundamental importance, they should disappear particularly among the Muslims of Calcutta.

The study is based on fieldwork carried out in Calcutta city between 1967 and 1968.[1] When I approached the field of my study I had no set notions about the problem although what I remembered of the village I came from in the southern suburb of Bhagalpur in Bihar had left an impression of the existence of a hierarchical pattern among Muslim groups that could not be explained in terms of Islam alone. The village is multi-ethnic.[2] Each group or *beradari* roughly occupies a *tola* or locality and observes strict endogamy and restricted commensal relationships. In the case of females it was extremely rigid, almost to the extent of inter-pollution. I had naturally to take note not only of the distinguishing features of the Muslims as a large social group but also of the larger matrix within which they were situated. Further, it was also necessary to take account of the historical background of the groups that composed Muslim society. The study had, therefore, to be both synchronic and

[1]The research on which this paper is based was carried out as part of a research project of the Anthropological Survey of India, Calcutta. I wish to express my gratitude to Dr. Surajit Sinha, Acting Director, Ahthropological Survey of India, for his guidance and help throughout this study as well as in the preparation of the paper. I am, however, solely responsible for any shortcomings in this paper.

[2]The term 'ethnic group' has been used here and elsewhere in this paper to mean groups which can be distinguished from other similar groups socially, biologically and in certain aspects of culture. For details see Sinha (1967) and Marriott (1960).

diachronic to the extent possible to yield profitable results. Considering the immensity of the subject, the present study is in the nature of a reconnaissance and I have relied for the present on the information elicited from the leaders and respected individuals of the various groups. These were often verified from other sources. Besides recording genealogies wherever possible, a random sample of a hundred families was studied to examine the extent of endogamy observed by the groups concerned. In the case of the smaller groups the occurrence of endogamy could be easily ascertained as the group members were familiar with most of those belonging to the group.

The City

Though the population of cosmopolitan Calcutta is predominantly Hindu, the majority of whom are Bengalis, Muslims form a substantial part comprising 12.70 per cent of the total population (1961 Census). About 70 per cent of the total Muslim population is Hindustani-speaking. The areas of their concentration roughly follow regional and linguistic affinities although there is one area where relatively affluent groups of different regional and linguistic backgrounds live together. This is around Mechuabazar, Colootola and Canning Street comprising wards numbered 23, 40 and 41.[3] Other concentrations are found in the central districts comprising wards numbered 50, 51, 53, 55, 57 and 60 around Park Circus up to Tapsia and the South-western districts extending from Kidderpur to Metiaburj (ward numbers 73, 74 and 75). Smaller pockets of Muslims in the city are situated in wards 31, 32 and 33, roughly comprising parts of Narkeldanga, Rajabazar and adjacent areas, and a little northwards in Belgachia and B.T. Road in ward 5. Smaller settlements are situated in Cossipur at the northern extremity and at the southern end in Tollygunj.

The Muslims of Calcutta belong to a number of different linguistic and geographical regions of India and beyond. In

[3]The ward numbers cited here correspond to those used in the 1961 Census of the city.

the course of their long association with the city extending over a century, a Hindustani dialect has emerged among the Muslims that contains elements of both Bengali and English vocabulary and syntax. This is spoken among the older inhabitants and has been termed 'Gulabi Urdu'.

Besides regional and linguistic affiliations, the Muslims of Calcutta are also divided into a number of groups on the basis of other factors such as common descent, common occupation or common origin. A broader division is on the basis of sects that often cuts across all other divisions, but sometimes coincides with regional and ethnic boundaries, making Muslim society more rigidly organized than otherwise.

The picture of the ethnic groups classified on the basis of their regional background or occupational pattern is as follows:

I. Foreigners

1. Afghans:
   - (i) Jalalabadi
   - (ii) Qandhari
   - (iii) Ghaznavi
   - (iv) Mazarsharifi
2. Iranians
3. Arabs
4. Tibetan, Chinese and others

II. Indians[4]

1. North-West Region
   - (i) Pakhtoon
   - (ii) Peshawari
     - (a) Sayyad (*pir*)
     - (b) Awan (muleteer)
     - (c) Kakazai (tribal)
     - (d) Kalal (transporters)
     - (e) Kashmir Peshwari (traders)
   - (iii) Kashmiri (divided into a large number of occupational subgroups)
   - (iv) Panjabi

[4]The word Indians here encompasses the people of the Indo-Pakistan subcontinent.

(a) Rajput
(b) Jat

2. Western Region
   (i) Rajasthani
   (groups wearing *ghaghra* of specified colours):
   (a) Shekhawati (red skirt—nilgar)
   (b) Madi (black skirt—nilgar)
   (c) Manihar (bangle-makers)
   (d) Sonar (goldsmiths)
   (e) Lohar (blacksmiths)
   (f) Dhobi (washermen)
   (Groups not wearing *ghaghra*):
   (g) Besati (hawkers and traders)
   (ii) Gujarati
   (Sectarian-cum-ethnic groups):
   (a) Dawoodi Bohra (traders)
   (b) Imami Ismaili Shia (traders)
   (Groups sharing sects with others):
   (c) Halai Memon (traders)
   (d) Kachi Memon (traders)
   (e) Sunni Bohra (traders)
   (f) Athna Ashari Bohra (traders)
3. Southern Region
   (i) Tamils
   (a) Maraykar (seafaring traders)
   (b) Rawther (horse-riding traders)
   (c) Labbai (agriculturists, servants, religious functionaries, etc.)
   (ii) Malayali
   (a) Thangal—Sayyads (very few in Calcutta)
   (b) Masalliyar
   (c) Mapilla
   (d) Rawther
   (e) Keyie
4. Northern Region (Consisting of the valleys of the Ganges and the Yamuna, extending from Haryana to U.P., Bihar and the Gangetic delta)
   (i) Groups claiming foreign origin (having no traditional occupation and not organized on the basis of caste

panchayat—represented in all sects and most regional groups)
(a) Sayyad
(b) Sheikh
(c) Mughal
(d) Pathan

(ii) Groups of indigenous origin (recruited from superior ruling and fighting castes coming from particular areas with some sort of caste organization, often taking the shape of formalized associations)
(a) Qaum-e-Panjabian (Delhi)
(b) Qaum-e-Panjabian (Anwla)
(c) Rajputs
(d) Jats
(e) Maliks

(iii) Groups with traditional occupations (with traditional caste organization of varying strength)
(Groups that do not pursue traditional occupations in Calcutta but continue to do so elsewhere):
(a) Momins (Ansari) (weavers)
(b) Ranki (Iraqi) Kalal (distillers)
(Occupational groups that continue to pursue traditional occupations though they have adopted other occupations and generally have a strong caste organization):
(c) Darzi (Bengali and non-Bengali—tailors)
(d) Kharadi (wood workers)
(e) Qasab or butchers (Qureshi)
(f) Chik (butchers of goat & sheep)
(g) Rai (greengrocers)
(h) Besati (pedlars of stationery articles, etc.)
(i) Mansuri (cotton carders)
(j) Churihar (shishgar—glass bangle-makers and dealers)
(k) Nikari (fish-mongers)
(l) Dafali (drum makers; priests of several castes and guardian-worshippers of special spirits)
(m) Hajjam (barber as well as surgeon)
(n) Dhobi (washermen)

(o) Mirshikar or Chirimar (trappers of and dealers in birds)
(p) Mirasi (musician)
(q) Qalandar (mendicant)
(r) Fakir (beggars and mendicants [Shah])
(s) Patua (painters)
(Pastoralists—dealers in animals and dairy farmers):
(t) Sheikhjee (*khatal* owners and dealers in milk, or dairy farmers)
(u) Meo (dairy men and dealers in milk)
(v) Ghosi (*khatal* owners and dealers in milk)

(iv) Groups engaged in 'unclean' occupations (on the borderline of Islam and Hinduism)
(a) Lal Begi (sweepers)

This classification covers, by and large, the decisive bulk of the Muslim population of the city. A few smaller groups might still have remained unidentified, yet the main factors in their ethnic composition have been shown. Separate population figures for the respective groups are not available but it is evident that numerically the most dominant group is that of the Momin followed by the Rai and the Qasab. The Imami Ismaili Shia, the Mirshikar, the Mirasi and the Nikari are among the smaller groups. Economically more dominant are the Gujarati groups—the Qaum-e-Panjabian, Dawoodi Bohra and the Ranki—the last mentioned virtually monopolizing the trade in hides and skins. The Momins have also attained substantial economic prosperity in recent years and have asserted themselves well enough to take their due share in the leadership of the community.

Before we go into an examination of the details of the various aspects of the groups relevant to the present study, it will be appropriate to present here a brief composition of the Muslim population on the basis of nationality, regional and linguistic affinity, and affiliation to sects and mystic orders.

Nationality

A major differentiation in Muslim society is between citizens and aliens in the political sense of the terms. The foreigners do not constitute a single homogeneous group but are divided on the basis of nationality. The Afghans alone are a sizeable group. They remain apparently unaffected by the changing spatial distribution of the Muslim population within the city due to the impact of the socio-political conditions of the country. Thus, they continue to inhabit the areas that the Muslims in general have had to vacate during the last two decades or so.

The Afghans are mostly money-lenders and appear to have little contact with others beyond the sphere of their business activities. Even where they live in predominantly Muslim localities, the stamp of foreignness on them does not allow the idea of neighbourhood (that the Islamic Great Tradition enjoins upon its followers) to develop between Afghans and the citizens of the country. Cases of marriage between Afghans and other categories of Muslims are very rare, and the few instances that are known show that such a marriage does not give the Afghans the full rights and obligations of a kin within the family of the bride; in fact, the woman gets alienated from the family of her orientation. The Afghans do not take part in any of the welfare activities of the Muslim community in the city and the two generally intermingle only in mosques and bi-annual congregations. The same pattern more or less holds good for other Muslims of alien nationality.

Regional Background

There is a considerable degree of exclusiveness on the basis of regional backgrounds. Regional groups with linguistic affinity interact a little more closely for obvious reasons. Thus, we find that Tamilians and Malayalis, who share a common Dravidian linguistic background, are closer to each other than to other Muslim groups. This affinity is mainly reflected in exclusive residence wherever possible, in collaboration or assistance in business and often rendering or abstaining from help in local welfare activities, etc. The language of inter-regional communication is Hindustani or some form of Urdu.

Sects

As a central discipline Islam does not encourage the emergence of sects within its fold, yet a variety of sects, sub-sects and socio-religious movements characterize the Muslim society of Calcutta. Being a metropolis of considerable importance, Calcutta serves as a centre for the dissemination of ideas including those based on religious trends of thought. Some of the more dynamic sects actively propagate their sect among other Muslims. I will briefly mention the main sects that exist and operate in the city and the popularity of these sects at different levels. The sects are as follows:

1. Sunni
   (i) Barelvi
   (ii) Deobandi
2. Shia
   (i) Atna Ashari
   (ii) Dawoodi Bohra
   (iii) Imami Ismaili Shia
3. Ahle-e-Hadith (Wahabi): A unified group, claiming to be strict followers of the Koran and the tradition (Shariat).
4. Ahmadia (Qadyani): The position of the Ahmadias as a sect within Islam has been controversial, since they are stated to undermine one of the fundamentals of Islam, namely *risalat*.

Besides these sects, there is a fairly prominent group of Muslims which believes in the futility of sectarian divisions and is critical of the system that vivisects Muslim society on flimsy grounds. The group derives inspiration from a few eminent scholars like Shah Waliullah who is particularly noted for toning down the animosity between the Shia and Sunni sects. Western education and the development of a feeling of unity among all Muslims in recent times are largely responsible for the emergence of this group. Yet it remains most unorganized and often appears in the form a collective consciousness at a sophisticated level only.

The Sunnis are by far the largest sectarian group, accounting for roughly 80 to 90 per cent of the Muslim population, followed by the Ahl-e-Hadiths and the Shias. The Ahmadias and Imami Ismaili Shias are the smallest, consisting of about 50 families each. The mosques or community centres, as in the case of Imami Ismaili Shias, serve as rallying points for the members of each sect. Generally, each sect has its separate mosque, some of which are more exclusive than others. This exclusiveness is more marked in the case of the three Shia sects as well as the Ahmadias. The last mentioned sect is the youngest of all and has a regular agency for propagating its religious peculiarities. The sects cut across regional and ethnic divisions and are a strong dividing force in the society in the sense that inter-sect marriages within the same ethnic group, though permissible, are often resisted. The emergence of new sects is also discouraged and often resisted.

Sectarian divisions are more marked among groups that are not wedded to a traditional occupation and are least organized on the basis of caste councils. The divisions are thus more marked among the Sayyads and Sheikhs than among the Mughals and Pathans, The groups drawn from higher Hindu castes are affected by sectarian divisions in a different manner. A few sects are exclusive to these groups. For example, the Dawoodi Bohra and Imami Ismaili Shia sects are almost exclusive to groups of this category. The Memons and the Qaum-e-Panjabian are almost exclusively Sunni. The present sectarian affiliation of the groups within the category is largely related to the history of their recruitment to Islam or the story of their origin. The subsequent categories consisting of groups with fixed occupational backgrounds are least affected by sectarian divisions. However, recent movements like Deobandism and Barelvism appear to be widely affecting the 'clean' occupational groups as they are affecting the categories above them.

The comparative numerical strength of the followers of these sects can be estimated from the number of mosques at the disposal of each. There is one mosque each for the Dawoodi Bohras, Imami Ismaili Shias and Ahmadias. The Atna Ashari Shia have five mosques (three in Metiaburj), the Sunni Deobandi about forty and the Sunni Barelvi have all the rest numbering around 500. The mosques of the last three sects are not exclusive though usually the members of the same sect use these mosques.

Thus it is evident that the decisive bulk of the Muslims belong to the Sunni sect of the Barelvi variety. This is highly significant because it is this sect that is least critical of the little tradition or the persistence of their pre-Islamic past, including the presence of caste-like elements. The Deobandis have however made considerable headway in improving their numerical strength in recent years (Siddiqui, 1974).

Khanquahs

Besides the sects, a number of hereditary mystic orders or *khanquahs* tracing their origin from, or affiliated to, various orders or *silsilahs* also characterize Muslim society in Calcutta. Most individuals either specially revere one of these *silsilahs* or register themselves as devotees of one of them. Some people do not consider attachment to a *silsilah* as being necessary; for others it is a must for individual salvation. The *silsilahs* are generally viewed as links through whom one must approach God; but the orthodox sects consider the belief in *silsilahs* to be against the very essence of Islam as they claim that Islam abolished all via media between man and God.

The mystic orders most prominent in the city are Qadria, Naqshbandia and Chishtia, named after their founder saints. The first has a large *khanquah* in central Calcutta and sub-centres at Kidderpur and Baniapukur. The chiefs of other *silsilahs*, known as *pirs*, visit the city from all parts of the country and rally their devotees, known as *mureeds*, around them. Certain ethnic groups specially revere certain *silsilahs*. The pastoralist groups, for example, generally revere the Naqshbandia and the Qalanders derive their name from the Qalandaria *silsilah* to which they are specially devoted. The Lal Begi derive their name from a Turkish saint, Lal Beg. Being a hereditary representative of his *silsilah*, a *pir* exercises considerable authority over the socio-religious life of his *mureeds* and serves as a rallying point for them as well as for a large number of Hindus. *Pirs* are mystics rather than theologians and are believed to have hereditary powers rather than acquired characteristics. Both these factors do not generally coincide in a single individual.

The history of the origin (or recruitment) of most ethnic groups in the second, third and fourth categories mentioned earlier is linked with one or other of the *silsilahs* in respect of which they perform special rituals either in the form of an *urs* or a *fateha*. It is worth noting that all the founders of these mystic orders belonged exclusively to categories that claim foreign origin—most of them are, in fact, Sayyads.

The nature of inter-relationship in the organization of the *khanquah* is based on a two-fold distinctions between the *pir* or the head and his disciples or *mureeds*. Among themselves the *mureeds* are equal and are known as *pir-bhais*. The inter-relationship between one order and the other is also not based on any hierarchical pattern. Theoretically, they all stand on the same footing (Siddiqui, 1974).

The Great Tradition

All Muslims share a belief in five fundamentals, namely, the unity of God, the prophethood of Muhammad, *namaz*, fasting in Ramadan and payment of *zakat*. The Shia sects add to these a sixth, i.e., a belief in the hereditary Imamate in one form or another.

It is difficult to estimate the proportion of people who actually perform the ritual aspects of these fundamentals, particularly the *namaz*, but a sense of belonging to a particular congregation as a unit exists. Except the Shias as well as the Ahmadias who, taken together, constitute a microscopic minority, all others come together at least in biannual congregations. The daily and weekly congregations of the Sunnis and Ahl-e-Hadiths are usually separate, but they can visit each other's mosques with greater freedom. The Shia mosques are separate and quite exclusive and the Sunnis and Ahl-e-Hadiths do not usually visit them.

There is no central agency for the levy and collection of *zakat* in Calcutta. Some charitable organizations, like orphanages, *madrasas* and welfare agencies, including hospitals, come forward with appeals for funds and these appeals are met with *zakat* funds. The bulk of the cost of religious primary education given in *madrasas* and mosques to children of the poor is largely met with *zakat* funds offered by individuals. At the primary stage such education is largely free from sectarian differences. A number of *maktabs* are run by the organizations or panchayats of various ethnic groups and preference is given in these institutions to the children of the group. The institutions run by organizations of a wider character also receive considerable attention from the community.

The recruitment of religious functionaries—like Imams or one who conducts the congregations in the mosque, and the *moazzin* who calls the faithful to attend prayers—is made on the basis of the capability of the individual for the job irrespective of the ethnic group he belongs to. Inside the mosque, or places where rituals within the sphere of the Islamic great tradition take place, distinctions based on birth or ascription are not evident.

Attributes of Caste

The ethnic groups are variously called *qaum*, *beradari*, *jat* or *zat* and *jamaat*. While these terms have various meanings, they are applied by the groups strictly in the sense of *jati*.[5] The difference in terminology reflects only regional and linguistic variations. *Qaum* is generally used by groups from the North-western region, including Delhi and Punjab. The Gujaratis from the northern region as well as Rajasthan use both *jat* and *beradari* to denote their groups. It is worth mentioning that the term *beradari* is also used to mean a small unit of kins inside an ethnic group within which marriage relationships are usually confined. It is in this narrower sense that the term is more often used within the groups in the first category, while all the rest use the term to mean the entire ethnic group in the city or elsewhere.

[5]'A *jati* is a named group usually spread over a wide territory roughly occupying, *vis-a-vis* other such categories, the same position in the caste hierarchy of a region. Members of a *jati* have roughly the same traditional occupation and may have such rituals and myths in common" (Cohn, 1968:3).

Nature of Ethnic Groups

The groups are of the nature of descent groups with or without occupational specialization. Even those members of a group who give up their traditional occupation to adopt a new one are bound together on the basis of their former occupational background and express unity with those sections of their group that continue to pursue the old calling. Each group has a name which its members use as a surname—a practice observed more frequently in the urban setting than elsewhere. A conscious attempt to adopt a suitable surname where it did not exist earlier is an interesting feature of many groups, such as butchers, cotton carders and grocers. Some other occupational groups have decided to adopt the surnames of groups in the higher stratum. Thus, the Maliks from Bihar have started claiming Sayyad as their title, and the Churihar and, even the Chirimar, have resolved to adopt Siddiqui as a title. Surnames are symbols of equality of status within the group and of prestige outside the group.

The members of most groups remain in contact with the area of their origin, though some do so more than others. South Indian groups generally maintain a more intimate relationship with the areas of their origin than the others. Except for a few families, the Malayalis in Calcutta remain detached from their families, and their marriages usually take place at home. The few cases of marriages between Malayali Muslims and others which have occurred in Calcutta are exceptions. The Tamilians, in spite of their long history of contact and relative prosperity, remain attached to their home where they go back for marriages and family rituals. The comparative attachment of a group to the area of its origin normally indicates a proportionate degree of detachment from the social environment of its habitat in the city.

Endogamy

Each ethnic group is endogamous and it is from amongst one's own group that actual or potential kins come. Class considerations enter into the establishment of marriage relationships, particularly where material advancement is not uniform, but marriages among subgroups are allowed by most ethnic groups. Inter-ethnic marriages, in spite of any similarity in class status, are severely discouraged. It is only at the higher levels, i.e., groups of the first block, that intermarriages take place more frequently, particularly among the smaller sects like the Shias or Ahmadias. At all other levels it meets with discouragement ranging from mere disapproval to ostracism depending upon the strength of the *jati* panchayat. Some sort of sanctity is attached to the purity of descent as is evident from the use of such terms as *sudh* as against *bisser* or impure, *najib-ut-tarfain* and *sahiun nasl* as against *birre* or *birrahe*, i.e., of mixed descent. The *sudh* or pure among all groups enjoy greater prestige than the *bisser* or mixed ones. The *sudh* and the *bisser* or *birre* have no other alternative but to remain within their subgroups.

Hypergamy is allowed among the groups of the first category, particularly the Sayyads and Sheikhs. But their progeny do not get the full status of their father and are known as 'Sayyadzada' or 'Sheikhzada'. They are supposed to establish kinship only with people of similar status. The material prosperity of such people in a city often appears to make good for the inferiority of their status but the social stigma is not removed easily.

The belief in the purity of descent presupposes that a violation of descent is impure or polluting. In spite of the emphasis on egalitarianism, the collective conscience is unfavourably disposed towards inter-ethnic marriages and generally disapproves of them, though, of course, in varying degrees at different levels. The rationale for this is varied at various levels ranging from mere compliance with customary practices and the necessity of occupational training to the permissive character of the Koranic verse which is interpreted to mean that groups are intended to demonstrate distinctions between one another.

Caste Councils

A *jati* council or panchayat is a normal prerequisite for a *jati*. In Calcutta we come across such panchayat organizations of varying strength at different levels. There is a striking absence of any such organization in all the groups of the first category which maintain themselves through collective sentiments and status consciousness. In the second category, group panchayats in the form of formalized group organizations are common and membership in them is compulsory. Leaders are elected. Economically dominant as the groups within this category are, their organizations generally combine welfare activities for the group with other regular panchayat activities. Linking the panchayat with larger councils elsewhere, collecting demographic details of group members and maintaining mosques and burial grounds belonging to the group are among their main functions.

Their organizational and functional features assume the pattern of guild-cum-caste councils although all of them do not necessarily follow a particular line of trade. Defiance and violation of caste norms are not very rare but the tradition of the respective groups are maintained by and large.

Amongst groups in the subsequent categories the panchayats are stronger. The groups that continue to pursue traditional occupations, at least partially, have the most effective panchayats dominated generally by hereditary leadership. As the members of each such ethnic group are drawn from a wide area in the region, they form several panchayats, each based on a particular village or group of villages. Several such panchayats form a larger council in a sort of confederation on the all-Calcutta level. The Qureshis have twelve such panchayats while the Rais have twenty-two. The head of the panchayat, called Sardar or Choudhri, is assisted by the Charidar or staff-bearer for corrective and other purposes. There are unwritten conventions relating to the convening of meetings and their deliberations. The Choudhri weilds enormous powers and in most groups, such as the Qureshi, Chik, Mansuri, Churihar, Dafali, Qalandar and also Lal Begi, this post is hereditary. A few groups, like the Rais, have recently started electing their leaders. The village or area based panchayats in Calcutta remain in living touch with the areas they come from and work as units of larger councils in the city. Among the Momin (Ansari) and Ranki (Iraqi) this institution has weakened considerably. However, the strong tradition of panchayat reasserts itself when an eventuality arises among the members of these groups. The purely Bengali groups, like Darzis and Nikaris, also have councils but they are not very strong.

At the regional level, the Rajasthani ethnic groups have strong panchayats that function when members assemble on occasions relating to the life cycle of a member and to ostracize and readmit members. The Malayalis have an association of a voluntary nature that assumes a certain amount of responsibility for the entire group. The Tamilians have no such formal association. The Peshawaris have a common panchayat for Awan, Kakazai, and Kashmiri Peshawaris. The Sayyads and Pakhtoons have none. The united panchayat of the Peshawari groups has come in vogue since these groups, have started intermarrying under the pressure of the political situation as a resnlt of which are more or less cut off from the areas of their origin.

In short, the caste panchayat is a must for all groups that follow a 'clean' or 'unclean' traditional occupation and are generally capable of asserting themselves effectively. It is also present among the groups drawn from superior Hindu castes though it is not very strong; while it is absent from groups of the first category.

Food and Pollution

The most common pattern of interdining is the one which is confined to one's kin group or known range within the ethnic group. The size of the ethnic group also determines the range and composition of usual commensal groups. The symbolic ritual equality of the members of an ethnic group is expressed in such terms as *tat* or *chatai* upon which members can sit, smoke and eat together. Expelled members lose the right to such equality. This phenomenon is observed among the Qureshi, Chik, Mansuri, Dafali and other occupational groups. Distinctions between *beradari* and non-*beradari* are usual, though not always in matters of seating arrangements which generally follows the class pattern. Among the economically higher classes, interdining in all aspects follows the class pattern with considerable bias in favour of one's kins and ethnic group. Among regional groups this is replaced by a regional bias, though the Rajasthani groups cannot ignore castemen.

The idea of pollution in matters of interdining is limited to 'clean' castes who will not dine with 'unclean' ones. Restrictions in interdining either among the groups in the first three categories or in respect of each other are not generally observed and are stated to be non-existent. Members of groups within these categories do not eat or drink with the Lal Begis. The latter can, however, receive all sorts of food from the former. The Dafalis, who work as priests for the Lal Begis, or the Qalandars, who sometimes live in their neighbourhood, refuse to accept food or water from the Lal Begis. Among groups in the other categories, the women are believed to observe more restrictions in interdining than men.

Ranking

Ranking is both a matter of a large measure of consensus and of practical operation. The realities of the urban setting tend to make their influence felt in this sphere and it will be futile to search for a perfect and consistent system of ranking on the basis of our model among the Muslims in Calcutta. The comparative numerical strength of the various categories is also an important factor in this connection. In the absence of exact figures for each category it is not possible to be precise, but it is not difficult for a careful observer to note the greater amount of concentration in the category consisting of groups with 'clean' occupational backgrounds who constitute over 80 per cent of the total. Despite these problems, it is possible to observe the presence of a fairly consistent system of ranking. Descent is an important factor in assigning rank, and those of foreign origin enjoy higher privileges and prestige. The Sayyads are by common consent assigned the highest position with the privilege of hypergamy. Those who enter into kinship with the Sayyads enjoy a similar status on the basis of descent. The position of *pirs*, who command the greatest respect and veneration of their disciples, is always and invariably occupied by the people of the first category. In this respect the remaining categories occupy the position of clients to the former (Table 1).

TABLE 1
Ethnic Groups with/without Caste Organization Hierarchically shown with Sect[6] Affiliation

Hierarchical Order	*Sect*	*Groups without Caste Organization*	*Groups with Formalized/ Weak Caste Organizations*	*Groups with Traditional Caste/Sectarian Organization of Considerable Strength*
1	2	3	4	5
I	Sunni Shia Ahl-e-Hadith Ahmadia	Sayyad Sheikh Mughal Pathan		
II	Sunni	North-Western Region Kashmiri	Northern Region (Gangetic Valley and Delta) Qaum-e-Panjabian (Delhi)	
	Ahl-e-Hadith	Northern Region (Gangetic Valley and Delta) Mallok	Qaum-e-Panjabian (Anwala) Panjabi (Rajputs)	
	Ahmadia	Southern Region (Tamil)	North-Western Region (Peshawari)	Western Region
		Maraykar	Awan	Dawoodi Bohra
		Rawther	Kakazai	Imami-Ismaili Shia
		Labbai	Kalal Kashmiri Peshawari Southern Region (Malayali) Musalliyar Mapilla Rawther Keyei	

[6]No hierarchical order has been shown within the sectarian organizations.

1	2	3	4	5
			Western Region Memon (Kachi) Memon (Halai)	
III	Sunni		Northern Region (Gangetic Valley and Delta) Momin (Ansari) Ranki (Iraqi) Darzi Nikari Patua Besuti	Northern Region (Gangetic Valley and Delta) Qureshi Chik Rai Mansuri Churihar Hajjam Dhobi Mirshikar Dafali Qalandar Fakir (Shah) Sheikhjee Meo Ghosi Western Region Nilgar (Shekhawati and Madi) Manihar Sonar Lohar Teli Dhobi
IV	Sunni			Northern Region (Gangetic Valley and Delta) Lal Begi (Sweeper)

Certain occupations are rated higher and others lower and in this respect the groups engaged in the occupations of ruling and fighting occupy the next highest position after the first category. Their economic position in the city often persuades them to assume a position only below the Sayyads and equal to the rest of the groups in the first category. Foreign descent, however, remains a matter of respect for most groups in this category and the fact that their position is that of clients to the former category, their place in the hierarchy comes only after the first category, about which there is a more or less general agreement.

Groups with fixed traditional occupations implying varying degrees of manual work and suggesting a large measure of dependence on others are assigned a low position in the social hierarchy. There is confusion in the hierarchical position of each group *vis-a-vis* others in the category but the position of the category as a whole is not much in dispute. Their influx in disproportionately large numbers into the city and the enormous swelling of their ranks tells its own story of suppression and depression both socially and economically. Considerable numbers in each group in this category, having freed themselves from the traditional bondage, have gained economic prosperity and due to changes in the political set-up have assumed the leadership of Muslim society. Yet, in spite of this change, their position of clients in relation to the *pirs* of the first category and the stigma of service to others attached to their traditional occupation, past or present, remains. It is at this level that some of the most virulent caste mobility movements are observable and manifest themselves in the adoption of pure Arab surnames and pedigrees, while the social systems of a few groups retain the basic structural elements of the *jati.* The Lal Begis, however, passively accept the lowest position in the last category on account of their being unclean and they often experience difficulty in getting their dead buried in the common Muslim burial ground.

Conclusions

Summing up we note that the Islamic Great Tradition does not attach significance to ascription of status and stresses the egalitarian mode of inter-relationships. This is true both of recruitment to the posts of religious functionaries and of the performance of rituals in accordance with the Shariat. In the sphere of the *tariqat*, however, the birth ascribed position of the *pir* in relation to the *mureed* is noticeable, though theoretically it is possible to attain the status of *pir* if a *pir* of the first block delegates his spiritual powers to one belonging to another block.

The structure of Muslim society bearing relevance to marriage, kinship and to political organization, characterized by the group panchayat, however, is mainly based on a number of ethnic groups whose members are recruited on the basis of birth. It is impossible for an individual to be legitimately called a Sayyad, a Momin, a Rai, a Qureshi, or a Lal Begi without having been born into the respective group. These are, therefore, closed groups in the form of *jatis*, known variously as *qaum*, *beradari*, *jamaat* or *zat*. Most of them have their own stories of origin and generally perform common rituals in the form of *fatehas*, *urs* or *taziyas*, etc. The relationship between these groups is basically tolerant.

Certain elements of restriction in interdining are present, though there is a good deal of laxity in interdining between the higher and the intermediate blocks and the ideal norms of the caste system in this regard are not elaborate. This is not only due to the egalitarian influence of the Islamic Great Tradition, but also due to the compelling factors of urban life in a cosmopolitan setting.

The basic elements of a system of ranking similar to the caste system are present. Most groups are aware of others, particularly in a regional framework, though not all of them know about each other. The four categories or blocks starting from the Sayyads and others of foreign origin are hierarchically arranged. The positions of the highest and the lowest are agreed to by more or less common consent. The position of the two intermediate blocks also becomes clear when we take into consideration the generally agreed principles on which the hierarchy is based—descent and nature of occupation.

The suggestion of the existence of an hierarchical order is generally overtly denied due to the influence of the Great Tradition, but it is observed in their covert behaviour as well as in certain aspects of the system of beliefs. However, when the anomalies between ideal and practice were pointed out, the

Muslim respondents agreed about the real situation.

Sectarian groupings align various groups cutting across ethnic and regional boundaries, but this is the characteristic feature of the upper categories, particularly the first one. Others remain largely unaffected. In spite of the existence of a caste-like hierarchy and sectarian segments, certain basic principles of the Great Tradition are reflected in the sphere of religion which, specially in the form of mass congregations, give a sense of unity to the decisive bulk of the Muslims in Calcutta.

A good deal of corporateness surrounds the mystic orders or *khanquahs* under the leadership of *pirs* who belong to the first block, particularly the Sayyads and the Sheikhs.

The *jati* panchayats or councils are absent in the highest block, they are present in a weak form in the next block and are generally very strong among the groups in the subsequent blocks.

Although there is a conspicuous absence of the myths underlying the Hindu *varna* system, the model is found to be unconsciously followed and is structurally operative in the Muslim society. Besides, the egalitarian character of Islam, with its own story of human origin and concepts of time and space, works against social and political iniquities which are found more in the urban situation than elsewhere.

The Muslim society in the field of our observation obviously exemplifies the meeting point of two systems—the cultural ideology of Islam and the social ideas of caste stratification, characterizing the pan-Indian civilization. The former prevails within the obligatory and tabooed ranges of the Shariat and the latter within the secular realm of socio-economic inter-relationships beyond the two ranges where the Shariat does not positively enforce a specified code of conduct. These two systems of a basically divergent nature interact in a way so as to make each adaptive of the other. For example, ethnic endogamy finds its justification from the pseudo-religious pre-Islamic concept of *kufv*, the meaning of which is extended at some levels to include the entire ethnic group. The violation of this ethnic purity termed as 'matching the bones' in case of at least several ethnic groups, resulting in the formation of sub-groups with considerable loss of social, though not ritual, status is a further example of this adaptiveness. It is argued that it is within the permissive range of Islamic egalitarianism to contract inter-ethnic marriages but desisting from such a practice and forming a sub-group for the purpose of marriage and kinship is not forbidden either. It is, however, clear that though the *letter* of the Shariat is not get grossly violated, the same cannot be said of the *spirit*, particularly in the sphere of the structural organization (Siddiqui, 1974).

Thus, the model of the society that emerges out of the interaction of the two systems does not bear perfect identity with the system of caste, yet the model has roughly harmonized some of the main structural features of caste and is obviously a variant of the caste system.

Bibliography

Ahmad, Zarina (1962), 'Muslim Caste in Uttar Pradesh', *Economic Weekly*, 14, pp. 325-36

Ansari, Ghaus (1956), 'Muslim Caste in India', *Eastern Anthropologist*, 9, pp. 104-11.

———(1960), *Muslim Caste in Uttar Pradesh: A Study in Culture Contact*, Lucknow, Ethnographic and Folk Culture Society.

Bose, N.K. (1958), 'Some Aspects of Caste in Bengal', *Man in India*, 38, pp. 73-97.

Cohn, B.S. (1968), 'Notes on the History of the Study of Indian Society', in Milton Singer and B.S. Cohn (eds.), *Structure and Change in Indian Society*, Chicago, Aldine Publishing Company.

Crooke, William (1906), *Tribes and Castes of the North-Western Provinces and Oudh*, 4 vols., Calcutta, Office of the Superintendent of Government Printing

Elliot, Sir Henry M. (1869), *Memoirs of the History, Folklore and Distribution of the Races of the North-Western Provinces of India*, 2 vols. London, Trubner.

Grunebaum, G.E. von (1961), *Medieval Islam: A Study in Cultural Orientation*, Chicago, Chicago University Press.

Gupta, Raghuraj (1956), 'Caste Ranking and Inter-Caste Relations among the Muslims of a village in North-western U.P.', *Eastern Anthropologist*, 10, pp. 30-42.

Hutton, John H. (1946), *Caste in India: Its Nature, Function and Origin*, Cambridge, Cambridge University Press.

Ibbetson, Sir Denzil Charles (1920), *Punjab Castes*, Lahore, Superintendent of Government Printing.

Iyer, L. Ananth Krishna (1909), *The Cochin Tribes and Castes*, Madras, Higginbotham.

Khan, Zillur (1968), 'Caste and Muslim Peasantry in India and Pakistan', *Man in India*, 47, pp. 138-48.

Marriott, McKim (1960), *Caste Ranking and Community Structure in Five Regions of India and Pakistan*, Deccan College Monograph Series No. 23, Poona, Deccan College Post-Graduate and Research Institute.

Nesfield, J.C. (1885) Brief View of Caste System of the North-West Provinces and Oudh, Allahabad, Government Press.

Risley, Sir Robert H. (1891), *Tribes and Castes of Bengal: Ethnographic Glossary*, 2 vols., Calcutta, Government Printing Press.

Rose, Horace A (1911), *A Glossary of the Tribes and Castes of the Punjab and the North-West Frontier Provinces*, 3 vols., Lahore, Government Printing Press.

Russell, Robert V. and Hiralal (1916). *The Tribes and Castes of the Central Provinces of India*, 4 vols., Nagpur, Government Printing Press.

Siddiqui, M.K.A. (1974), *Muslims of Calcutta: A Study in Aspects of their Social Organization*, Calcutta, Anthropological Survey of India.

Sinha, Surajit (1967), 'Caste in India: Its Essential Pattern of Socio-cultural Integration', in Anthony de Reuck and Julie Knight (eds.), *Caste and Race: A Comparative Approach*, London, Ciba Foundation.

Srinivas, M.N. (1964), 'Social Structure', *The Gazetteer of India*, vol. 1, Delhi, Manager of Publications, Government of India.

Thurston, Edgar (1909), *Castes and Tribes of South India*, 7 vols., Madras, Government Press.

Weber, Max (1947), *From Max Weber: Essays in Sociology*, H.H. Gerth and C.W. Mills (eds. and trans.), London, Routledge and Kegan Paul.

12

The Concept and Ideology of Caste among the Muslims of Rural West Bengal[1]

Ranjit K. Bhattacharya

There is a widely held view that the system of caste stratification is a characteristic feature of Hindu social organization, and that other religious communities in India are organized on the basis of egalitarian principles. There is some truth in this view, especially since the Hindu social philosophy and ideology alone endorse the rigid status inequalities inherent in a caste system. Other religious traditions are egalitarian in their ideology and decry gradation of social groups on the basis of birth. Nevertheless, the ideological egalitarianism propagated by several of the non-Hindu religious traditions, such as Islam and

[1]This paper is based on research carried out by the author in connection with a research project of the Anthropological Survey of India on the Changing Social Structure and Cultural Pattern of the Muslims of Rural and Urban Bengal. I am grateful to the Survey for the grant of a Senior Research Fellowship which made this study possible and to Dr. Surajit Sinha, Deputy Director of the Survey, for his continued guidance throughout this research and for helpful suggestions and advice in the preparation of this paper. I am also thankful to Dr. D.K. Sen, Director, Anthropological Survey of India, for providing me with excellent research facilities during my tenure as Fellow in the Survey. An earlier version of this paper was presented at a seminar in the Anthropological Survey of India in 1969.

Christianity, has been compromized in varying degrees in the Indian social setting and their adherents have come to share certain attributive notions of high and low so elaborately formulated by the Hindus. Even while rejecting the hierarchical gradations inherent in the system of caste stratification, they have come to accept the social segmentation of the caste system as practised among the Hindus as natural and abide by its numerous restrictions. In this paper, I shall describe certain caste-like features in the social stratification system of the Muslims of rural West Bengal.

Since the system of social stratification analyzed here shares certain features of the caste system but is not quite like it, I have chosen to designate it as a system of inter-ethnic[2] stratification in order to distinguish it from the caste system proper. I shall first begin with a general discussion of the different phases of fieldwork through which my understanding of the Muslim system of inter-ethnic stratification evolved, and the methodological and conceptual difficulties I encountered in grasping its precise nature and character. Then, I go on to describe the system as it is generally verbalized and conceptualized by the local people. Lastly, I explore the caste-like features of that system and compare it with the caste system as it has been found to exist among the Hindus of rural West Bengal and elsewhere in the country. I should like to add that the paper has been written somewhat autobiographically not because the facts observed could not be presented otherwise, but rather because this mode of presentation seemed to offer a fruitful way of setting out the difficulties faced and the solutions attempted during the course of study.

Tackling the Problem

My understanding of the system of inter-ethnic stratification

[2]I use the term 'ethnic group' in this paper in the same sense as Marriott. According to him, 'An ethnic. . . is a hereditary group within a society which is defined by its members and by others as a separate people, socially, biologically and culturally; it need not be distinguishable in objective fact by any unique complex of cultural or biological traits' (Marriott, 1960:2).

among the Muslims of rural West Bengal evolved through three phases of field experience.[3] The first phase began in January 1966, and lasted unfil middle of that year. During this period, I carried out a study of how production was related to the socio-economic organizations of the different religious communities in three adjacent village communities called Bergram, Debagram Manjhi Para and Khiruli under the Bholpur police station of the Birbhum district in West Bengal. These villages are located in a predominantly Hindu cultural zone, but they are characterized by the presence of three distinct cultural and religious traditions. Bergram is a predominantly Hindu village and closely resembles the other Hindu villages of this area. Debagram Manjhi Para is a tribal village and is dominated by a tribal cultural tradition belonging to the Santal tribe. On the other hand, Khiruli is a Sheikh dominated Muslim village and is characterized by the presence of an Islamic religious tradition in an otherwise Hindu dominated cultural milieu.

Quite early in the course of this study of the relationship between production and socio-religious organization, I came to realize that each of the three villages studied was characterized by the presence of a distinct pattern of social stratification. Bergram, with its predominantly Hindu population, contained seven named, endogamous caste groups arranged according to a local version of the *varna* order into a locally accepted social hierarchy. Each caste group observed certain restrictions on commensality with the other groups and membership in the caste was based on birth. Besides, the system of castes in Bergram had a characteristic division of labour associated with specific caste vocations (*brittis*). Specialization of occupations by castes was openly emphasized in the local situation by requiring certain castes to engage in particular occupations and by prohibiting the higher castes from direct involvement in manual labour and certain other agricultural activities (Bhattacharya, 1968). Moreover, the members of the different caste groups tended to live in separate parts of the village, and this spatial

[3]These three phases of fieldwork were spread over a period of three years between January 1966, and February 1969. The first phase lasted from January to May 1966; the second from February to May 1967; and the third from November 1967 to February 1969.

segregation of castes was graphically reflected in the physical structure and layout of the village.

The seven caste groups of Bergram were again grouped together according to prescribed ways into two larger categories called the *bhadralok* (gentry) and *chhotolok* (lowly). These categories were formed by stratifying the caste groups into two main blocks, namely, high or clean and low castes, and formed a highly functional and structurally simple division of the village society. But the boundaries of the *bhadralok* and *chhotolok* categories were quite fixed and permanent and depended on caste status. For one thing, membership in these categories was based on a person's caste status which depended on birth and heredity (Bhattacharya, 1968; Sinha and Bhattacharya, 1969). Secondly, the categories closely followed a differential pattern of wealth and power distribution in the village and in this respect they were again closely linked to caste status. It was, thus, nearly impossible for anyone to change one's status from one category to another without a corresponding change in caste status.

The tribal village of Debagram Manjhi Para presented no observable distinctions comparable to the rigid caste stratification found in Bergram. The Santals of the village were divided into eight clans (*khuts*) which were arranged into a traditional hierarchy based on the mythological notion of the order of their appearance on earth. But this traditional hierarchy had no concrete social function in the village, and it certainly did not serve to stratify the population of the village in any definite order of social precedence. There were also no observable economic class distinctions among the residents of the village since they all belonged to the class of agricultural labourers. In sum, the clans could not be equated to the caste groups found in Bergram and they could also not be said to be linked in any formal system of economic or social interdependence so characteristic of Bergram. Even while belonging to eight different clans, all the residents of Debagram Manjhi Para thus operated as a socially undifferentiated and homogeneous tribal group within the context of their village (Bhattacharya, 1968).

Khiruli presented a social situation which seemed at first to be somewhat similar to that of the Santals of Debagram Manjhi Para. The Khiruli Muslims were all Sheikhs and they lacked any clear-cut social stratification comparable to the system of castes in Bergram. They were economically stratified into *baralok* (rich) and *garib* (poor), but these categories were more economic than social in nature. Moreover, unlike the categories of *bhadralok* and *chhotolok* among the Hindus of Bergram, the categories of *baralok* and *garib* were quite fluid and flexible. The somewhat fluid character of the *baralok* and *garib* divisions among the Khiruli Muslims and their repeated assertions that they did not stratify their society into a hierarchical order so characteristic of the Hindus of the area, suggested the absence of a rigid system of social stratification among them. Indeed, with all the Muslims belonging to the single Sheikh category, the village had an aura of castelessness and created the impression that the Muslims constituted, like the Santals of Debagram Manjhi Para, an undifferentiated and unstratified community.

Nearly a year after the first phase of fieldwork, I returned to the village of Khiruli and stayed there for another period of three-and-a-half months. This time I confined my attention almost entirely to the social structure and cultural patterns of the Muslims with a view to gathering some more detailed information about the system of social stratification obtaining among them. During this phase of fieldwork, I came to know about the existence of a few other Muslim ethnic groups who lived in villages around Khiruli, but not more than two such ethnic groups were found to live in any single village in the entire region. Scattered over a number of villages, these different ethnic groups naturally lacked any systematic and regular hierarchical interaction amongst themselves. Furthermore, my Muslim informants once again tended to emphasize their egalitarian Islamic tradition and ideology and asserted that, unlike the local Hindu population, they did not stratify their social organization into a hierarchical order of high and low castes. Lack of systematic hierarchical interaction among the different ethnic groups and the emphasis placed by the local Muslims on social egalitarianism in their social life thus confirmed my earlier impression about the absence of social gradations in the local Muslim society. I concluded, therefore, that the Muslims in the area did not possess a system of caste stratification comparable to the caste system among the Hindus.

Later on I had the opportunity of revisiting Khiruli several times and stayed there for a further period of seven months to further explore the nature of social stratification among the local Muslim ethnic groups. During this prolonged stay in the village it became gradually evident that the extreme emphasis placed by the local Muslims on the ideas of Islamic brotherhood and social equality was actually a social mechanism designed for the promotion of their communal solidarity and for the preservation of their separate social identity *vis-a-vis* the other religious communities in the area, especially the numerically and culturally dominant Hindus. In sharp contrast to their claim of adherence to an egalitarian Great Tradition and social ideology, they shared an attributive notion of highness and lowness regarding their different ethnic groups and roughly graded the local Muslim population into an hierarchical order. Each Muslim ethnic group was ranked into a definite social hierarchy, and the social rank accorded to a group depended on certain ascriptive criteria associated with its general style of life. Even though the specific criteria applied in the evaluation of each ethnic group were not the same, the social stratification system was nevertheless sufficiently closed, thereby disallowing rapid social mobility so characteristic of open and relatively egalitarian social systems.

Usually one tends to see a new social situation in terms of certain preconceived notions. The initial error in my understanding of the real nature of the system of social stratification among the Muslims of rural West Bengal arose from such a misconception. My endeavour from the very beginning had been to understand the system of inter-ethnic stratification among the Muslims in the area in relation to the system of caste stratification as it was found among the Hindus of Bergram. This led me into certain initial difficulties, especially since the different Muslim ethnic groups in the local area were scattered discretely over a number of villages and did not operate in terms of a specific and systematic hierarchical interaction. Moreover, as I found out later, the consciousness of an egalitarian Great Tradition made the Muslims avoid any explicit and direct reference to social facts which were considered contrary to Koranic texts and Islamic ideology. This attitude was yet another unfavourable factor in conceptualizing the real nature of the system of social stratification among the local Muslims. Nevertheless, these initial difficulties led me to a creative exercise of exploring the field situation from as many different angles as possible in order to overcome the earlier error of judgment, namely, that the Muslims of the area constituted an undifferentiated and homogeneous community. It showed that the social stratification among the Muslims had a somewhat illusive quality about it and it could be analyzed and understood only outside the framework of the philosophy and ideology of the Great Tradition.

Ethnic Categories

Let us now turn to a consideration of the different ethnic groups of Muslims in the area and the system of social stratification prevalent among them. It has already been pointed out that Khiruli has an exclusively Sheikh population and no other Muslim ethnic group lives there. Nevertheless, the Sheikh residents of the village are quite familiar with members of some other ethnic groups who live in neighbouring villages in the area. For example, during informal discussions on the ethnic divisions among the local Muslims and their hierarchical positions, my Sheikh respondents at Khiruli mentioned that there were four ethnic groups among the Muslims in the local area. These four main ethnic groups were said to be the Sayyads, Sheikhs, Pathans and Mughals. Each of these ethnic groups is referred to as a *jat*, a colloquial abbreviation of the word *jati* meaning caste. Each ethnic group also lives in a separate village though there are some villages in which more than one ethnic groups live together. There are, however, significant differences in the proportion of the different Muslim groups in the local population.

The Sayyads are a small numerical minority in the entire region and are confined to only one village within a radius of about fifteen miles from Khiruli. It is called Khastigiri and lies about ten miles West of Khiruli under the Sainthia Police Station. There are two families of Sayyads in that village and they claim to be the linear descendants of a very prominent local Muslim saint who is supposed to have come from the family of a Persian king some generations ago. There are no other Sayyad families anywhere else in the whole region, and the local Muslims' information about the Sayyads is based only on their contact with, and knowledge of, the Sayyads of Khastigiri. My single Sayyad informant also belonged to the same village. A very sophisticated and educated person with a graduate degree from Calcutta University, he avoided any clear-cut reference to the apparently anti-Islamic inter-ethnic inequalities among the local Muslims. However, in his daily life he quietly conforms to caste prejudices and conventions of inequalities implicit in the local social organization.

The Sheikhs are a somewhat more numerous group and are dispersed fairly widely throughout the area. For example, apart from the inhabitants of Khiruli who are all Sheikhs, the members of that ethnic group also live in the majority of the villages in the surrounding region. There are seven villages within the immediate neighbourhood of Khiruli wherein the Sheikhs constitute an almost exclusive ethnic group of Muslims, while in four other villages they live along with other Muslim groups and Hindu castes. The Sheikhs at Khiruli are, therefore, naturally better informed about the relative social standing of their own group and its social customs and practices, and they tend to assert their importance over the other ethnic groups in the area, especially the Pathans and Mughals whom they regard as somewhat lower in social position.

The Pathans and Mughals are much less numerous than the Sheikhs and are confined to only a few villages in the region. For example, there are only two families of Mughals (locally known by their surname Mirza) in a village at a distance of about five miles from Khiruli. The Pathans too are similarly confined to a single village situated in the neighbourhood of Khiruli. It has a Pathan population of about forty families and the Pathans of the village celebrate Muharram together with the Sheikhs of Khiruli and Kasba, a mixed Hindu-Muslim village adjoining the Pathan village of Keshabpur. The Sheikhs of Khiruli are much more aware of the presence of the Pathans than they are of the Mughals. The Pathans are bi-lingual and speak both a corrupt form of Urdu and the local form of Bengali unlike the local Hindus and other Muslims who speak only Bengali. Moreover, they are also somewhat distinctive in their physical features and differ from local Hindus and Muslims in their physical appearance. However, these distinctive physical features are generally overlooked by the local population in their evaluation of the Pathans and they are treated as indigenous to the area as the other Muslim ethnic groups.

To begin with, the Sheikh respondents at Khiruli had mentioned the existence of the Sayyads, Sheikhs, Mughals and Pathans as the Muslim ethnic groups found in the area, but during the latter part of my stay in the field I came to know about the presence of three other Muslim ethnic groups. These were the Shahs or Shah Fakirs, the Momins or Julahas, and the Patuas or Potos. The Shah Fakirs, as their name implies, are religious mendicants and engage in the traditional occupation of religious begging. The Momins are traditionally weavers, but in this region they do not engage in their traditional calling any more and are agricultural labourers. The Momins are not indigenous to this area. Originally belonging to Bihar where the weavers are found in large numbers, they came to this area as agricultural labourers and settled here as time passed. The Momins work largely as agricultural labourers while their womenfolk either engage in agricultural work as labourers or are itinerary vegetable-sellers.

The Patuas or Potos are usually regarded as half Muslims and half Hindus by the local people. In fact, local respondents say that the Patuas serve as a bridge between the members of the two religious communities as they are a Muslim group but perform services which are utilized largely by the Hindus. The Patuas' anomalous position in the local social structure is partly a consequence of their traditional occupation—they are engaged in the traditional occupation of painting Hindu gods and goddesses used for ceremonial worship. The Patuas, however, are believers in Islam and they consider themselves to be Muslims like everybody else. Their women are itinerary traders in cosmetics.

The fact that the Sheikhs of Khiruli knew about the existence of these ethnic groups but refrained from mentioning them suggested to me the possibility that a clear-cut line of social distance separated them. In order, therefore, to be able to gather some information about these ethnic groups and to personally contact some of their members, I found it necessary to extend my fieldwork to thirteen neighbouring villages. Even though these villages could not be studied intensively, some basic genealogical and demographic data were collected regarding their caste composition, their size, and the general economic condition of the castes or ethnic categories residing in them. Some of these data are presented in Table 1.

Social Hierarchy

Each ethnic group described above is also a status group, that is, it is ranked and occupies a position of social superiority or inferiority in relation to other ethnic groups. But while the idea of hierarchy is commonly shared by all the Muslims in the local area, the precise position of each ethnic group in the social hierarchy is not always clear and well-defined. In fact, there is often considerable disagreement among the members of the different ethnic groups regarding the relative social standing of their group. This disagreement arises from two somewhat closely related reasons. Firstly, except for the Sayyads whose social position as the highest in the social hierarchy is widely recognized, the different ethnic groups in the area are not ranked according to any definite and rigorous set of criteria. Secondly, the members of the different ethnic groups are geographically dispersed and live in different local hierarchies. Under the circumstances, they naturally do not form an interacting social field and their members are not bound by common obligatory behaviour toward one another. Each ethnic group in the region therefore sees the social hierarchy and its own position in it somewhat differently than the others.

The Sheikhs of Khiruli whom I interviewed first regarding the relative social ranking of the different ethnic groups in the area roughly divided the seven ethnic groups mentioned above into two strata resembling the Hindu stratification of the castes in the region into the *bhadralok* and *chhotolok* categories. The ethnic groups are distributed into the following strata:

(a) The upper stratum, analogous to the *bhadralok* among the Hindus, includes the Sayyads, Sheikhs, Pathans and Mughals.

(b) The lower stratum, analogous to the *chhotolok* among

the Hindus, includes the religious mendicants called the Shah Fakirs, the Momins, and the painter Patuas (Sinha and Bhattacharya, 1969:55).

The similarity between these strata and the *bhadralok-chhotolok* division among the Hindus of rural West Bengal is clearly indicated by the line of social distance that divides the four ethnic groups of the upper stratum and the rest. Nevertheless, the interaction between the members of these two strata is not built up systematically into any hierarchical order of relationships. This is so partly because the ethnic groups belonging to the upper and the lower strata do not usually live in the same village in the region,[4] and partly because they are not organically linked with one another like the Hindu *bhadralok* and *chhotolok* castes in building up the structure of local social and economic life. Moreover, apart from the factors of residential pattern and economic relationships, the egalitarian teachings of the Koran and the Hadith also seem to have prevented these status analogues of the Hindu *bhadralok* and *chhotolok* from gaining far too much strength among the Muslims.

Within each stratum, the different ethnic groups are again ranked in a hierarchical order. Thus, the Sheikhs of Khiruli ranked the four ethnic groups of the upper stratum into a hierarchy as follows: Sayyad, Sheikh, Pathan and Mughal. In conceptualizing this hierarchy, my Sheikh informants emphasized the position of the Sayyads as the highest in the hierarchy and suggested that it rested on two significant criteria: (a) they are direct descendants of the Prophet Muhammad through his daughter Fatima and Ali; and (b) they are saints (*pirs*) and therefore entitled to deferential treatment from other Muslims. Both these factors seem to set the Sayyads and their social position apart from the other ethnic groups.

The high social standing of the Sayyads in the hierarchy is often compared to that of the Brahmins in Hindu society.

[4]Cf. Schwartzberg: 'Villages or hamlets tend to be, on the whole, clearly Muslim dominated or clearly Hindu dominated, Muslim villages having far fewer castes in general than those dominated by Hindus. The non-Muslim groups who are most commonly found in large numbers in Sheikh villages are depressed Hindu castes or tribal or semi-tribal people, who are, for the most part, petty cultivators, fishermen, and agricultural labourers' (Schwartzberg, 1968:108).

TABLE 1

Muslim Ethnic Groups in Thirteen Villages in Birbhum District[1]

No.	Village	Approximate distance from Khiruli	Muslims Ethnic groups	Religious sects[2]	Approximate No. of Muslim families	Economic Condition of the Muslims within the Village (rough estimate)[3]	Remarks
1	2	3	4	5	6	7	8
1.	Khiruli	—	Sheikh	Hanafi	71	Richest Muslim holding 20 acres of land. Number of landless families is 20.	Predominantly Muslim village with 8 Dom and 1 Hadi families. The Dom and Hadi are Hindu low castes.
2.	Keshabpur	1 mile south-east	Pathan	-do-	40	3 rich families holding 17 to 33 acres of land each. There are 14/15 landless families.	Half Hindu, half Muslim (i.e., Pathan) village. But both the Hindus and Muslims have separate hamlets of their own within the village.
3.	Kasba	$1\frac{1}{2}$ miles south-east	Sheikh	-do-	25	No rich Muslim in the village. Half of the population is landless or 'semi-landless', i.e., holding 1 acre or less cultivable land.	Predominantly Hindu village with a Muslim section.
4.	Kendradangal	3 miles north	Sheikh	-do-	100	Richest Muslim village in Bholpur Thana	Predominantly Muslim village with a few

					(police station) is Kennagal. Some of these families have 67 to 100 acres of land. Approximate number of landless families is 20/21.	Hindu low castes residing there.
5. Sattor	½ mile north-west	Sheikh and Momin (Julaha)	-do- Sect of the Momins not ascertained	50 (Sheikh) 4 (Momin)	No really rich Muslism family there. Half of the total number of families are landless. All the Momins are landless. Quite a good number of the Sheikhs are involved in cattle-trade (*paikar*, a local term for the trade in cattle).	Hindu-Muslim mixed village where one part of the village is Muslim dominated and the Hindus exclusively dwell in the other part.
6. Lohagore	6 miles north-west	Sheikh	Ahl-e-Hadith as well as a good number of Hanafiites	65	No rich family. More than a third of the population is landless.	Muslim village with a few Hindu families of low caste.
7. Bheramari	4 miles south-west	Sheikh	Hanafiites	45	No rich Muslim family in the village. The Muslims of the	Hindu-Muslim mixed village.

1	2	3	4	5	6	7	8
						village constitute an economically poor class.	
8.	Bholagore	6 miles south-west	Sheikh	50% Hanafi, rest Ahl-e-Hadith	80/85	There are quite a few rich Muslims whose landholdings vary from 20 to 50 acres. Less than a third of the total number of families is landless.	Muslim village with a few Hindus of low caste.
9.	Digha Shah Para (the Shah section of Digha village)	5 miles south	Shah Fakir	Hanafi	24	Richest family owns 7/8 acres of land.	Cf. Serial no. 10 of this table.
10.	Digha	5 miles scuth	Patua	-do-	8	A third of the total families of the Patuas have 1 acre or less of land. The rest are poor, mostly landless.	A Hindu multi-caste village having 8 Patua families clustered within the village.
11.	Dhanai	5 miles south	Sheikh Mughal	-do-	6 (Sheikh) Out of these 6 Sheikh families, 2 belong to the Mallick	The Mughals are rich while the Sheikhs are poor.	Predominantly Hindu village with a Muslim sub-section.

				'subcaste'. 2 (Mughal)		
12. Purandar-pur	10 miles south	Patua and Sheikh—I did not contact the Sheikhs	-do-	6	The Patuas are all landless.	Large village with a very old marketing centre, populated mainly by Hindu trading castes.
13. Khustigiri	10 miles west	Sayyad Sheikh	-do-	2 (Sayyad) 40 (Sheikh)	The Sayyads are very rich. The Sheikhs' economic condition not ascertained.	Muslim village.

[1]Villages from 1 to 7 fall within the Bholpur Police Station under which Khiruli is also located, while the remaining villages lie under the Sainthia Police Station.

[2]Locally, the religious sect of a group is known as *mujab* which appears to be a corruption of the Urdu word *mazhab*. There are two prevalent religious sects among the local Muslims: the Hanafis and Ahl-e-Hadith. Members of each of these sects are not endogamous. Thus, it is common to find a few members of the Ahl-e-Hadith group living in Hanafi dominated villages or vice-versa as affinal kins. It is noteworthy, however, that all the Muslims of the area surveyed were Sunni.

[3]Throughout this region the Muslims are less well off in comparison to the numerically dominant Hindu high castes. It is striking, however, that the Muslims as a community are economically better off than the Hindus of low castes. Low caste Hindus as a whole and tribals are the poorest in the area.

Indeed, the Brahmin's social status among the Hindus is so overwhelmingly evident to the Muslims that on seveal occasions I found a fervent enthusiasm among the Muslims for describing a Hindu convert, especially one having a knowledge of the Koranic texts and whose Hindu caste-status is not clearly known, as a Brahmin. Persons having a sound knowledge of the Koranic and other Islamic texts are highly esteemed in Muslim society and such persons are not frequently met with in rural West Bengal. Given their background as very religious people, the Sayyads naturally correspond to the literate Brahmins (Dumont, 1970:207). The superior position of the Sayyads in the hierarchy is also frequently reinforced by the single fact that, like the Brahmins, Kayasthas, and a higher sub-group of the Sadgop (Konar Sadgop or simply Konar) among the Hindus of the locality (Bhattacharya, 1968), they avoid ploughing the fields with their own hands and are supposed to desist from manual labour associated with agriculture.

The Sheikhs place themselves next to the Sayyads followed in that order by the Pathans, the Mughals and the remaining ethnic groups of the lower stratum. The Sheikhs look down upon the Pathans as they feel that the latter's way of life does not correspond closely to Islamic injunctions. For example, they allege that some of the Pathans indulge in drinking toddy (*tari*) which is considered taboo (*haram*) according to strict Islamic principles. Again, some of the Pathans keep moustaches which is also not considered proper, for, any food consumed after having been touched by the moustache would also become tabooed (*haram*). The Pathans do not accept these allegations or the rank accorded to them by the Sheikhs. On the contrary, they claim that their own ethnic status is higher than the Sheikhs though they are aware that the latter do not concede superior rank to them. Likewise, the Mughals also claim that they are superior to the Sheikhs and Pathans and place themselves next to the Sayyads in the hierarchy, followed by the Sheikhs and the Pathans. Both the Pathans and the Mughals nevertheless accept the superiority of the Sayyads in the same way as the Sheikhs.

Considering the fact both the Pathans and the Mughals concede the third position to the Sheikhs while they are themselves in disagreement about who among them occupies the second rank, it would seem that the social hierarchy as conceptualized by the Sheikhs represents a fair approximation of social reality. The disagreement over the precise position of each ethnic group arises from the fact that, as already indicated, each ethnic group lives in a different local hierarchy and its members are not bound by common obligatory behaviour toward the members of the other groups.

The ethnic groups of the lower stratum are ranked merely by extending the four-fold hierarchical inter-ethnic order of the groups of the upper stratum and they are placed in a separate block below the latter. The overall social hierarchy of all the ethnic groups in the area is, then, as follows:

TABLE 2
Social Hierarchy of Muslim Ethnic Groups

Stratum	*Rank*
Upper	Sayyad
	Sheikh Pathan Mughal
Lower	Shah Fakir Momin Patua

The Shahs or Shah Fakirs are ranked below the four upper Muslim ethnic groups. Although begging as an occupation is generally regarded as low among the Muslims, yet they do make a distinction between religious and profane begging, and the relatively higher status of the Shahs is rationalized by the fact that they are religious mendicants. This, however, does not raise their status to the level of the four upper Muslim groups. The Shahs, on the other hand, claim that they rank below the Sayyads. In claiming high status, they place importance on their distinctive way of life, namely, a highly difficult and dedicated life of religious mendicancy and also suggest that, like the Sayyads, they avoid ploughing. The concept of a dedicated life as mendicant friars is the central theme around which the Shahs have developed an other-wordly value system. They, however, feel that they are regarded low by the high status Muslims because the common Muslims have no ability to appreciate their sophisticated philosophy of life and consider them not much above the class of ordinary beggars.

The Shah claim that they do not engage in ploughing is not commonly accepted. In fact, the Sheikhs at Khiruli frequently ridicule the Shahs about this claim. The Sheikhs argue that the Shah pretentions about not ploughing the fields is not so much due to their aspiration for a higher status, but rather to get more and more alms from the villagers. This may not be entirely true, but there are definite indications that the Shah claim is not entirely accurate. I found that the Shah families did plough the fields in the villages where they owned land. They, however, rationalized this fact by maintaining that they were all poor people so it was not practicable for them to employ labourers for tilling the soil.

The Momins and Patuas are regarded as the lowest in the hierarchy of Muslim ethnic groups. Literally, the word 'Momin' means believer, and each pious and believing Muslim is terminologically a Momin. However, in local parlance the word 'Momin' is used to refer to the Muslim weavers. A few high ranking Muslim informants in and around Khiruli said that the Momins would enjoy a fairly high social status according to the Arabic meaning of their name if their women folk would only observe purdah. Purdah is an Islamic practice requiring women, according to local Muslims, to cover all parts of the body in public, except their feet below the ankles and their hands up to the wrists. In rural West Bengal the socially superior Muslim families observe purdah merely by disallowing their womenfolk to undertake outdoor work. However, the Momin women, as noted above, do not observe purdah. Both the Momins and Patuas are ranked low because their women do not observe purdah in public and engage in outdoor work. The Sheikhs and Pathans observe restrictions on commensality with the Momins and Patuas, but there is no bar, at least in theory, to praying together.

The Momins are poor and do not belong to the area. They do not voice any overt protest about the low status accorded to them by the other Muslim groups. The Patuas denounce any kind of social hierarchy among the Muslims and claim equality with other Muslims. They claim that the discriminatory behaviour shown toward them by other Muslims is a consequence of their poverty. The Patuas, however, regard the Sayyads as superior in status to all the other Muslims. They are also aware that they are regarded as low by other Muslim groups.

Hierarchical Interaction

The different Muslim ethnic groups of the area conceptualize their notions of the social hierarchy as discussed above. However, these groups are spatially separated from one another and the demographic situation does not offer much scope for systematic interaction among them. It is, therefore, difficult to concretize their notions of hierarchy in interactional terms. It is, nevertheless, certain that the interactional pattern of the Muslim ethnic groups of the area is a loose one in comparison to that prevalent among the Hindus.

Each Hindu caste has, or is at least supposed to have, a specialized occupation and the Hindu castes are interdependent. The services of priests, artisans, cultivators, traders, barbers, midwives, washermen, drummers, etc., are all caste-based among the Hindus. Although the system of caste-based services is dwindling among the Hindus in practice, ideally the *jati*-based hereditary as well as hierarchic division of labour exists in the minds of the Hindus. In fact, they still conceptualize their caste hierarchy in terms of this idealized model. In Bergram, the services of priests, barbers, midwives, drummers, blacksmiths and leather workers are, even today, hereditary and caste-based and rendered under traditional arrangements in return for annual payments in kind. Except for the drummers and priests who belong to the village itself, the services of the other specialists, like barbers, midwives, blacksmiths and leather-workers, are obtained from the appropriate caste in neighbouring villages. Besides, itinerary artisans like carpenters, bell-metal smiths and traders and leatherworkers also visit the villages in the area and thus provide the villagers with their respective caste services usually in lieu of money. Some of these artisans and traders come from as far as the neighbouring districts of Burdwan and Murshidabad. However, most of them are from the towns of Bholpur and Suri[5] and from the market centre of Purandarpur.

The interaction among the different Muslim groups of the area is not as elaborate and interdependent as among the local Hindus. In fact, the number of Muslim ethnic groups, being only seven in the area, is too low for the local Muslims to divide their society in terms of a *jati*-based hereditary division of labour to any great extent. But while the Muslim ethnic groups do not operate in terms of a complex *jati*-based division of labour among themselves, they do nevertheless form part of the system of caste interdependence prevalent among the Hindus and play their limited role in it either as patrons or as clients.

For instance, the Hadi midwife of Khiruli serves her Muslim as well as Hindu clients of the area. Similarly, the Hindus of Bergram and the Muslims of Khiruli get their agricultural implements repaired from the members of two families of Hindu Kamar (blacksmith) caste. Itinerary leatherworkers of the Hindu Muchi caste, Hindu bell-metal smiths of Kansari caste, etc., also visit all villages and provide the villagers with their services without considering the villagers' social and community status. In Rahamatpur, a multi-caste Hindu village adjacent to Khiruli, a Bayen works as a leatherworker. The Muslim villagers of Khiruli often bring him a goat-skin, specially when a goat is being slaughtered in the village, to get it mounted on a *mora* (sitting stool made of bamboo splits). On the other hand, the local Muslims as a community are regarded as dealers in cattle and this particular trade is more or less their monopoly. On the whole, however, the structure of inter-ethnic stratification among the local Muslims is not highly ramified,[6] and the 'inter-

[5]Suri is the headquarter of Birbhum district and is situated about fifteen miles south of Khiruli.

[6]Marriott (1960) has noted that population density and settlement pattern were important determinants for the elaboration of caste ranking in any particular region His findings are confirmed by the present study. It is clear that the lack of elaboration of inter-ethnic hierarchy among the Muslims of the area is directly linked to the small number of Muslim ethnic groups present in this region and the small size of the communities resident in any single village. See Schwartzberg (1968:108-9) for a further discussion of the linkage between the number of castes or ethnic groups found in the villages of this region and the absence of elaboration and ramification of the social hierarchy.

mixing of Hindu-Muslim communities commonly yields a local caste pattern with a very high level of heterogeneity' (Schwartzberg, 1968:109).

Caste Characteristics

A formal system of interdependence through ritual service which links the different strata of a locality together in the economic, political and religious fields is a characteristic feature of caste stratification. It would be quite obvious from the above discussion that such a formal system of interdependence is somewhat lacking in the case of the Muslim ethnic groups and their hierarchical interactions are not particularly ramified. Nevertheless, the Muslim ethnic groups in rural Bengal seem to share some other caste-like features and frequently use them in determining their relative social standing. Some of these strikingly common Hindu caste-like features found among the local Muslim ethnic groups are endogamy, restrictions on commensality and hereditary occupational specialization, and the relative merit of the different occupations. I shall now briefly discuss the relevance of these features in the inter-ethnic hierarchy of the local Muslims.

Endogamy

Like the Hindu castes, the Muslim ethnic groups of the area are endogamous, corporate patrilineal descent groups. There have been no marriages across ethnic boundaries in Khiruli within the living memory of the informants (genealogical data also confirm this). However, cases of intermarriage between ethnic groups of roughly the same social status occasionally occur.[7] For example, the Muslims having the surname Malick in the area claim to belong to the Sheikh ethnic group. In answering

[7]Intermarriages between Sayyads and any of the other ethnic-groups of the upper stratum are permissible, but such marriages do not appear to have been made in the area. Rules regarding intergroup marriages appear in any case to be largely theoretical as there is no empirical evidence to suggest that these rules have ever been put to a test.

my query regarding the ethnic status of the Malicks the Sheikh informants said: 'The Malicks are Sheikhs, no doubt. The Malicks and the Sheikhs belong to the same *jat*, but they (the Malicks) enjoy low status among the Sheikhs'. It would appear, thus, that from the Sheikh viewpoint the Malicks are a 'sub-caste' within the Sheikh ethnic group. There have been some hypogamous marriages between the Sheikhs of Khiruli and the Malicks of Dhanai (see Table 1) and of other villages.

Some cases of marriages across ethnic groups were noted in villages around Khiruli. In Sattor there was a case of inter-marriage between a Julaha woman and a Sheikh, and two Pathans of Keshabpur village had married two Sheikh women. The local Muslims, unlike the Hindus of the area, do not categorically decry such unions. As mentioned earlier, they attempt to rationalize these inter-ethnic unions with the help of their Islamic egalitarianism. But in reality and in their day-to-day social interactions, such unions were considered somewhat derogatory to the members of the higher status group involved in such inter-ethnic unions. In fact, inter-ethnic marriages seldom take place and local Muslim ethnic groups may conveniently be regarded as endogamous units.

Commensality

Commensal relations are not as elaborately structured among the local Muslim ethnic groups as they are among the local Hindus, but certain restrictions on commensality and inter-dining are nevertheless prevalent among them. In the course of informal discussions, the Sheikhs of Khiruli clearly admitted that while their menfolk take food with the Pathans and the Mughals, neither their menfolk nor womenfolk would dine with the Shah Fakirs, Patuas or Momins. The Sayyads, Pathans and Mughals also admit indirectly that they do not dine with the members of those three ethnic groups. It is clear, then, that while there is no restriction on inter-group commensality insofar as the four ethnic groups of the upper stratum are concerned, restrictions on commensal relations with the three ethnic groups of the lower social stratum are uniformly observed by all the higher ethnic groups among the Muslims.

These commensal restrictions are rationalized on considerations of social hygiene and personal cleanliness. For example, the higher ethnic groups suggest that whether one would dine or not with a person or with all the members of a particular ethnic group depends on one's personal taste or liking (*ruchi*). They maintain that the Patuas and Momins are poor, lack cleanliness and a sense of hygiene and will make one sick if one dines with them. However, the fact that many well-to-do Sheikhs of Khiruli dine with very poor families whose general standards of cleanliness are not particularly better than the Patuas and Momins shows that considerations of hygiene and cleanliness are not at the root of their commensal behaviour.

The notion of hygiene and cleanliness in a person is related to his social position or status and not to his economic condition, or even to the fact of his objectively being clean or hygienic. To a certain degree this notion provides indirect evidence of the existence of a concept of purity and pollution in inter-ethnic relationships. In fact, some Sheikh informants of both the sexes indicate that the Patua and Momin are regarded as low groups in the same sense of the phrase that the local Hindus use to specify their different castes of low status, e.g., *chhotolok* or *chhotojat*. Similarly, the Sheikhs of Khiruli consider the Muslims belonging to the ethnic groups of the lower stratum as *chhotojat*. For example, during a discussion of different Muslim ethnic groups and their social status, one of the Sheikh women of Khiruli maintained: 'The Patua, Momin or Julaha belong to *chhotojat*.' Furthermore, the Khiruli Sheikhs in general maintain that they refrain from dining with Patuas and Momins simply because they are lowly-placed in terms of their social standing.

The emphasis placed by the high 'castes' on cleanliness and sense of hygiene as reasons for their refusal to inter-dine with the Momins, Patuas, and Shahs is a way of rationalizing social behaviour patterns which are inconsistent with Islamic social values. In reality, they have a concept of purity and pollution. However, their concept of purity aud pollution does not enjoy any sanction in the literature of their Great Tradition.

Occupations

The upper Muslim ethnic groups do not claim any hereditary occupation and live mainly by agriculture. The Shahs, Momins and Patuas are associated with hereditary caste occupations of mendicancy, weaving and painting, although they are also deeply involved in agricultural activities like many of the local Hindu castes who have specialized hereditary occupations but also depend on agriculture. The Shahs and Momins regard their traditional occupations as worthy. The Patuas, however, feel embarrassed to admit that they are traditionally involved in painting Hindu gods and goddesses. They do not like to disclose this for they know that their occupation lowers their social prestige in the eyes of fellow Muslims.

However, the occupations of the Shahs, Patuas and Momins are considered low by the members of the four upper Muslim ethnic groups. But these different lowly occupations are further categorized into different degrees of lowliness by the Muslims. The hereditary occupation of the Shahs, viz., religious mendicancy, is given a relatively higher status than the occupations of the Patuas and Momins. On the other hand, the occupation of painting Hindu gods and goddesses is graded lowest by local Muslims. The Patuas are themselves aware of the fact that they occupy the lowest occupational status. For this reason they generally avoid disclosing the practice of their traditional occupation to other people. For convenience, the hereditary and traditional occupations of the different local Muslim ethnic groups of the area are arranged below according to their locally accepted degree of lowliness:

TABLE 3
Hereditary Occupations of Muslim Ethnic Groups

Traditional Occupation	*Ethnic Group Hereditarily and Traditionally Related to the Occupation*	*Relative Status of Occupation*
Religious mendicancy	Shah	Comparatively higher
Weaving	Julaha (Momin)	——
Painting	Patua	Lowest

Although the Patuas hold the lowest status occupationally, their ethnic status is actually considered by the local Muslims to be equivalent to the Momins. This seems to be due to the fact that, as an indigenous group enjoying a better economic condition and having greater numerical strength than the Momins, the Patuas have a better standing in local Muslim society. Moreover, unlike the Momins who are indifferent to the status accorded to them, the Patuas are anxious to claim a higher social status.

If any member of the four higher Muslim ethnic groups engages in a service occupation, he is expected not to extend his services to the so-called low 'caste' Muslims, namely, the Patuas, Momins and Shahs, as well as to the Hindu low castes. For example, an old Sheikh informant, expected to leave for Haj (pilgrimage) soon, complained that a Sheikh of Khiruli, who had a hairdressing saloon at the market centre of Panrui (5 miles south of Khiruli under Sainthia Police Station), clipped the hair of both the Hindu and Muslim low castes. He appreciated the fact that another Sheikh who also served as a barber did not extend his services to any low caste, Hindu or Muslim.

Operational Model

Despite the existence of these features of caste behaviour in their local inter-ethnic stratification, the Muslims of this area tend to deny the existence of caste among them. As a matter of fact, they argue that caste is a feature of Hindu social organization and their own social life is ordered on the basis of equality. However, when someone points out the presence of caste-like behaviour in their social life, they explain that away as a Hindu influence. By and large, the Muslims are quite distinct and point to the fact of caste as a basis of that distinction. It seems to me, however, that the Muslims fear that by admitting that Hindu social features are present among them they will be betraying a basic similarity of their society to that of the Hindus and thus their distinct social identity will be compromized. Furthermore, on account of the lack of frequent interaction among the different Muslim ethnic groups in the area, they can afford to ignore these features of stratification which can thrive only on the basis of close and continuous intergroup interaction. But the fact remains that the different Muslim ethnic groups are not on equal footing within the local society of the Muslims.

There is an attempt on the part of Muslims to explain these observable inequalities in the status of different local Muslim ethnic groups in terms of features that can adequately be correlated to their Islamic tenets. Thus, it would seem that they are in search of a model of an operational value system of their own to justify the inequalities of social status in their stratification of the local Muslim society. To my mind, inequalities in social status of different Muslim ethnic groups, in contrast to their conscious Islamic model of an egalitarian society, make them mentally insecure. They try to overcome this mental dilemma caused by the sharp contrast between their ideology and their practices by rethinking the undeniable social fact of status inequality in terms of suitable idioms that can successfully be related to their traditions. However, even these idioms are inadequate to explain their complex social hierarchy and the presence of certain caste-like features in their social life.

Purdah

The most common ground on which the Sayyads, Sheikhs, Pathans and Mughals deny equal status to the Shahs, Patuas and Momins is the failure of the women of these ethnic groups to observe purdah. However, there is considerable evidence that even the Muslims of the upper four ethnic groups cannot often maintain purdah in the strict sense. Observance of purdah depends on one's economic condition. This is not to deny that some families do observe strict seclusion for their women. The Sheikhs of Kendradangal village observe strict purdah and consequently avoid marrying with families who fail to do so. Genealogical data show that the Sheikhs of Khiruli, who by their own confession cannot afford to maintain their women in seclusion, have formed no marital unions among the Sheikhs of neighbouring village of Kendradangal. Nevertheless, the failure of the traditionally upper Muslim ethnic groups to observe purdah is rarely held against them in the evaluation of their status.

A middle aged woman of Khiruli claims that she observes strict seclusion and this claim is accepted by others. She actually runs a grocery store in the village and comes frequently in contact with the men of the village. Another old lady similarly claims that she observes purdah though she frequently looks after the grocery store run by her family. However, the deviations on the part of upper Muslim ethnic groups are overlooked while the failure to observe purdah on the part of the low ranking Patua and Momin women is emphasized. It is obvious that observance of purdah is more of a symbolic than an empirical fact. If a person wishes his womenfolk to observe strict purdah he will be required to put walls around his homestead and arrange for facilities for bathing, washing, toilet, etc., within his homestead so that the women of the family can lead their day-to-day life comfortably without having to move out. The majority of the Muslims in the area cannot afford to create conditions necessary for the observance of purdah. Yet, while the inability of the traditionally superior ethnic groups to provide these facilities for their womenfolk is not held out against them, the members of the lower ethnic groups are considered lower because they do not observe purdah.

Pollution

The Muslims of the four upper ethnic groups also assign low status to the lower three ethnic groups because they claim that the latter do not observe certain ritual practices (*paksaf*). For instance, they claim that the Muslims belonging to the lower three ethnic groups do not perform ablutions after urination and thus generally do not maintain *paksaf* or purity according to Islamic traditions. By *paksaf* (locally pronounced *paksak*) the local Muslims mean physical purity or cleanliness. However, observation shows that this allegation on the part of the upper ethnic groups is a popular stereotype. It is comparable to another widely prevalent stereotype that the Muslims of the lower three ethnic groups do not regularly say their *namaz*. However, it was found that the majority of the Muslims belonging to both upper and lower ethnic groups do not pray according to Islamic Shariat nor do they observe rules of ritual cleanlinesss. It is clear, then, that these features do not help us to understand the social hierarchy of the higher and lower social strata among the Muslims of the locality.

Wealth

Wealth has a direct relationship with the differential position of an ethnic group in the hierarchy. For example, the Sayyads are the richest group in the area studied. The Shahs, Julahas and Patuas are a poor class of people by and large. But wealth is not a determinant of ethnic status. Many Sheikhs, Pathans and Mughals are not particularly better off than the Shahs, Patuas and Julahas and their general style of life is quite different from the more affluent members of their ethnic groups. They are frequently illiterate, belong to the class of agricultural labourers, live in wretched huts and do not observe purdah. Nevertheless, a direct correspondence between caste position and wealth is generally assumed by the people. Thus, all high ethnic groups are considered well-to-do, while all low ethnic groups are regarded as poor.

Caste among the Muslims

Caste among the Hindus is traditionally associated with so much mythology, tradition and religious beliefs that one at first tends to feel somewhat uneasy about considering the local Muslim inter-ethnic stratification as really comparable to the Hindu caste system. For one thing, unlike the Hindu practice of disallowing low castes from directly performing certain rites and rituals, the Muslims of all castes, high and low, can enter the mosque, provided their clothes are clean, and can perform prayers shoulder to shoulder in the same row (locally called *katar*). No high caste person would mind saying his prayers behind a Julaha or Patua or Shah who may happen to come first and stand in the front row. Secondly, like free entry into the mosque, *maktabs* (elementary Islamic educational centres) and *madrasas* are open to all members of the society. If a low Muslim becomes a *mulla* (Muslim theologian) by dint of his perseverance and merit and conducts *namaz*, even the members of the highest ethnic group would not grudge considering him an Imam (Imam means the person who conducts a *namaz*). Even so, the observable fact was that, in the religious congregations, the Muslims of low ethnic status usually tried on their own not to stand in the front rows. Furthermore, an old Sheikh at Khiruli, finding the behaviour of a newly appointed *Khatib* (officially 'priest' of the village mosque) somewhat callous, ridiculed him in his absence as a member of the Julaha caste. There are, thus, unmistakable signs of a caste-like behaviour in their day-to-day social interactions.

The fundamental difference between the Hindu caste system and the Muslim ethnic hierarchy is that the former is based on the traditional Hindu system of *varna* while the latter has no systematic mythological and theological basis. Moreover, the egalitarian concept of Islamic brotherhood contradicts a social arrangement in terms of inter-ethnic stratification. Besides, each Hindu caste or *jat* has, or is supposed to have, a specialized occupation, while the upper four Muslim ethnic groups are not associated with any specific 'caste' occupation.

In sum, the Muslims of the locality operate very much like the local Hindus in a *jati*-based hierarchy in their interactions. This hierarchic model of the Muslims is not a product of their Great Tradition. The Muslim ethnic hierarchy described above is a 'situational' one, while the Hindu social hierarchy of castes is basically a traditional system. This situationally derived model of social hierarchy is inconsistent with the ideal Islamic view of social life and it has created much confusion in the mind of the Muslims in conceptualizing the reality of their social hierarchy. For this reason the Muslims, rather than considering their inter-ethnic stratification a normal social condition, take pains either to deny or to rationalize it. Nevertheless, the different Muslim ethnic groups of the locality maintain social distance among themselves by practising certain Hindu caste features like endogamy and restrictions on commensality. Each of the three Muslim ethnic groups of lower social status in the area also has, or is supposed to have, a specialized hereditary occupation. Moreover, the local Muslims have devised certain special rationalizations in an attempt to maintain status discrimination among their different groups. Considering all this, the non-*varna*-based, situationally derived inter-ethnic stratification of the Muslims in rural West may be regarded as a system of inter-ethnic stratification analogous to the Hindu caste system.

Bibliography

Bhattacharya, Ranjit K. (1968), 'Social and Cultural Constraints in Agriculture in Three Villages (Hindu, Muslim and Tribal) of West Bengal', *Journal of Anthropological Society*, 3, pp. 79-108.

Dumont, Louis (1970), *Homo Hierarchicus: The Caste System and its Implications*, Delhi, Vikas Publications.

Marriott, McKim (1960), *Caste Ranking and Community Structure in Five Regions of India and Pakistan*, Deccan College Monograph Series No. 23, Poona, Deccan College Post-Graduate and Research Institute.

Schwartzberg, Joseph E. (1968), 'Caste Regions of the North Indian Plains', in Milton Singer and B.S. Cohn (eds.), *Structure and Change in Indian Society*, Chicago, Aldine Publishing Company.

Sinha, Surajit, and Bhattacharya, R.K. (1969), 'Bhadralok and Chhotolok in Rural Areas of Bengal', *Sociological Bulletin*, 18, pp. 50-66.

Glossary

Ahl-e-Hadith, a member of the Sunni sect claiming adherence to the precepts and practices of the Prophet Muhammad.

Ahmadia, Modern Muslim sect divided into an older group, Qadiani, and a newer group, Lahore party, heretical in that it denies, at least to some extent, the finality of Muhammad's prophethood, subscribes to a mythology of Christ's sojourn and burial in Kashmir and advocates a 'loyalist' theory of *jihad* which it equates with proselytization and missionary work.

ajam, non-Arab.

ajlaf, a convert Muslim, especially from a lower Hindu caste.

Allah, God, so-called in Islam.

amin, a revenue official.

amir, rich.

Arya Samaj, modern reformist Hindu sect which advocates return to the Vedas.

asabiyyah, spirit of kinship.

ashraf, a Muslim claiming descent from any of the four groups of foreign extraction, viz., Sayyad, Sheikh, Mughal and Pathan.

ashrafization, process of social change involving raising of status through claiming of descent from any of the four groups of foreign extraction.

Atna Ashari, Shia subsect that recognizes twelve imams the last of whom, Muhammad al-Muntazar, is believed to have disappeared between A.D. 873-877 and will return on the day of judgment.

avatar, incarnation.

baal, religious discourse.

baitha, devotional singing.

baralok, aristocracy; people of high status.

barat, marriage party or procession.

Barelvi, an adherent of the religious philosophy as interpreted by Ahmad Raza Khan of Bareilly in Uttar Pradesh.

beradari, caste brotherhood.

bhadralok, a socially privileged group of Bengali society which kept its distance from the masses by its acceptance of high caste prescriptions and its literate culture, sharing a pride in its language and history.

bhumidari, right or title to land; the system of land tenure whereby a tenant-cultivator could acquire title to land under his cultivation upon payment of a specified amount to the Government.

bibi, lady.

birrahe, of mixed descent.

birre, of mixed descent.

bisser (corrupt form of Arabic *bi-shar*), Irreligious or impure.

britti, traditional occupation, usually caste-based.

burka, loose garment covering the entire boby and having veiled openings for the eyes, worn by Muslim women.

charava, gifts from the bridegroom to his bride.

charidar, staff-bearer.

chatai, mat.

chavarikyam, custom requiring matrilineal kinsmen of the deceased to abstain from work for a stipulated number of days.

chhotolok, gentry.

chhotojat, low castes.

chilam, earthen pot used for smoking tobacco.

Chistia, Sufi order which advocates ontological monism and whose mystical practices include liturgy (*dhikr*), regulation of breadth, which was probably an Indian influence, concentrated seance, and secluded worship for forty days, an exercise of undoubted yogic origin.

chunam, lime

cowle, leasing of Government land.

churidar pyjama, pleated trousers, usually narrow round the ankles.

daff, tambourine.

Dasavatar, religious book of the Khojas which describes Ali as the tenth and the most important incarnation of Hindu God Vishnu.

Deobandi, an adherent of the religious viewpoint represented by the Deoband Theological Seminary situated at Saharanpur in western Uttar Pradesh.

dharma, the proper way of life, righteousness; duty as prescribed by the sacred scriptures.

dhikr, liturgical recitation.

dwija, twice-born.

fateha, an offering to God, the Prophet or a Muslim saint, so-called because the first chapter of the Koran called sura fateha is usually read as part of the ritual.

garib, poor.

ghagra, petticoat.

gharara, long flaring lower garment.

gotra, a Hindu clan tracing descent from a common ancestor, usually a saint or sage.

gram panchayat, lowest of the three-tier system of elective institutions of rural government in India.

hadith, report of a statement the Prophet is alleged to have made.

haj, pilgrimage to Mecca which every Muslim is supposed to make at least once in a lifetime.
halal, permitted in Islam.
Hanafi, a follower of the Hanafi school of Islamic jurisprudence which recognizes analogical deduction and consensus among jurists as important roots of Islamic jurisprudence.
Hanbali, a follower of the Hanbali school of Islamic jurisprudence which rejects the consensus of learned Islamic opinion as an unlawful innovation and depends upon the actual wordings of the traditions as a source of Islamic jurisprudence.
haram, forbidden in Islam.
har gor, ritual purity of blood and bone.

illam, Nambudiri house.
imam, leader, in Shia doctrine the hereditary head of the community in line of succession from Muhammad through his daughter Fatima and son-in-law Ali.
Imami Ismaili, Shia subsect that recognizes Ismail as its imam.
Islamization, cultural process whereby individuals and groups distinguish themselves from non-Muslims by purifying themselves of the so-called un-Islamic customs and practices.
jahiliya, period of Arab history before the advent of Islam.
jajman, patron.
jajmani, system of exchange of goods and services among castes in rural India.
jamaat, caste council.
jamaatkhana, Khoja hall of worship.
jami, pertaining to *juma* (Friday).
jat, corrupt form of *jati*.
jati, the effective endogamous unit in the caste system.
jenmi, landlord.
jenmom, tax free land.
juma, Friday, a day considered auspicious by Muslims.

kalava, coloured thread supposed to ward off evil.
kamin, artisan and menial; a member of a serving caste.
kanam, superior tenancy right.

karanavar (also *karnavar*), head of a *tharavad* or one of its segments, usually the oldest male.
karma, the law of action and causality.
karyakar, agent of a ruler.
katar, line or row.
kazi, the Islamic judge.
khanquah, a Sufi hospice.
khatal, dairy.
khatib, lit. reader of sermons, hence also a priest.
kootam, a group of matrilineally related *tharavads* usually comprising a number of matrilineages.
kuccha, uncooked.
kudambam, a collection of matrilineages.
kudian, tenant.
kufv, kin.
kutchery, district court.

Maliki, a follower of the Maliki School of Islamic jurisprudence which regards traditions, either that of the Prophet or local customs, as having first claim to consideration after Koran as the root of Islamic jurisprudence.
mancheel, hammock slung to a pole.
marumakkatayam, law regulating matrilineal descent and inheritance.
masjid, Muslim house of prayer.
masawat, equality.
maulood, religious discourse, usually by recitation, held to commemorate the birth anniversary of the Prophet as well as on other socio-religious occasions.
mawali, a Muslim of non-Arab origin.
mazar, tomb of a Muslim saint.
milad, religious discourse held to commemorate the birth anniversary of the Prophet or on other socio-religious occasions.
millat-e-Islamiyah, the community of Muslims.
mithqual, a measure of gold.
moazzin, the official attached to a muslim mosque whose duty it is to announce the hours of prayer.
mohalla, ward of a city.
moktessor, juror.

mokhyastan, an influential person.
moopan, elder.
mora, sitting stool made out of bamboo splits.
maalim, leader of a crew.
Muharram, the first month of the Islamic calendar; the festival held to commemorate the martyrdom of Hasan and Hussain sons of Ali.
mulla, Muslim priest and teacher.
mujab, (corrupt form of Urdu *mazhab*), religion, faith.
mujawar, keeper of a shrine.
mureed, devotee owing allegiance to a Muslim saint, living or dead.

naib, deputy.
najib-ut-tarfain, of impeccable descent.
namaz, prayer, the Islamic form of worship supposed to be performed five times daily.
napaki, impurity.
Naqshbandia, Sufi order influenced at the beginning by certain Mahayana Buddhist features, although it was a Sunni movement aiming at the integration of external ritual and inner spirituality, advocating the doctrine of phenomenological monism or 'unity of witness' which has been defined as 'a belief in God witnessing to Himself in the heart of this votary'.
nikah, the Muslim marriage contract.

odam, large sailing vessel.

paksaf, purity and cleanliness.
panchayat, council, caste or village.
panchayat samiti, middle level of the three-tier system of elective institutions of rural government in India.
pandaram, Government land.
pankti, line or row.
pap, sin.

Parsurama, mythological Brahmin protagonist who sought to exterminate the whole of the Kshatriya race.
parwim, non-Gaddi.
patwari, village land record-keeper.
pir, Muslim saint.
purdah, veiling of women.
pucca, cooked; also solid, made of bricks.
purohit, Hindu priest.

Qadiria, Sufi order, heretical in that it believed in freedom of the will.
qalandar, wandering mendicant; follower of a heterodox Sufi order.
Qualandaria, a heterodox sufic order which accepted a number of Indian influences including the use of intoxicants and whose members shaved their head and hair on their face and went about wrapped in blankets so that the word qalandar underwent a lowering of meaning and now denotes a wandering mendicant.
quam, lit. 'nation', in colloquial Urdu the effective endogamous unit in the Muslim social stratification system.
qurankhani, reading of the Koran.

Ramadan, the ninth month of the Islamic calendar; the daily fast from dawn until sunset that is rigidly enjoined during the month.
rathib, religious rite wherein persons get into a trance and lacerate different parts of the body.
risalat, prophethood.
ruchi, preference or inclination.

sadhu, holy man, monk or ascetic.
sahiun nasl, of impeccable pedigree.
salwar kamiz, pantaloons and tunic.
sambandham, alliance or marriage.
sari, long piece of cotton or silk worn round the body with one end draped over the head or over one shoulder.

sarih, full-blooded bedouin who regarded himself superior to the converts to Islam outside Arabia.
sarkar, lit. government, hence also lord or master.
sayyadzada, son of a Sayyad (used in contempt).
Shafi, a follower of the Shafi School of Islamic jurisprudence which frowns upon the unlimited use of arbitrary opinion as a root of Islamic jurisprudence and insists that, before any valid deductions can be made, the underlying motive in the Koranic 'premises' must be taken into account.
shariat, the sacred law of Islam.
sheikhzada, son of a Sheikh (used in contempt).
sherbat, sherbet, sugar and water.
sherwani, long tight-coat.
shetia, rich trader or business magnate.
Shia, a member of that Muslim sect which maintains that Ali, first cousin of Muhammad and husband of his daughter Fatima, was the first legitimate successor of the Prophet, rejecting the three caliphs of their opponents, the Sunnis, as usurpers.
shijra, family tree.
silsilah, a Sufi order.
sudh, pure.
sunna, precepts and practices of the Prophet.
Sunni, the name commonly given to orthodox Muslims, because in their rule of faith the *sunna*, or traditional teachings of the Prophet, is added to the Koran.
sura, any of the chapters of the Koran.

Tabligh, religious movement seeking to enforce a rigid practice of Islamic principles.
taqiyya, disguise or subterfuge, Shia practice allowing a believer to disguise his real faith in order to escape persecution in a hostile environment.
tala, custom requiring sixteen persons of a lineage to eat from the same plate.
taluk, administrative sub-division of a district.
tari, toddy, palm beer.
tariqat, road, path; within sufism, the proper mode of acting or manner of conduct.

tasht, brass tray.
tat, gunny.
taziya, representation of the tombs of Hasan and Hussain, sons of Ali.
tola, ward or locality.
tehsil, administrative sub-division of a district.
tehsildar, official incharge of a tehsil; administrative head of a tehsil.
tharavad, matrilineal residence group.
tola, or ward locality.

unchi, high.
urs, lit. 'marriage', hence also the anniversary of a saint's death which is regarded as his union with God.

varaha, gold coin.
varna, classification of Hindu society which places all castes into four major categories, *viz.*, Brahmin, Kshatriya, Vaishya, and Sudra.
vattelutu, the script of old Malayalam.

Wahabi, a follower of Abd-al-Wahab, opposing all practices not sanctioned by the Koran.

zakat, a tax, supposedly 40 per cent of personal income of every kind, levied on Muslims for the relief of the poor.
zamindar, hereditary landlord.
zat, Urdu equivalent of *jati*.

Index